"A Clown
 in a Grave"

Complexities
and Tensions
in the
Works of
Gregory Corso

"A Clown
in a
Grave"

Michael
Skau

Southern Illinois University Press
Carbondale and Edwardsville

Frontispiece: Photograph of Gregory Corso by Arthur Winfield Knight

Library of Congress Cataloging-in-Publication Data
Skau, Michael, 1944–
    A clown in a grave : complexities and tensions in the works of Gregory Corso
/ Michael Skau.
    p. cm.
Includes bibliographical references (p.   ) and index.
1. Corso, Gregory—Criticism and interpretation. 2. Beat generation. I. Title.
PS3505.0763Z87 1999
811'.54—dc21   98-47515
ISBN 0-8093-2252-8 (cloth : alk. paper)   CIP

Contents

Preface

This book has been a project of love spanning more than thirty-five years, the length of time I have enjoyed reading Gregory Corso (b. 1930), admired the pithy comedy of his works, and appreciated the personal warmth, the heart at the heart, of his writing. Corso's work, however, forces the critic to face considerable difficulties not always encountered with other writers. Divorcing Corso's ridiculous, self-applauding posturing as Captain Poetry from the self-effacing, vulnerable Everyman who bares his flaws and weaknesses with absolute candor is a challenge. Attempting to provide analysis and insight for the works of a poet who treasures the mystery of his writings, claiming that "[n]o thing of beauty was meant for inspection" ("'Let Us Inspect,'" *HB* 18), also poses problems. In addition, accurately citing sources is difficult in the treatment of a poet whose poems vary in form from volume to volume and who recycles phrases and images in a variety of poems. Even locating many of his writings is a demanding task, because many of them (particularly the prose works) remain uncollected and were published in less-than-traditional outlets, and because no thorough bibliography of Corso's works has been published since 1966.

Nevertheless, the poet who claims, "I've new delight—and eternally toward delight / I've a possession to assume / to bestow" ("Greece," *LL* 27), has seldom failed to bestow that delight to this particular reader. I can only hope that this book effectively conveys that pleasure and can entice other readers to indulge in the same satisfaction that I have gained from Corso's writing.

My approach has been essentially thematic, rather than to present a chronological treatment of his published volumes, which usually collect poems originally appearing erratically over an extended period of years. I have also depended heavily on offering relevant supporting materials from Corso's own writings instead of simply making unsubstantiated generalizations about his attitudes and beliefs. Because so many of his passages recur—often in only slightly different form—in several different publications, I have incorporated more complete source citations into my text in order to provide precise and immediate identification. The danger here is that such citations will interfere with the flow of the prose; but I trust that the parenthetical signals are clear enough that intelligent readers may skip over them, if they so desire, with a minimum of disruptive effort. The parenthetical source citations seem to me to be more useful than would documentation in notes relegated to the end of the volume. Unless otherwise noted, the idiosyncrasies of Corso's punctuation, diction, and spelling have been retained throughout this volume. For in-text citations, source information for Corso material can be found in the bibliography of Corso's works; source information for all other material can be found in the works cited.

I have also provided notes that identify Corso's allusions. This seems appropriate for a writer who, in "Marriage," suggests that the modern world no longer acquaints its young with classical knowledge. The classical allusions are brief identifications, because they may be easily accessible through such reference works as encyclopedias; for more contemporary allusions, especially those from the more evanescent realm of popular culture, I have been slightly more elaborate. The poems originally published in *The Vestal Lady on Brattle* and *Gasoline*, Corso's first two books, were published bound together by City Lights in 1976; I have used this *Gasoline/Vestal* volume as the reference for these poems because the double volume is so much more readily available now than either of the single volumes.

Acknowledgments

I would like to express my appreciation for the support of my parents, my brothers and sisters and their families, and my friends and colleagues, particularly Ray Rogers, Kurt Austin, Dr. Susan Naramore Maher, Dr. Gordon Mundell, and Dr. Gregory and Francoise Sadlek. I also wish to thank Jeffrey Weinberg, Robert Wilson, Bill Morgan, Mitch Corder, and Kyle Roderick for their assistance. In addition, the University of Nebraska at Omaha has granted me valuable research support. I also appreciate the assistance provided by the following libraries: the Bancroft Library, University of California; the Rare Book and Manuscript Library, Columbia University; the Humanities Research Center, University of Texas; the Kenneth Spencer Research Library, University of Kansas; and the Interlibrary Loan staff, University of Nebraska at Omaha.

I acknowledge the following periodicals, which published earlier, abbreviated versions of two chapters of this book: "'Elegiac Feelings American': Gregory Corso and America." *The McNeese Review* 32 (1989): 38–48. Published by permission from *The McNeese Review*; "'To Dream, Perchance to Be': Gregory Corso and Imagination." *University of Dayton Review* 20.1 (Summer 1989): 69–78. Published by permission from the *University of Dayton Review*.

I also offer gratitude, especially to Gregory Corso, for permission to reproduce the following copyrighted materials.

From *The American Express*. Copyright © 1961 by Gregory Corso.

From *Elegiac Feelings American*. Copyright © 1970 by Gregory Corso.

From *Gasoline/The Vestal Lady on Brattle*. Copyright © 1976 by Gregory Corso.

From *The Happy Birthday of Death*. Copyright © 1960 by New Directions Publishing Corporation. From *Long Live Man*. Copyright © 1962 by New Directions Publishing Corporation. Poems by Gregory Corso appear with the permission of New Directions Publishing Company.

From *Herald of the Autochthonic Spirit*. Copyright © 1981 by Gregory Corso. "Honor if you can" from *Sitting Frog*. Copyright © 1976 by Gregory Corso. From *Mind Field*. Copyright © 1989, Gregory Corso. All rights reserved. From *Mindfield: New and Selected Poems*. Copyright © 1989 by Gregory Corso.

"Piffle." Copyright © 1980 by Gregory Corso.

From *Selected Poems*. Copyright © 1962 by Gregory Corso.

"All Survived" from *Wings, Wands, Windows*. Original printed in Ashes #2 (Howling Dog Press, 1982). "Wings, Wands, Windows" by Gregory Corso.

Abbreviations

EF	*Elegiac Feelings American*
G	*Gasoline*
G/V	*Gasoline/Vestal Lady*
HA	*Herald of the Autochthonic Spirit*
HB	*Happy Birthday of Death*
LL	*Long Live Man*
M	*Mindfield*
MF	*Mind Field*
SP	*Selected Poems*
VL	*Vestal Lady*
WW	*Wings, Wands, Windows*

"A Clown
 in a Grave"

1

Introduction

On 1 July 1975, Chögyam Trungpa, Rinpoche (an honorific term meaning the dear or beloved one), lectured to students from an elevated stage at the Naropa Institute in Boulder, Colorado. Trungpa (1939–87), a brilliant and remarkable man, was raised since childhood to be supreme abbot of Eastern Tibet's Surmang monasteries and escaped to India in 1959 when the Chinese Communists took over Tibet. He went on to England, where he studied at Oxford University, and in 1970 he came to the United States, where he founded several Buddhist contemplative communities, including Naropa. About halfway through his lecture during that summer of 1975, a commotion erupted in the rear of the hall, and a member of the audience interrupted to say, "There's too much killing. You want to kill ego too. You want to say that I peaked and killed culture and I made it in America. You dumb ass. You're one of the best foreigners that came here when this country was gone sick." Trungpa thanked the heckler, who continued, "Trungpa, sufi, you picked on me that night when I read poetry. You're doing things with my head. Look, look around . . ." At this point the Rinpoche interrupted him to say, "I think you better shut up, sir, please, if you don't mind." The heckler persisted, "Do I mind? I would like to get an ambulance. My girlfriend's eye is bleeding." Trungpa, perhaps misunderstanding, commented, "That's good for you," and continued, "Watch your step, please," as the man and his friend were being conducted out of the lecture hall. As they reached the doors, Trungpa rather superfluously yelled, "Get out!" A last, resigned "Fuck you" came from the exiting figure. The heckler was Gregory Corso, who was there as part of the faculty for Naropa's Jack Kerouac School of Disembodied Poetics, a program founded by Allen Ginsberg and Anne Waldman. Trungpa's lecture was titled "Compassion" and focused on ego and authority as impediments to the expression of true compassion.

This incident seems representative of Gregory Corso's role in the Beat Generation. Like the Native American figure of Coyote, the Trickster, he has served as a disruptive force—self-centered, as unpredictable as a summer storm, unsettling the comfortable patterns of convention, and provoking those in contact with him to reassess their values, often much against their will. But Corso's impetuosity and spontaneity could work against him as well. During that same summer of 1975, stories were going around Naropa about Corso's meeting with a Japanese American student at a social gathering, where, echoing a line from his poem "Marriage," he said to her, "When are you going to stop people killing whales?" She flabbergasted him with her response: "When are you going to stop people killing Vietnamese?" Whether this story is apocryphal or not, Corso's public behavior has often been as irritating as that of a spoiled, or neglected, adolescent; the various symposia in which he participated and the recordings of his performances identified in the bibliography provide evidence of these exasperating patterns. He is enough to try the patience of a saint or an angel, or of a Trungpa or a Ginsberg. Jack Kerouac's portrayal of him as Yuri Gligoric in *The Subterraneans* and as Raphael Urso in *Desolation Angels* provides further evidence of the manic, incorrigible, and irrepressible nature of the fellow; and yet Kerouac, in a cover blurb for Corso's *Gasoline*, endorses him (along with Ginsberg) as one of "the two best poets in America," one "who rose like an angel over the rooftops and sang Italian songs as sweet as Caruso and Sinatra, but in *words*." Obviously, this poet is a tangled man.

Gregory Nunzio Corso was born in New York City on 26 March 1930. His mother, just sixteen years old when Gregory was born, abandoned the family a year later and returned to Italy, after which Corso spent his childhood in orphanages and foster homes. When the boy was eleven years old, his father remarried and brought Gregory into his home. But Corso repeatedly ran away, as he did also from a boy's home to which he was later removed. By his own accounts, Corso spent several months in the Tombs, the New York City jail, held as a material witness in a case involving a radio he stole. He also underwent three months of observation in Bellevue before being returned to his father's home, from which he ran away again.[1] Later, after living on the streets, he was convicted of theft at the age of seventeen and sentenced to Clinton State Prison for three years. Despite brutal treatment by the inmates, he benefited from his experience, reading widely from the prison library. Released in 1950, he met Allen Ginsberg in a Greenwich Village bar and formed a friendship, testy over the course of time, which lasted until the latter's death; through Ginsberg, he met William Burroughs and Jack Kerouac, as well as other New York literati and artists. In 1952, he worked for the *Los Angeles Examiner* and then shipped out as a merchant seaman. Returning to America, he went to Harvard University in 1954 as a drop in, and students in the area funded publication of his first volume of poems, *The Vestal Lady on Brattle and Other Poems*. In 1956, he joined Ginsberg in San Francisco, and

Lawrence Ferlinghetti solicited poems that City Lights published as *Gasoline*. Since then, he has traveled extensively, particularly in Mexico, North Africa, and Eastern Europe, though frequently returning to New York City as his home base.

In 1957, Corso joined Kerouac and Ginsberg for raucous and madcap readings, press conferences, and interviews. He taught at the State University of New York at Buffalo in 1965, but his appointment was terminated when he refused to sign a state-required loyalty oath. His major publications after *Gasoline* include *The Happy Birthday of Death* (1960), *The American Express* (1961), *Long Live Man* (1962), *Elegiac Feelings American* (1970), and *Herald of the Autochthonic Spirit* (1981). Corso's heroin and alcohol problems, which he confronts in a number of his poems, have apparently limited his poetic output since 1963, but the 1991 volume *Mindfield: New and Selected Poems* renewed interest in his materials.

Corso's reading while in prison provided him with a lifelong appreciation for the established poets of what is commonly called the 'canon,' and his association with the emergent Beat writers introduced him to the more emancipated poetry of the spontaneous and unconventional avant-garde. Throughout his career, his poetry provides testimony to a collision between these two forces. His early efforts were supported by Mark Van Doren, Randall Jarrell, and William Carlos Williams, all of whom recognized potential in the undisciplined talent of the earnest young writer. Corso's career seems characterized by the conflicting tensions of his ragged life, his autodidactic education, and his disparate influences. Childishly innocent, he crosses the boundaries of legality; his independence of spirit challenges the rigidity of his Catholic upbringing; and he seems as comfortable with Whitmanesque long-line indulgence as with the lapidary precision of Emily Dickinson—as relaxed in surreal juxtapositions as he is in prosaic diatribe.

Corso became especially infatuated with the British Romantic poets, particularly with the figure of Percy Bysshe Shelley, whose role as a writer and as a prototypical rebel cannot be underestimated when examining Corso's work. He has fondly and repeatedly cited "beloved Shelley" ("Columbia U," *HA* 4) as his poetic master and model: "With a love a madness for Shelley" ("I Am 25," *G/V* 36); "Shelley is my ichor" ("After Reading," *LL* 89); "that is why I like Shelley so much, . . . he did know how to blend the fanciful with the real, he was above all a true man, a goodly man, I feel he did honor to human kind" ("Dear Fathers" 11; ellipsis added); "And my heart has always held to Chatterton, Rimbaud, Shelley" ("Between" 39); "No, the only writing I like is Shelley, and Poe. It's weird. Rimbaud, of course, but I'm giving up on him now. I'm dwindling down now to Shelley and Poe" ("Sources" 2); "That's a good thing in life to find Shelley when you're a kid" (qtd. in Cherkovski 195). Dom Moraes recounts a comically characteristic anecdote about Corso's visit to Oxford:

> I took Gregory to look at Shelley lying obscene in white marble at
> University College. He inquired whether he was allowed to kiss the
> statue's foot. I said probably not. He then demanded to know where
> Shelley's rooms were. I had not the faintest idea but indicated the
> nearest door. I hadn't dreamed that he would want to enter, but he
> did; he flung open the door and crawled over the carpet, kissing it
> reverently, inch by inch, while its occupant, who prior to his arrival
> had been making tea, stared at him in dumbfounded silence. (66)

As early as 1959, Corso indicates that his appreciation of Shelley stems from the Romantic poet's use of imagination to transcend the bleakness of ordinary life: "Shelley is a good example of a poet who, conscious and heartfelt for social conditions remedied such dour by ethereal inspiration" (Letter to Editor, *Cambridge*). Corso's interest in Shelley is also reflected in titles of his poems: "I Held a Shelley Manuscript" and "On Gregory Being Double the Age of Shelley." Furthermore, in a 1959 letter to the editor of the *Nation*, written with Ginsberg and Peter Orlovsky, Corso signed himself "in respect to Shelley." In addition, Corso strongly identifies with the poetic role of the herald cited by Shelley, and he repeatedly celebrates this mission: "the America I heralded" ("Elegiac," *EF* 9); *Herald of the Autochthonic Spirit*. His adoption of this role was clear to his fellow Beat writers: in a linked-verse poem written by Ginsberg and Corso, the latter writes, "In ready ritual trumpet blown Herald! Herald!" and goes on to offer "Herald!" three more times in his next four entries, leading Ginsberg to respond amusingly, "How many Heralds must I suffer, ear-aflame, O Horn?" (Corso and Ginsberg, "ALGREINORSO" 313). Such self-proclamation is undoubtedly also responsible for Kerouac's cover-blurb reference to him as "the one & only Gregory the Herald" (*G/V*). Corso even suggests that he is fated for this role, citing his middle name as evidence: "I abide by my name I have a very unique name, one that almost marks me, I was born on the annunciation, I was named Nunzio, plus Gregory plus Corso, which means Watchful Announcer—The Way" ("Dear Fathers" 8); "Thank you, Gregorio Nunzio Corso—my full name, which means: The Watchful One, The Announcer, The Way" ("In This," *New Directions* 161);

> I am Nunzio
> today my birthday Annunciation Day
> I am bathed, dressed, and doted upon
>   by the pigs of prophecy . . .
> I've one final message to deliver.
>
>   ("I am rich")

Additional passages from a number of Corso's works show a thematic indebtedness to those of Shelley, particularly to "Ode to the West Wind," about which

Corso enthusiastically comments, "That poem, 'Ode to the West Wind' is one of the greatest poems ever written" (Interview with R. King 19):

> *And winter does come*
>
> ("You, Whose," *G/V* 89)

> Though the West Wind seemed to harbor there not one
> pure Shelleyean dream of let's say hay-
> > like universe
>
> ("Ode to Coit," *G/V* 13)

> There goes my hair! shackled to a clumping wind!
> Come back, hair, come back!
> I want to grow sideburns!
> I want to wash you, comb you, sun you, love you!
> as I ran from you wild before
>
> ("Hair," *HB* 15–16)

> And these apples whose certain death breeds more
>
> ("Apples," *M* 219)

> Time, I'll treat you as you are
> I'll not Ah Autumn you anymore
> Though I've a feeling lyric heart
> And by the feeling I know the lyre
>
> ("Written While Watching Lenny Bruce" 56)

> There was a time plenty of time
> running ahead so fast the wildcarefree
> flight seemed a standstill
>
> ("Eleven," *EF* 33)

> The clarion for departure *blew over the dreaming earth—*.
> > (*American Express*, 235)

Despite these allusions and borrowings, Jim Burns asserts,

> His [Corso's] enthusiasm (and that is, I think, the right word) for
> Shelley, although undoubtedly genuine in its appreciation of the
> poems, had much to do with the way in which the Romantic poet
> flouted convention, dedicated himself to poetry, and was a leading
> light of a group of brilliant individuals. (53)

Burns here articulates a position shared by other critics of Corso, and Bruce Cook even titles his chapter on Corso "An Urchin Shelley." Corso himself has lent support to such a position: "The one who really turned me on very much was Shelley, not too much his poetry, but his life. I said, 'Ah, a poet then could really live a good life on this planet'" (Interview with R. King 6). Corso has also repeatedly indicated that he values Shelley for his role as a "revolutionary of the spirit" (Interview with G. Selerie 28, 42, 43).

The Romantics are a clearly discernible influence on the themes and concerns of the Beat poets, most of whom (especially Ginsberg, Kerouac, Corso, and Ferlinghetti) can be seen as urban Romantics of the twentieth century. For Corso, the Romantic celebration of the innocence and naturalness of childhood is particularly evident, even in the poems that bemoan a hazardous upbringing (Kerouac too shares this fascination with the innate purity of the child), a nostalgia that seems to depend on the child's very helplessness. On a larger scale, that nostalgia can also involve what Corso sees as the more innocent periods in human civilization, treasuring classicism and the noble savage of prerational, primitive culture.

The one factor on which any child can depend is imagination—a versatile Romantic tool that can, at an extreme, offer a bittersweet escape. Like Keats's narrator in "Ode to a Nightingale," Corso can find himself "half in love with easeful Death," can call it "soft names" and wish it a "Happy Birthday," or he can dismiss it like the Keats of "Ode on a Grecian Urn" as a "Cold Pastoral"—and even recognize that he is doing both at the same time. The very precariousness of such an existence leads to a Romantic celebration of experience, a desire to capture life in all its fullness of Faustian/Byronic intensity, and a sense that unless life has been thrown into jeopardy, the ultimate gamble, it is not worth living. As a result, the rebels, the ones who risk all, become the models, the champions—even Lucifer (whose name originally means light-bearer) suggests a Promethean illumination and vitality for mortals. They seize the day, *carpe diem*—or more precisely, they twist the maxim to *carpe noctem* (seize the night), when one is free of the labors of the day, when forbidden delights and pleasures are made available. The hero becomes a Goethean Werther, tormented by the disillusionment of the age; a wild Heathcliff storming the moors in a passion and intensity bordering on murder or suicide; a visionary or a psychopath—and sometimes both.

The rejection of the norm, of complacency, leads to another important parallel to Corso's writings: Surrealism. In the introduction to Corso's *Gasoline*, Ginsberg calls attention to the "weird haiku-like juxtapositions" and his "jumps of the strangest phrasing" (7). Corso also offers evidence of this quality in the "Saleable Titles" provided opposite the title page of *The Happy Birthday of Death*: "Fried Shoes," "Radiator Soup," "Gargoyle liver" (2). In an accelerated age of scientific and technological innovation, the efficacy of artistic production often seems, if not suspect, at least beside the point. For many artists, surrealism offers to alleviate creative anxiety in several ways. First, surrealism defies rationality, demanding to be measured by the caliper of the imagination rather than that of logic. Secondly, its emphasis upon spontaneity and automaticism safely attributes the source of artistic inspiration to the as-yet-unplumbed depths of unconscious or subconscious thought. The Romantics differentiated between brain and mind, with the former limited to rational analysis and the latter expanding to include fancy, imagination, and dream; thus, in "Ode to a Nightingale," Keats finds that "the dull brain perplexes and retards" (*Poems* 370). Similarly, the Surrealists privilege fantasy and dream, investing their capriciousness and unpredictability with value, and the Beats, Corso in particular, follow them in prizing oneiric ventures beyond the province of analysis and precise definition.

André Breton's prescription for the Surrealist creative process bears significant similarities to the methods of the Beats, particularly those recommended by Jack Kerouac, even with a road metaphor that anticipates Kerouac's imagery and tone:

> After you have settled yourself in a place as favorable as possible to the concentration of your mind upon itself, have writing materials brought to you. Put yourself in as passive, or receptive, a state of mind as you can. Forget about your genius, your talents, and the talents of everyone else. Keep reminding yourself that literature is one of the saddest roads that leads to everything. Write quickly, without any preconceived subject, fast enough so that you will not remember what you're writing and be tempted to reread what you have written. (29–30)

> SET-UP. The object is set before the mind, either in reality, as in sketching (before a landscape or teacup or old face) or is set in the memory wherein it becomes the sketching from memory of a definite image-object. (Kerouac, "Essentials" 69)

> Submissive to everything, open, listening

> No fear or shame in the dignity of yr experience, language & knowledge

> Accept loss forever. (Kerouac, "Belief" 72–73)

> PROCEDURE. Time being of the essence in the purity of speech, sketching language is undisturbed flow from the mind of personal secret idea-words, *blowing* (as per jazz musician) on subject of image.

> SCOPING. Not "selectivity" of expression but following free deviation (association) of mind into limitless blow-on-subject seas of thought, swimming in sea of English with no discipline other than rhythms of rhetorical exhalation and expostulated statement, like a fist coming down on a table with each complete utterance, bang! (Kerouac, "Essentials" 69)

As casual, generalized directions, the prescriptions become parodies of the controlled scientific experiment. Surrealist experiments anticipate many of the procedures of the Beats. The cut-up techniques of William S. Burroughs were prefigured by the surrealists, most notably by Tristan Tzara (Sami Rosenstock, 1896–1963), the Rumanian-born Dadaist who "had pulled cut-up words out of a hat at a Surrealist rally and made a poem out of them" (T. Morgan 300). Lawrence Ferlinghetti's plays are influenced by surrealist performances, and he specifically acknowledges Breton's *Nadja* as an inspiration for *The Victims of Amnesia* and describes his novel *Her* as a "surreal" book. Kerouac's "spontaneous bop prosody" and Corso's spontaneous and automatic poems also stem from the surrealist limb. However, most important for the Beats, especially for the poets, is the influence of the surrealist image, which Breton clearly associates with spontaneous creation: "It is true of Surrealist images as it is of opium images that man does not evoke them; rather they 'come to him spontaneously, despotically. He cannot chase them away; for the will is powerless now and no longer controls the faculties'" (36).[2] Breton continues, using imagery that again evokes the pseudoscientific dimension:

> It is, as it were, from the fortuitous juxtaposition of the two terms that a particular light has sprung, *the light of the image*, to which we are infinitely sensitive. The value of the image depends upon the beauty of the spark obtained; it is, consequently, a function of the difference of potential between the two conductors. (37)

The classic pattern of this image (and language) was established by the precocious Comte de Lautréamont (Isidore Ducasse, 1846–70), who in 1890 presented "the fortuitous encounter upon a dissecting-table of a sewing-machine and an umbrella" (263). The success of the image depends upon the startling, imaginative displacement of commonplace objects, resulting in a pattern of irrationality ideally reflecting aspects of the subconscious mind.

What makes Corso preeminent among the Beats influenced by surrealism is his effective use of humor, ranging from the unusual structures producing gentle smiles of the mind to whole poems that seem to exist only for the radical displacement, or punch line, which brings the work to closure. Corso is ever alert for the natural surrealism of the times, whether it be the found-poem quality of "Direction Sign in London Zoo" or the more profound concept of a country bombing itself in "Many Have Fallen." As halfhearted as it may have been, his participation in the cut-up experiments of William Burroughs, echoing the tactics of Tzara, nonetheless influenced the imagery and structure of many of his most mature and important works.

In terms of American literary influences, at times Corso seems to have skipped the first half of the twentieth century, deriving much of his influence from the poets of the nineteenth century (particularly those most likely to be found in a prison library, and Whitman and Dickinson, as unlikely as the pairing of the two seems to be on a formal level). In a true Romantic vein, he yearns for simpler times, particularly those that viewed America as a frontier with Edenic possibilities.[3] But he also recognizes that his yearnings are sentimental and so rejects conventional values, throwing Truth, Love, "Faith Hope Charity," and Beauty out the window—though he does rescue the latter value ("The Whole Mess," *HA* 48). Maturity teaches him the sobering truths of existence, but he continues to esteem the ideals of what those abstractions could mean and how they could make lives valuable. This spirit too is essentially American in its rebellion against traditional authority and its nostalgia for less complicated, idealized times, when traditional values could meaningfully direct human behavior.

Especially noteworthy are the similarities between the Transcendentalists and the Beats. Both involved a loose group or community of participants in a movement rather than strict adherents to a systematized set of doctrines. Both groups were reacting to what they perceived as a cold, mechanical, and stifling stagnation of ideas and beliefs, and in each case they sought to revitalize the spirit and the intellect. Each movement sought a "new consciousness" that would elevate individualism and discover the divinity immanent in the human being. They rejected orthodox authority and, with Romantic idealism, favored social reform. Finally, both groups rebelled against the dominant rationalism of their times and replaced it with a trust in intuition and spontaneity. In particular, Corso reflects many aspects of the Transcendentalists, but his limited formal schooling and eclectic reading experience suggest that the connections could more appropriately be seen as parallels rather than as influences.

With the exception of the references to Shelley's influence noted earlier, little critical attention has been focused on the Romantic, Transcendental, and Surreal links to Corso's work; but then critics have devoted little attention to Corso at all. What is available tends to focus on biography and reminiscence, which is a pattern that has long been true of approaches to other Beat writers as well. Most analysts seem to consider the primary contribution of Beat writers to be sociological rather than literary. Two notable exceptions are the analyses by Marilyn Schwartz and Gregory Stephenson. Schwartz's essay, one of the few to really engage Corso's poems, examines the dialectic of creative and destructive elements in his works, and she offers insightful treatment of several specific poems, especially "Bomb," "Power," and "Eleven Times a Poem." On the other hand, she discerns a chronological development in Corso's books, but only by being terribly selective in her focus on poems in successive volumes, and she completely ignores his novel, *The American Express*. Stephenson's slender monograph, *Exiled Angel*, is the only book previous to this one devoted to Corso's work. Published in 1989, it explores Corso's individual volumes, as well as his plays. *Exiled Angel* and Stephenson's essay "The Arcadian Map" in *The Daybreak Boys* are the stoutest recent attempts to show how certain themes recur with variations throughout Corso's work. Stephenson's book also devotes a chapter to *The American Express*, but he fails to focus on the parallels between the novel's characters and the members of the Beat Generation. Thus far, few critics have attempted to explore Corso's prosody in depth. The manuscripts of poems available in research libraries as well as the publication of variant stages of individual poems offer evidence of the attention that Corso devotes to the language and shape of his poems. Perhaps this study will help open the door to further examination of Corso's craft.

Corso's writings offer a surprising range of ideas and self-revelations. His poetic voice encompasses mawkish sentimentality and boisterous rambunctiousness, but always with an emotional honesty that is disarming. Even his moments of posturing seem strangely genuine, allowing the reader access to his rationalizations and his misgivings. He confronts the standard themes of great poetry, but with an idiosyncratic approach that offers fresh perspectives. At their best, his literary probes provide unique contributions that rank high among the productions of the Beat Generation writers and deserve closer attention than they have yet received.

2
The Uses of Imagination

To know is nothing at all;
  to imagine is everything.
              —Anatole France, *The Crime of Sylvestre Bonnard*

The increasingly personal and confessional quality in American poetry of the 1950s and 1960s was at least in part a reaction to a perception of the diminishing role of the individual within society and to a feeling of helplessness in the face of this loss. Thus, Seymour Krim describes the modern age as "a period when the terrifying bigness of society makes the average person resort to more immediate and practical oracles (psychiatrists, sociologists, chemists) than to the kind of imaginative truth that the artist can give" (126). Many artists attempted to reassert the primacy of individual worth, assuming that the artist's role had also been adversely affected. For Gregory Corso, the poetic attack on the forces that obscure or deny the value of the individual is especially important: he recognizes that "the world is changing therefore man must change, and the poet, who sooner than most becomes aware of the changing, must blow the trumpet" ("Some of My Beginning," *Poets* 177), no doubt the "trumpet of a prophecy" from Shelley's "Ode to the West Wind."[1] Corso's visionary poetic voice celebrates the inviolability of the human spirit, subsuming strengths and vices, weaknesses and virtues. Like Walt Whitman, he glories in his self-contradiction, a quality that is most evident in the consistency of Corso's vacillation. He sings the uniqueness of the human being in terms of the nonrational imaginative capacity and of the indefinability of the human mind.

In an age in which the industrial criterion of maximum efficiency too often predominates, Corso deliberately extols the idiosyncratic imperfection of humanity. The mad, deviant, and criminal elements, those who disturb the smooth functioning of conventional society, exert an especially romantic appeal for him because they resist assimilation by the standards and values of the established civilized world: they are round pegs that will not fit into square holes. Steve Dossey recalls Corso's expression of a principle relevant to this neo-Romantic position:

> The poet, he [Corso] said, is by necessity in opposition with society. If society is insane, the poet must bring it to reason. Then he concluded with sparkling eyes, if society is rational, the poet must create an insane sensibility to render that society meaningful.

Unpredictability and amorality represent to Corso a refusal or an inability to surrender to the disabling and standardizing forces of modern times. Chandler Brossard provides a model in *Who Walk in Darkness*, his provocative and influential 1952 novel, when he describes a character whose "ideal is to look like a street-corner hoodlum and be the finest lyric poet in America at the same time" (74). Corso, constantly aware of the disheveled appearance that he cultivated as well as his humanistic concerns, fits this projection well. Bruce Cook also notices this disposition in Corso: "Corso, the poet, is self-invented, a fantasy projection of his own John Garfield self, the slum kid who wants all, takes all, only to feel it trickle through his fingers as he grasps it tight in his hands" (134).[2] Similarly, Kenneth Rexroth describes Corso as "a genuine *naif*. A real wildman, with all the charm of a hoodlum Le Douanier Rousseau, a wholesome Antonin Artaud, or a 'sincere' Tristan Tzara" (*Assays* 194).[3] In fact, Corso's incarceration in New York City's infamous Tombs and in Clinton Prison might even suggest that he comes by his reputation honestly. Jeff Nuttall points to the contrast between this background and the middle-class experience of the other Beat writers and observes that

> the delinquent came to be revered not only as a creature liberated of morality and superego but also as a person whose way of life served as a protection against the massive public guilt of the Korean war and the H bomb. He, like the hipster whose descendant he was, showed an alternative way of life to that of society. Gregory Corso and Ray Bremser, therefore, excellent poets though they both are by any standards, were both adopted by the group largely for their delinquency and the special frisson which it created. (111–12)[4]

This frisson of the dangerous and forbidden experience manifests itself in Corso's poetry in its spirit of daring recklessness and the trembling bravado of a dead-end kid who tweaks the nose of authority—religious, social, or national—and then races around the corner:

> Summoning Death and God
> I'd a wild dare to tackle Them
>
> ("Writ on the Steps," *LL* 77)

> I care nothing for my blood
> and dare the things I most fear
> when I do not care if truth is forever
>
> ("Dear Villon, Dear Milarepa," *Unmuzzled Ox* [#22] 104)

> I could never understand Uncle Sam
> his red & white striped pants his funny whiskers his starry
>   hat:
> how surreal Yankee Doodle Dandy, goof!
>
> ("America Politica," *EF* 95)

Imagining being challenged by the proposition that "you are governed by laws of society," he responds, "But I'm trying to avoid that" ("Variations," *Casebook* 89). Corso ignores the sensational material that might be of special interest to many of his readers, usually avoiding direct exploration of his prison experiences as poetic material: "If one must climb a ladder to reach a height and from that height see, then it were best to write about what you see and not about how you climbed. Prison to me was such a ladder" ("Some of My Beginning," *Poets* 173). Nevertheless, risk, jeopardy, and danger are staples of his poetry, and he recognizes a constant attraction and vulnerability to forces of which he cannot intellectually or morally approve:

> I know I'm one who
>   even if he does see the light
> still won't be completely all right
>   and good for that.
>
> ("Writ in Horace," *LL* 84)

Such awareness of the tensions between his enlightened understanding and his promiscuous behavior provides the foundation for identity as complicated and tangled as a pile of wire clothes hangers; the conflicts presage a life of alternating apology and defensiveness.

Corso indicates that his self-recognition, coupled, of course, with experiential knowledge of the world, results in conflicting views of humanity: "thus i know man as best i can, and thru myself i know him, and when i trust myself i trust him, but never held i complete faith in him, complete trust" (Letter to William Burroughs 160–61), for he believes "[w]hat makes man man is both the beauty and the monster in him. . . . If he dances with a rose in his mouth, he must also be ready to march with a gun in his hand" ("Berlin Impressions" 83; ellipsis added). In poetic form, this ambiguity reveals itself as vacillation:

> Yesterday I believed in man today I don't
> and tomorrow
> tomorrow's a toss-up
>
> Somedays I see all people
> in deep pain with life
> And other days
> I see them victors.

("Writ in Horace," *LL* 84)

The source of this uncertainty is self-analysis, examination of his own forked being. The frequent result of his uncertainty is that his assertions can be simultaneously authoritative and hesitant: "Stooped and hushed Chronicleleer of Spenserian gauderies / Is surely maybe my Power" ("Power," *HB* 79). Uncertainty is seldom celebrated as a literary strength, but it is "surely maybe" an accurate characteristic of the human condition. At times, Corso even prides himself on the discrepancy between his principles and his feelings: "I am able to contradict my beliefs" ("Writ on the Steps," *LL* 77); "It were best to contradict" ("To Die Laughing [?]," *LL* 58); "But I am constantly changing! Contradiction will rescue me, I am sure, and as I can not dislike anything for long I am sure that I will change my mind about this, but I must change it honorably, nobley" (Introduction 252). At its worst, this stance suggests the aggravating presumption of Rumpelstiltskin delighting in the fact that no one knows his name; at its best, it provides a valuable and probing comment on the tensions between individual integrity and the patterns, themselves often conflicting, prescribed by social convention. "Hair" and "Marriage," two of Corso's more popular long poems, offer extended studies of these clashes and of each narrator's attitudes as they erratically collide with stereotypes and norms like pinballs bouncing off stationary bumpers, providing what he calls in a later poem "a multitude of variable thought" ("Field Report," *M* 256).

In "Hair," the narrator begins by mourning the fact that he is balding. He recalls earlier days when he devoted careful and loving attention to his hair and regrets his baldness as an indicator of waning youth—"And when I dream I dream children waving goodbye"—and of the loss of the accoutrements of innocence and intensity so often associated with the young: "Now how can old ladies cookie me? / How to stand thunderous on an English cliff / a hectic Heathcliff?" (*HB* 14). The second stanza of the poem concludes with tongue-in-cheek resignation based on the assumption that energy and sexual attractiveness are the provinces of youth: "Bald! I'm bald! / Best now I get a pipe / and forget girls." The next stanza begins by linking the loss of hair with the loss of identity: "Subways take me one of your own / seat me anybody / let me off any station anyman" (15). The identification of hair loss with personal anonymity in a civilized urban environment is based on the superficiality of physical appearance.

The narrator continues his regrets and then suddenly interrupts with a preposterous attempt to rationalize his plight: he exclaims, "Wrestlers are bald / And though I'm thin O God give me chance now to wrestle." The syntactical ambiguity here conjures an image of the speaker wrestling with Chance for a prize of hirsuteness. However, he recognizes the absurdity of this projected career and in an exaggerated gesture of despair begs for "even a nose hair, an ingrown hair." In the fourth stanza, he passionately pleads for the return of his hair and again highlights social values as he betrays a self-consciousness regarding his image and appearance:

> I thought surely this nineteen hundred and fifty nine of now
> that I need no longer bite my fingernails
> but have handsome gray hair
> to show how profoundly nervous I am.

(16)

By the last stanza, his despair is transformed into a furious denunciation of the intrinsic value of hair: "Damned be hair! / Hair that must be plucked from soup! / Hair that clogs the bathtub!" The poem concludes with an ironic litany of hair-associated images: "Veronica Lake Truman Capote Ishka Bibble Messiahs Paganinis / Bohemians Hawaiians poodles."[5] The fact that these images are stereotypical and/or derivative of popular culture is crucial, for the theme of the poem concerns neither the desirability nor the undesirability of hair. Instead, the poem explores the situation of the narrator in terms of a superficial social signifier, a phenomenon recognized by many harassed beats and hippies and later exploited in the popular Broadway musical *Hair*. Thus, Abbie Hoffman can refer to "what we as long-hairs experience all the time—the experience of living in a police state and the beauty of our alternative society" (65), capturing in a radical sense the ambiguities of Corso's poem. "Hair" follows the vacillating moods of the speaker caught in a blind alley of convention. In this sense, the poem reaches no conclusion—it simply stops. One could well imagine the narrator ricocheting interminably between helpless regret and defensive recalcitrance.

In similar fashion, "Marriage" comprises variations on a theme, continually sliding from one assumed attitude to another, refusing to offer a definitive stance regarding its ostensible object. The opening line of the poem provides the thematic crux: "Should I get married? Should I be good?" (*HB* 29). The poem then takes off on a comical ride through the ritualized conventions encountered in such a decision: courtship, obligatory and uncomfortable meeting with the intended's parents, wedding and reception, honeymoon, housekeeping, childbirth, and parenthood. The speaker imagines himself within stock cinematic images of marital settings (rural Connecticut suburb, bleak New York City apartment "seven flights up," sophisticated New York penthouse) and rejects them all, while still recognizing their seductions and embodying his ambivalence in a memorable oxymoron: "No, can't imagine myself married to that pleasant prison dream" (32). The narrator's reluctance stems from his inability to imagine himself forsaking the unpredictable and unconventional outlook upon which he prides himself. He conceives of himself in wildly imaginative and surrealistically disruptive patterns:

> So much to do! like sneaking into Mr Jones' house late at night
> and cover his golf clubs with 1920 Norwegian books
> Like hanging a picture of Rimbaud on the lawnmower
> like pasting Tannu Tuva postage stamps all over the picket fence
> like when Mrs Kindhead comes to collect for the Community Chest
> grab her and tell her There are unfavorable omens in the sky!
> And when the mayor comes to get my vote tell him
> When are you going to stop people killing whales!
> And when the milkman comes leave him a note in the bottle
> Penguin dust, bring me penguin dust, I want penguin dust—.[6]

(30–31)

These projected actions become a nonviolent assault on the equanimity of dull, routine modern life. The speaker can anticipate joining the mainstream only if he can retain his penchant for roiling that stream, destroying its placid stability, and investing it with an energetic unpredictability to prevent it from becoming stagnant. Thus, in a world estranged from classical culture and values, he imagines himself as an ideal father eager to give his child

> for a nipple a rubber Tacitus
> For a rattle a bag of broken Bach records
> Tack Della Francesca all over its crib
> Sew the Greek alphabet on its bib
> And build for its playpen a roofless Parthenon.[7]

(31)

However, as Richard Howard points out, "the prospect of withholding himself from the common fate is just as painful for Corso as the doom of conformity" (82). The rebellion against current standardized norms also threatens projected isolation for the rebel: "what if I'm 60 years old and not married, / all alone in a furnished room with pee stains on my underwear / and everybody else is married! All the universe married but me!" ("Marriage," *HB* 32). Finally, yearning for a form of integration, yet unwilling to sacrifice his own values, the persona can only retreat into the fantasized safety of an ideal "SHE," the eponymous, timeless H. Rider Haggard goddess whose integrity matches his own.[8] The speaker is unable to resolve in a practical, realistic manner his vacillation between assimilation by the human community and preservation of the idiosyncratic self. As Jim Burns notes, "It is the indecisiveness that gives the poem its humanity" (55). The indecisiveness also gives the poem its form, structure, and strategy.

"Hair" and "Marriage" provide models for many of Corso's poems. Typically, he deliberately courts disjunction and ambivalence, explaining, "Their clarion-warnings discord / the rhythms I walk to hear" ("Cambridge, First," *G/V* 97). Often this discord results in "[c]ontradiction, that good virtue" ("Writ in Horace," *LL* 84), which Corso repeatedly invokes and celebrates. Of course, the virtue also has a rich pedigree in American literature, most famously in Whitman's "Song of Myself"—"Do I contradict myself? / Very well then I contradict myself, / (I am large, I contain multitudes.)" (88)—and in Emerson's essay on "Self-Reliance":

> A foolish consistency is the hobgoblin of little minds, adored by little statesmen and philosophers and divines. With consistency a great soul has simply nothing to do. . . . Speak what you think now in hard words and to-morrow speak what to-morrow thinks in hard words again, though it contradict every thing you said to-day. (33; ellipsis added)

Similarly in *The American Express*, one of Corso's characters offers what appears to be Corso's own praise: "What makes a man not dead, to me at least, is his ability to contradict what he a moment ago believed with all his heart" (161). The sources of the "virtue" lie in the poet's view of existence, which he provides by explaining "that is why I admit contradiction, I am contradictory because I am of life and life is contradictory" ("Dear Fathers" 11), and in his self-knowledge: "A drunk dreamer in reality / is an awful contradiction" ("Getting," *HA* 34).[9] In an essay he wrote with Allen Ginsberg, Corso goes so far as to suggest that this quality and his vocation as poet are inseparable: "I am a poet, therefore I am apt to contradict myself" ("Literary" 193). What might at first seem a form of schizophrenia is actually a Whitmanesque expansiveness of vision that allows the poet to acknowledge opposite extremes. Corso rather narrowly asserts that the recognition of such duality is one of the contributions made by the Beat writers: "The Beat Generation is because truth rests on the contradictory rattans of the soul" (Corso, Ginsberg, and Orlovsky 30). Thus, as much as Corso desires to believe that "[m]an is the victory of life," he is forced to admit that "[t]he fall of man stands a lie before Beethoven, / A truth before Hitler" ("Man," *LL* 10) and to endorse the evaluation provided by his character Rodger in *The American Express*: "I think I know the makeup of man, and I feel he is both monster and angel" (218). The acceptance of these contradictions, both in himself and in humanity, corresponds to Keats's "*Negative Capability*, that is when man is capable of being in uncertainties, Mysteries, doubts, without any irritable reaching after fact & reason" (*Letters* 193). Corso feels no need to resolve the contradiction and ambiguities his poems discover, for "[p]oetry is seeking the answer" ("Notes after," *HB* 11), not finding the answer; reflecting the principle that the job of the writer is to present a problem, rather than to solve it, the poem then is a process, an exploration, not a resolution. In fact, he indicates his objection to didacticism in poetry:

> it is not the poet's duty to be serious about condition because the poet lacks remedy, it is the politician's duty, the doctor's duty, the lawyer's duty, they have the remedy, their seriousness is justified, the poet's is not, the only thing the poet need be serious about is beauty, the unknown, the magnificent dream. ("Literary" 193)

As a result, much of his poetry lacks a conventional sense of closure, making many of his poems seem like fragments, jottings, rather than finished products. Readers accustomed to a neat resolution in poetry—a pithy solution to uncertainties—are likely to find unsatisfactory many of Corso's poems that refuse to reach a conclusion, settling instead for a judicious acceptance of the contradictions and conflicts of life.

A similar double vision appears in Corso's self-characterization. He portrays his mixed patriotic feelings about America, revealing an ambivalence characteristic of many of the Beat writers:

> O whenever I pass an American Embassy I don't know what to feel!
> Sometimes I want to rush in and scream: "I'm American!"
> but instead go a few paces down to the American Bar
> get drunk and cry: "I'm no American!"
>
> ("America Politica," *EF* 95)

In the peculiar position of having mixed feelings about ambivalence, he also seems unable to decide whether his vatic role is that of savior or con man: "I dark mad ah solace dreams grace miracle quack awful O!" ("Death," *HB* 41);

> Ah,
>   this surfeit of charlatanry
> will never leave my organic pyx
>   thank God.
>
> ("Clown," *HB* 61)

Bruce Cook suggests that "[f]or Gregory Corso, the simple act of choosing has always provided profound difficulties. It is a theme that runs through his poetry—decision-making or, alternatively, refusing to decide—and it can be read even more plainly in the record of his life" (133); similarly, Richard Howard sees "Marriage" as a poem "about the impossibility of choosing" (82). One is reminded of the fabled Buridan's ass, which starved to death because it could not choose between two equivalent stacks of hay. However, Corso's choices are hardly the "simple" ones Cook alleges, even though they may be common, and the poet feels that human complexity obviates easy decisions: "Mine the true labyrinth, it is my soul, Theseus; / try a ball of string in *that*!" ("Paranoia," *HB* 51); conflicting but equally powerful values and principles support each alternative, each possible corridor in the maze of life.

Corso's response sometimes has all the earmarks of facile paradox. Howard has perceptively noted that "[t]he great thing, for Corso, is *not to choose*, not to settle for the possible, but to take everything" (80). Thus, evoking Robert Frost's "The Road Not Taken," Corso suggests, "No choice of two roads; if there were, / I don't doubt I'd have chosen both" ("Writ on the Eve," *LL* 93); "If you have a choice / between two things / and cannot decide / —take both" ("Getting," *HA* 34).[10] Corso is apparently serious: for him, goals can be accomplished, and, therefore, dreams and reality are not by necessity mutually exclusive. Mere accessibility cannot be the determinant if values are to remain intact: "And all around are apples ripe for the picking / but I go for that out of reach one / and quite make it" ("There Can Be," *LL* 74). This is the imaginative power to which Corso so often returns in his poetry—the ability to create human possibilities despite restrictions, frustrations, and denials. Reality, which can so often shackle life, is irrelevant to the strength of the imaginative powers. As he asserts in "Power," "Since I contradict the real with the unreal / Nothing is so unjust as impossibility" (*HB* 75). For Corso, ideals are not unreal—they are simply not yet realized, not yet chosen.

Most often Corso's choices lean in the direction of imagination. Allen Ginsberg has noted that Corso maintains "[a] rare sad goonish knowledge with reality—a hip piss on reality also—he prefers his dreams" (Introduction, *G/V* 8). Thus, his preference provides an escape from life's harshness:

> I would a tinkler of dreams be
> deluded in zodiacal pretence
> than have to wonder such reality
> as human violence.

> ("Eleven," *EF* 32)

On a smaller scale, a major drawback of the very real responsibilities of "Marriage" is that the narrator feels it would be "[i]mpossible to lie back and dream Telephone snow, ghost parking" (*HB* 31). The core of his objection parallels that in W. B.

Yeats's "The Song of the Happy Shepherd": "Of old the world on dreaming fed; / Grey Truth is now her painted toy" (7). Corso's preference for imagination springs from a distrust of tawdry reality and from a fear that modern society threatens to extinguish fantasy—and with it individuality. In "Mutation of the Spirit," he makes his complaint explicit:

> TRUTH ABOVE ALL the demand
> I am a wreck of truth Damn such demand
> I cried I would rather my value be true
> than truth be my value.
>
> (*EF* 23)

His objection is that reliance on and subservience to abstract truth and reality can lock human beings into enervated acceptance of the status quo. Thus, he apostrophizes, "Truth why has man Frankensteined you / You are the *big lie* Truth / It is you who stops man from outstepping himself" ("Greece," *LL* 26). What Corso endorses instead is a Keatsian truth that maintains a symbiotic relationship with beauty: "We came to announce the human spirit in the name of beauty and truth" ("Elegiac," *EF* 5); "beauties and the joys of them / superimpose their truth upon all the lies" ("Eyes," *HA* 37). He refuses to "make beauty miserable with horrible truths" ("Dear Villon, Dear Milarepa," *Unmuzzled Ox* [#22] 104); the beauty with which Corso involves himself celebrates the unfettered imagination, free to frolic, sing, and dance.

Corso asserts that imagination, rather than contemporary objectivity, provides the vital key to understanding and perception: "Since I observe memory and dream / And not the images of the moment / I am become more vivid" ("Power," *HB* 75). Furthermore, the combination to which he refers becomes creative, fashioning its own reality:

> The occurence is in the remembrance
> Whenever from dreams I awaken
> the dream I cannot recall
> is like no dream at all
> Remembering that which happened
> makes happen.[11]
>
> ("occurence")

However, he believes that the modern world discourages the tendency to indulge in imagination. Thus, in his brief play, "Standing on a Streetcorner," a woman complains against the protagonist, "Action, not talk! Not dreams!" (457). Corso suggests that the discouragement from engaging the world of dreams in any meaningful capacity begins at an early age:

Look at the babe born today in this age—as soon as he is able to walk, his Liberace loving parents wouldn't think of giving him Latin and Greek, no because that doesn't make money, so they send him off to school for a terrible knowledge. If once in school he dreams, if once he tires of trivial things, "lazy lazy!" the teacher screams, while all the while in his little heart an ocean sings . . . they're educating kids to-day to do anything but dream.[12] ("In This," *New Directions* 154; el-lipsis added)

Furthermore, the "dreamless world" of materialistic and practical values im-poses severe punishment on those who will not or cannot conform to it: "in America most all the young impractical dreamy emotional genius angelic poets are or have been in a madhouse" ("Literary" 193). Though these demographics may be exaggerated, the point is that the American pursuit of success stigmatizes sensitivity and imagination as pointless and unproductive, even shameful. For Corso, such damage is especially to be regretted because he associates imagina-tion with youthful health, granting it a crucial role in the process of maturation:

The imagination in its infancy is born of a young man's mind. A child need not imagine, to a child life is imagination—but to a young man, a young man face to face with inexorable truth, suffering the pangs of surging suicidal romance, and a trickster Fate's injustice, to this new soul the realist's real is not real enough. His intense sense of reality, without the grace of the imagination, would present him a life im-possible to live. ("Between" 39)

Thus, in the midst of youth's darkest moments of disappointment, loss, or trag-edy, imagination is the vehicle for the projection of alternatives to disillusionment, for intimations that gloom need not be permanent, and for hopes that can tran-scend the rational recognition that human pleasures fade. Corso regrets that "THINK signs will never give way to DREAM signs" ("Power," *HB* 76): he be-lieves that an artificial world has already been imposed on humanity, and unfor-tunately it does not spring from intrinsic values: "[Louella Parsons is] a dictator of the mind, that's why. She whores you off to a phony dream world that oozes over with a gush and sentiment, a peaches and cream world that doesn't even have a john in it—when she shows you the moon she shows you an Alice Faye moon, not the moon" ("In This," *New Directions* 152–53).[13]

Obviously Corso puts his trust in a different quality of dream world. He con-siders the peculiarly modern, mass-produced false dream as dangerous and sub-versive and suggests that his friend Jack Kerouac was a victim of "that unreal fake America, that caricature of America, that plugged in a wall America" ("Elegiac,"

EF 10): as Kerouac's visions began to be adopted by a generation that revolted against the artificial dream, Kerouac himself was absorbed by the very forces he criticized, surrendering his exaltation for mundane bleakness. On the other hand, Corso's preference for imagination over reality is not necessarily a rejection of truth for falseness: "Though truth is no longer my master / I will not entruth lies" ("The Doubt of Truth," *M* 222). Corso pleads "for that madness again that infinitive solitude where illusion spoke Truth's divine dialect" ("Ode to Coit," *G/V* 13). This is the dream world that penetrates the thick cell walls of the ordinary, exposing the radiance of pure perception, the world generated by the mind, not by the brain: imagination, traveling "by mindrocket" ("With Proxima"), need not take orders from reason, and what the conventional world may call madness can be a fresh mode of perception.

The "madness" of Corso's discordant mixture of "memory and dream" attributes considerable potency to the creative abilities of imagination. Even in poems that carry the aroma of what the Beat writers called "goofing,"[14] that is, playing around with words and images, as in "Food" and "Poets Hitchhiking on the Highway," the poems rise above the game; Jim Burns indicates that in the latter poem Corso "took a simple scene of two poets trading nonsense phrases, and transformed it into a celebration of imagination and humour, and of being alive to all the possibilities of life and language" (56). Similarly in "Bomb," Corso asserts that "if I felt bombs were caterpillars / I'd doubt not they'd become butterflies."[15] He immediately illustrates this tendency for image to evolve into illusion:

> There is a hell for bombs
> They're there   I see them there
> They sit in bits and sing songs
>   mostly German songs
> and two very long American songs
> and they wish there were more songs.

An imaginative speculation creates its own setting and characters in a surreal poetic vision. The playful pleasures of imagination are repeated ingredients in Corso's poetry. He recalls

> How happy I used to be
> imagining myself so many things—
>   Alexander Hamilton lying in the snow
>   shoe buckles rusting in the snow
>   pistol shot crushing his brow.[16]

("How Happy," *HB* 12)

Although one might be tempted to see this as a neurotic death wish, the tone of the poem suggests instead that it embodies the melodrama that allows children in their fantasy games of make-believe to take as much pleasure in pretending to be shot as they do in pretending to shoot. This probability is reinforced by his poem "Uccello," where, despite the stylized horrors of war in the painter's *Battle of San Romano*, the narrator exclaims, "how I dream to join such battle!" *G/V* 29).[17] The explanation for his desire depends on a Grecian Urn situation of frozen time and action. The thrill of battle here entails no cost and offers glory without threat, for "[t]hey will never die on that battlefield / . . . never to die but to be endless / a golden prince of pictorial war" (29; ellipsis added). On another level of whimsicality, imagination can play a more practical role:

> Thank God one's thoughts
> excite as much as flesh
> Thank God there's a place
> in all this he and she
> and he and he
> and she and she
> for a me and me.

> ("God Is a Masturbator," *EF* 112)

One can only regret that Corso does not deign to cite the role of imagination even in the he-she, he-he, and she-she relationships—the sexual fantasies people indulge when they are not alone, as well as when they are. Nevertheless, in Corso's poetry, fantasy continuously spurts onto reality, altering its colors and shapes. "Alchemy" offers creatively visual transformation: "A bluebird / alights upon a yellow chair / —Spring is here," as two primary colors blend into a completely imaginary spring green (*HA* 50).[18] In "The Sacré-Coeur Café," the speaker's imagination transforms a bland Parisian setting into a scene thrilling with tension and excitement as he overlays it with the romance of Victor Hugo's *Les Misérables*.

Too often, however, his fantasized projections of foreign locales butt up against an implacable reality:

> Like the touching of snow
> > Athens was no longer Athens.
> Must one keep home to keep Rome Rome?
> Surely then this England visit
> will spoil whatever dream I have of it.

> ("How One," *SP* 58)

On the other hand, in "Vision of Rotterdam," his narrator, arriving in Rotterdam in 1957 "filled with despair" (*G/V* 16) finds that the city, in classic fashion of the pathetic fallacy, partakes of his feelings as it reverts to the wartime of 1940; and the Venice of "I Where I Stand" is reconstructed through transhistorical fancy as "[t]he outskirts of a dreamed map" (*LL* 41). In "Errol Flynn—On His Death," the actor is totally and hopelessly confused with his cinematic roles, a confusion that also occurs with Humphrey Bogart in "Was Papa Haydn Born April 1st?"[19] Corso's imagination frequently incorporates cinematic images and performers into mundane reality. In "How Not to Die," he explains that when he feels oppressed by his own mortality he goes "[t]o the movies—to the movies / that's where I hurry to / when I feel I'm going to die" (*HA* 17), as cinema provides the relief of escapism through the release of the imagination.

For Corso, however, the power of the imagination is more than whimsically perceptual. It has been suggested that in the modern age people have dreams rather than visions, and Corso sees himself as trying to reinculcate the visionary capability. In the footsteps of Blake, Shelley, and Whitman, he sees the poet as instrumental in the redemption of this lost aspect of humanity, the recovery of which will restore forgotten dimensions to life:

> What we are witnessing is a delicate shift of total consciousness in America. . . . The shift and new recognition can only be incarnated and commenced thru great works of Art (as Whitman rightly demanded from poets to come)—Art to stand beacon like Statue naked and courageous, individual statement of private actual, uncensored individual perception. . . .

> —The total alteration, personal work social political poetic, emotive—demanded by alteration of consciousness—enforced by alteration of facts: the arrival on the world of the great bomb of the apocalypse, the journey from our world to others now unknown but visionarily reachable. ("Variations," *Casebook* 95–96; ellipses added)

For Corso, the visionary capacity promises human fulfillment. The surrender to it must be total in order to break free from the bondage to trivial self-consciousness and thereby to attain a new level of consciousness. This new plane encompasses the marvel and delight of the mind's preoccupation with its own complexity and the surreality made possible when fantasy and imagination are viable lenses for apprehension, enabling the perceiver to witness a unique reality too long denied to humanity. Thus, Corso is capable of celebrating his apparent flaw:

> O God! God!
> I'll never see things as they are!
> Debauched of dream,
> I've an eye impure for sight.

> ("On Palatine," *HB* 63)

Mere visual perception is a mechanical behavior of the human physiological system. Corso exalts what goes beyond sensual awareness. He explains,

> There is no mouth no eye no nose no ear no hand enough
> The senses are insufficient
> You need Power to dispel light
> Not the closing of the eye.

("Power," HB 75)

Thus, the perception he endorses is more than visual and not merely solipsistic; it is the imaginative vision that exceeds the apprehension of the limited senses. The ability to perceive both levels can provide the quality that Gavin Selerie notes when he explains that one of Corso's poems, "*The Geometrician Of Milano*, looks at the relationship between microcosm and macrocosm, natural bodies and natural forces" (11). Similarly, "Proximity" focuses on the twin perceptions in a directly and aphoristically visual image:

> A star
> is as far
> as the eye
> can see
> and
> as near
> as my eye
> is to me.

(HA 26)

His repeated focus on ocular visualization and its limitations emphasizes Corso's conception of a vision surpassing the senses:

> Eyes project mental images
> upon the elemental screen
>
> It's only there when seen there
> There's nothing behind
> until the eyes turn around
>
> Sight brings life to what's seen
> What's unseen waits to be born
> by the breath of sight.

("Shots" 8)

The visionary propensity offers humanity the hope to circumvent its usually mundane existence and to liberate itself from customary human limitations.

In "Man," Corso suggests that this notion of circumscribed power is a relic of primitive times: "Poor caveman, so scared of the outside, / So afeared of its power and beauty, / Created a limit, and called that limit God" (*LL* 9). This issue is even more complex as Corso indicates later in the same poem: "King of the universe is man, creator of gods" (10). Thus, the very creation of the human limits that Corso connects with the idea of a god reveals the power of primitive imagination. In fact, the invention of an eternal, omnipotent creator by a mortal human may arguably be the most sublime act of imagination conceivable. Corso's shift within that single poem from the uppercase *God* to the lowercase *gods* is reflective of an interchangeability he employs throughout much of his writing. At times, the effect can have a witty humor: realizing that he has lived longer than the supposed thirty-three years of Christ, he exclaims, "Ye gods! in the Catholic sense / I am 15 years older than God!" ("Feelings on Growing" 144), a combination of polytheism and monotheism that can recall Wordsworth's irony in "The World Is Too Much with Us": "Great God! I'd rather be / A Pagan suckled in a creed outworn" (19).

The God of modern Western civilization—and of Corso's Roman Catholic upbringing—is simply one of the many deific creations of the human imagination, a process that he sees as still continuing. In "The Makers of God," the makers referred to in the poem's title range from "the Gypsyan hag," through a "Calabrian Virgin-Mary maker," to "the Haitian maid" engaged in voodoo (79); for each person, the god manifests itself in an individual way. Corso even goes so far as to expand the conventional Western gender and race possibilities of divinity: "God? She's Black" (*LL* 44); "Queen God" ("Purple"). In addition, he feels free to intermingle qualities associated with mythology and those associated with monotheism: he imagines poets "with their God-given / Petasus, Caduceus, and Talaria" ("Destiny," *HA* 46). Corso goes on to suggest that continued religious belief still springs from anxiety and fear of the unknown:

> The love one has for the God
>   sensed by all humankind
>   is unsure, by faith enjoined,
>   An answer to the impermanence
>   of things and oneself.
>
> ("Money/Love," HA 36)

Corso's own uncertainty reveals itself in his qualified phrasing: "Man still suffers; his compassion, his broken heart cries out 'O God' perhaps to no God— man seems to be a god-minded creature without a god" ("Some of My Beginning," *Poets* 180–81). As valuable as such a belief may once have been for the safety and health of human beings, for what he calls "the warmth / and secure / of God-embracement" ("Fire Report," *M* 234), Corso indicates that the modern age demands an adaptation of the nature of divinity. Thus, in *The American Express*, asked by the Cardinal, "What will you do without God?" the rebellious Carrol answers, "I will find a better representation of Him! I will find a God fitting for me! A God of the new consciousness! The Catholic Church is done—your God has not changed. Man changes, therefore God must change" (31).[20] In the second half of the twentieth century, a person no longer need bow to primeval beliefs:

> Must I dry my inspiration in this sad concept?
> Delineate my entire stratagem?
> Must I settle into phantomness
> and not say I understand things better than God?
>
>   ("1959," *HB* 91)

The syntactical ambiguity of the final line (i.e., better than God understands things, better than I understand God, or things that are better than God) underlines the obsolete nature the poet attaches to the concept.

In his later poems, Corso's rejection of the concept of God is emphatic, and, in a 1993 interview with Danny O'Bryan, he flatly states, "I've never accepted God." In "I Gave Away . . . ," his narrator crowns his independence by giving the gods away, and in "The Whole Mess . . . Almost," he throws God out the window. In "Fire Report—No Alarm," he celebrates himself for the fact that he is "God-free":

> And that I did not adhere
>   to any man's God
> neither a comprehensible
>   Absolute
> nor the inexplicable
>   unseen breath
>   of Omnipotent power.
>
>   (*M* 235, 234)

In "Field Report," he sees himself as having traveled through life with "no dio" (*M* 242), but concludes the poem by asserting that "like Holderlin sayeth I am closer to god / away from Him" (268).[21] For Corso, this is no real ambiguity: his resentment is toward the obeisance so often expected by organized religion; if he can feel no need to "fall to / my knees / in abject piety" ("Fire Report," *M* 234), his relationship to the concept of a god can be faced with equanimity. However, Corso sees the idea of God as inimical to the integrity of individual identity: "I can find nothing human about heaven" ("After Another," *LL* 73). Although some might find such a nonhuman condition attractive, Corso clearly does not. In "Transformation & Escape," the speaker arrives in heaven and finds "God a gigantic fly paper" (*HB* 19); the poem describes the speaker's rebellion against the fragmentation and loss of self in an "oppressively sweet" heaven and his determination to assert his personal identity and preserve his human spirit at all costs. Concepts of rewards and punishments destroy the freedom of individuality and "pollute the sky / with heavens / the below with hells" ("The Doubt of Lie," *M* 223). In "When I Was Five I Saw a Dying Indian" and "Youthful Religious Experiences," Corso recounts his own firsthand acquaintance with this dogma: at five years old, he had a vision of God with two books, one black and the other white. A priest explained to him,

> The black book is for all the bad you do
> the white book for all the good
> If the black book
> at the end of your life
> weighs more than the white book
> you'll go to hell and burn forever!
>
> (*HA* 22)

He blames such spiritual pollution on humanity's conception of a god, but his response to the possibility of infernal punishment by a wrathful God of retribution bears similarities to that of Charles Péguy (1873–1914), the French Catholic writer who refused absolution, preferring eternal damnation if an omnipotent God were inclined to condemn any sinners. As Corso recognizes, "There's a divine discontent / in some sinners" ("Shots" 6). He declares, "Were such a He able to damn me / Such damnation I'd" ("6 Poems"). He complains of divine unfairness, characterizing the creator as "a stingy creep who got great kicks / out of not telling you when and how and why life" ("Clown," *HB* 59), lines that parallel the resentment articulated in *The Rubáiyát of Omar Khayyám*:

> Into this Universe, and *Why* not knowing,
> Nor *Whence*, like Water willy-nilly flowing;
>   And out of it, as Wind along the Waste,
> I know not *Whither*, willy-nilly blowing.
>
> What, without asking, hither hurried *Whence*?
> And, without asking, *Whither* hurried hence!
>   Oh, many a Cup of this forbidden Wine
> Must drown the memory of that insolence!
>
> (FitzGerald 18–19)

To kill the god he sees as the cause of human misfortune, the "drear" that recurs antiphonally throughout "Satyr's Chant," Corso's satyr-narrator imagines that "[t]his knife aimed at Zeus might do the trick" (*HB* 73).

Nevertheless, Corso's criticism can be tempered by the recognition of a need to be just. After blaming God for the symptoms of human mortality—"To lie in bed and be hairless is a blunder only God could allow" ("Hair," *HB* 14)—he prepares his deposition: "I am here to tell you various failures of God / The unreasonableness of God" ("Power," *HB* 76). He can, however, immediately qualify his attack: "There is something unfair about this / It is not God that has made Power unbearable it is Love / Love of Influence Industry Firearms Protection." Although *lust* might seem a more appropriate word than *love*, the reservations are significant, particularly in terms of the God-consciousness that seems to persist in Corso's writing. In fact, one is tempted to echo Cranley's comment to Stephen Dedalus: "It is a curious thing, do you know, . . . how your mind is supersaturated with the religion in which you say you disbelieve" (Joyce, *Portrait* 240). In a 1962 letter to William S. Burroughs, Corso provides a telling revelation about his preoccupation:

> i once had this dream, bill, that a man came up to me and handed me a piece of white paper and said God wants to see you, here is his address; i compulsively impulsively refused the paper, saying I KNOW THE ADDRESS, and indeed i felt i did know, so i ran to where i thought God lived, and when i got there, i was lost, i did not know, and the man with the paper was gone and i awoke—so you see bill, i damn well could have seen God, even if it be a god of my own imagining, a catholic god whatever, i missed the opportunity— that dream dreamnt in new york five months ago, upset me very much; i felt i had been denied; i asked one drunken night a protestant minister if i were denied having told him said dream, he said no, not denied, warned.[22] (160)

In a 1963 letter about his religious background and beliefs, Corso cites this dream as "proof that I am not far from my religious heritage" ("Dear Fathers" 10), from the God-haunted consciousness of his childhood.[23] As when one's tongue worries the gum from which a tooth has been lost, Corso returns to the vacancy left by his abandoned religion:

> O would there a god I might love
> One to offer prayers of marvel to
> One in whom I may endow all such wonders
> as greatworks of love allow
> Were such a god mute

and I blind
I'd embrace the very air
and breathe the breath of its beauty.

("Field Report," M 260)

At times, Corso's delight in the wonders of life draws him toward an assertion of faith:

Yet it's all so beautiful
isn't it?
How perfect the entire system of things
The human body
all in proportion to its form
Nothing useless
Truly as though a god had indeed warranted it so.

("For Homer," *HA* 13)

However, even here the concluding dependent clause is qualified and hesitant, and the same poem continues by citing life's "inequities," until the narrator decides, "I've no religion / and I'd as soon worship Hermes."

Although Corso's self-acknowledged "strict Catholic upbringing" ("When I Was Five" 87) may help to explain his lingering attachment to the God he has rejected—"that god and devil / I inherited from catholic parentage" ("Lines Between")—an equally important motive is his belief that his role as a poet entitles him to a favored connection with whatever deity may exist. Most often he portrays this role in terms of the mythological Greek, Roman, and Egyptian gods for whom the poet becomes the privileged herald or messenger, but he also celebrates that poetic role in terms of the uppercase God: "They [poets] deliver the edicts of God / . . . The Messenger-Spirit / in human flesh" ("Destiny," *HA* 46; ellipsis added). The familiar role of the poet as a divinely inspired medium conveniently attributes the blame or the credit for the poet's production to the deific source while still allowing the poet the endowed position of agent. Moreover, Corso's poetic role parallels God's role as creator:

I am the architect of elsewhere world
and the way the Lord built this here world
is the way I, in dreams build . . . I think therefore it is
or I dream therefore I build (?).

("30th Year," *Residu*)

The concept bears significant similarities to Wallace Stevens's aphorism that "[t]he mind that in heaven created the earth and the mind that on earth created heaven were, as it happened, one" (*Opus* 201). The human-divine parallel is instructive: human imagination generates varieties of gods just as God's imagination creates varieties of human beings. The created world may include human mortality, crises and frustrations, and human imagination creates the "monsters" of the zodiac, missed opportunities to contact God, and heavens and hells—for Corso points out that "everything imagined about hell is imagined by man" ("Some of My Beginning," *Poets* 181).

Corso recognizes that the products of imagination are not always Edenic. In "A Difference of Zoos," he catalogues imagined horrors: "hoary ligneous Brownies," gnomes, midges, the bogeyman, Medusa, Polyphemus, the chimera, the gargoyle, the sphinx, the griffin, Rumpelstiltskin, the Heap, Groot, the mugwump, Thoth, the centaur, Pan, the werewolf, the vampire, Frankenstein. In fact, Corso sometimes seems vulnerable to de Tocqueville's complaint against poets in democracies: "they perpetually inflate their imaginations, and expanding them beyond all bounds, they not infrequently abandon the great in order to reach the gigantic. . . . and poets, not finding the elements of the ideal in what is real and true, abandon them entirely and create monsters" (82–83; 2: Book 1, Chap. 18). However, in this particular case, Corso puts a twist on the observation through his narrator's response: surrounded by the monsters, he finds his environment "unbearable" and concludes, "I went to the zoo / and oh thank God the simple elephant" (*LL* 62). An earlier version of the same poem makes his point didactically:

> The joys I receive from my seldom zoos
> are the lovely reallive animals
> and not the fake fiends and furies
> caged in the mind.

> (*SP* 57)

Reality, for which he can "thank God," here offers a relief from the frightening terrors of the imagination.

Corso believes that imagination can provide the power to transcend limits through the "new consciousness" to which he refers in *The American Express*. This "new consciousness" is dependent upon an expanded sense of freedom, the emancipated power of humanity's recognition of the individual as God. In *The American Express*, Simon preaches, "All the consciousness is waiting for the Messiah to make a break. We are the God we always longed for" (44), and Carrol corroborates the message: "You long for God and don't know that you're already God! What's all this nonsense about looking for Power outside yourselves? It's in YOU!" (45). Accepting traditional limits on the power of human awareness and consciousness becomes the equivalent of guaranteeing those restrictions. The visionary capacity, on the other hand, offers limitless possibilities to humanity, for "[h]is dream can go beyond existence" ("Man," *LL* 10). Thus, discussing Corso's "Greece," John Fuller notes, "The climax of this poem is Corso's rejection of Death . . . in favour of the power and eternity of the human imagination" (75). For Corso, imagination can offer a form of immortality.

The exploration of the complex regions of dream, imagination, and vision constitutes Corso's poetic mission:

> There are no more lands to explore, to conquer—Christopher Columbus must now traverse the sea of the mind and who can doubt he'll not discover some kind of wondrous continent there? . . . the wider the expanse of the mind the greater our possibility to learn and enjoy the adventures it holds for us. ("Some of My Beginning," *Poets* 180; ellipsis added)

The image and thrust of Corso's statement parallel André Breton's comment that

> the human explorer will be able to carry his investigations much further, authorized as he will henceforth be not to confine himself solely to the most summary realities. The imagination is perhaps on the point of reasserting itself, of reclaiming its rights. (10)

The indomitability of the human spirit, the universal integrity of a personal and subjective response to beauty's truth, and the vast richness of the uncharted imagination—these are the lessons of the new art that Corso champions.

3
Elegiac Feelings American

> The most unfailing herald, companion, and follower of the
> awakening of a great people to work a beneficial change in opinion
> or institution, is Poetry.
>
> —Shelley, "A Defence of Poetry"

The writers of the Beat Generation rejected attempts to project them as
a political movement and characteristically eschewed political affiliations. Invok-
ing a theme of *carpe diem*, Corso explains the reasons for their refusal to enter this
arena: "the American young and the German young live for the moment, they are
not concerned with politics; in that moment they find the joy and meaning of life,
for they have seen the joylessness and meaninglessness of politics" ("Berlin Impres-
sions" 74). Nevertheless, despite their political reluctance, the Beat writers were
thoroughly involved with and concerned about the direction and fate of America.
Beat writings that begin as strident diatribes against the distortion and corruption
of the American dream frequently conclude as love poems to America. Expressing
the peculiarly American short-term cultural nostalgia, the Beats celebrate the
length, breadth, and spirit of the American nation and declaim against the forces
that they feel are perverting it, desiccating it into a sterile and polluted wasteland.
They proclaim the innocence and energy of the American people and berate the
forces that betray and impoverish American values. Their writings are registers of
a vast distance between the real and the ideal America, between the fact and the
promise of America, what Corso calls "American disappointment of a cherished
hope" ("Variations," *Casebook* 90). As Gregory Stephenson points out, "America,
for Corso, was to have been the new Arcadia, but it has instead become merely
another empire, mad with material greed, obsessed with military power, denying
its own vision and ideals" ("'Arcadian'" 86). Corso and many of the other Beat
writers are patriots of a visionary America and are continually disappointed by the
refusal or inability of America to live up to its own professed goals.

Corso especially concerns himself with what he sees as the falseness of the American situation. He is indignant over the failure of the nation to accomplish or sustain the principles upon which it was founded:

> All we had was past America, and ourselves, the now
> America, and O how we regarded that past!
> And O the big lie of that school classroom! The Revolutionary
> War. . . all we got was Washington, Revere, Henry, Hamilton,
> Jefferson, and Franklin. . . never Nat Bacon, Sam Adams,
> Paine. . . and what of liberty? was not to gain liberty that war,
> liberty they had, they were the freest peoples of their time; was
> not to *lose* that liberty was why they went to arms—yet, and yet,
> the season that blossomed us upon the scene was hardly free; be
> there liberty today? not to hear the redman, the blackman, the
> youngman tell.[1]
>
> ("Elegiac," *EF* 7)

Corso claims that early American heroes, many of them uncelebrated, fought for an ideal that modern America has not preserved, citing what have become the conventional examples of disaffected groups (with the significant omission of women[2]): the result is "The Failure of America to generate the energy of Freedom—The Fall of America" ("Variations," *Casebook* 96). In addition, as his complaint continues, he asserts that the honored heroes were often less than exemplary models, despite the stature they have been accorded in the American educational system:

> And in the beginning when liberty was all one could hear;
> wasn't much of it for the poor witches of Salem;
> and that great lauder of liberty, Franklin, paid
> 100 dollar bounty for each scalp of the wild
> children of natural free; Pitt Jr. obtained most of the city of
> brotherly love by so outrageous a
> deception as stymied the trusting heart of his
> red brother with tortuous mistrust; and how
> ignorant of liberty the wise Jefferson owning the
> black losers of liberty; for the declarers of
> independence to declare it only for part of the
> whole was to declare civil war.[3]
>
> ("Elegiac," *EF* 7)

His factual errors notwithstanding (in fact, at times even illustrating his point), Corso's observation that most Americans remain unaware of the hypocrisy of their forebears provides evidence of the historical deception by which Americans have been victimized, especially in the first two-thirds of the twentieth century, when the histories of America's growth seem to have been so programmatically celebratory. In fact, when Corso recalls his early schooldays, such as in "P.S. 42," his memories are replete with nostalgic reverie for the conventional heroes of American history: Washington, Franklin, Lincoln, and Hamilton. Encountering the American educational system a little later than Corso, Abbie Hoffman points to a similarly selective perspective: "Can you believe I was eighteen before I even knew this country had a Depression but at thirteen I could list with correct dates all Revolutionary War battles and discuss in detail the battle of Lexington and Concord which took place just thirty miles from my hometown?" (53). By contrast, in contemporary America Corso finds the "Statue of Liberty standing surrounded by the garbage of materialism, a sea of humanity starves in the water outside her" ("Variations," *Casebook* 95). The historical American heroes begin to seem irrelevant when these inequities can be ignored by those successful enough to insulate themselves against them.

Corso blames the mass media, "a controlled voice, wickedly opinioned, and directed at gullible" ("Elegiac," *EF* 4), for misconceptions that many Americans hold regarding their own country and its history and for the gloss applied to tarnished historical figures. Having grown up before the advent of television, Corso frequently focuses his attack on the print medium:

> the PRESS
> they're the voice of people
> not of the people
> these redundant chronicleers
>   of events daily
> whose opinionations
>   veer society
> toward their
> hypocritical morality.
>
> ("The 5th Estate," *MF* 54)

An innocent naiveté or a guileless blindness on the part of the American populace insures the perpetuation of false perceptions, especially among those Americans most infatuated with the espoused ideals and goals of their country, and consequently the most reluctant to bring critical intelligence to bear on disseminated information. Corso sees his friend and fellow Beat writer Jack Kerouac as representative of those people who have been too willing to see only what they wished to see. He addresses Kerouac, then recently deceased, and admonishes his spirit: "When you went on the road looking for America you found only what you put there" ("Elegiac," *EF* 11). Too often what Kerouac found was his own innocence projected on the land, its people, and its history. This propensity can result in hero worship of authoritarian leaders unworthy of adulation:

> Thrice I've seen the two-gunned ghost of Patton
> waxing wars in the backroom   whitehaired and mad
> his fat thumbs pressing violence with schoolboy gaud.
> He hates God he has alchemy cannons aimed at Him!
> Badgered angels (wine-soaked rags) slaughtered by his orders
> by his battalions of exorbitant drunks
> hang (not as sweet Alexander would have it hang)
> like rags in the bombblotched air of God.
>
> ("Army," *HB* 81)

> And miles and miles away Shades MacArthur
> wets his knees in tropic water
> the mangled children of Buddha floating pass his eagled belly button.[4]
>
> ("Army," *HB* 84)

However, even though modern warfare has escalated the carnage of conflict, contemporary generals are hardly any more brutal, insensitive, or self-aggrandizing than those (including Alexander the Great) of more remote times. Nevertheless, Corso's point is that Hollywood and the print media have largely ignored or minimized the vicious brutality that sacrifices human beings to the Moloch of egoism and vanity and that they have foisted on the "gullible" American public such heroes, who prefer "gaud" to "God."

Corso especially regrets that the media mythology seems to have displaced the values and culture that characterized the ancient civilizations of the Egyptians, the Greeks, the Romans, and the Native Americans, all of which play prominent roles in his poetry. He is particularly sensitive to the loss of the precepts and traditions that disappeared with these civilizations. His condemnation of the devastation and despoliation of the highly ritualized Native American culture is pronounced. Gavin Selerie sees Corso's contrast of past and contemporary societies as part of the poet's "search for wholeness" (12), and Corso's portrayals certainly decry the fragmented anomie of modern culture. "A Spontaneous Requiem for the American Indian," a plaintive and moving dirge for the disappearance of the proud, natural, and independent Native American spirit and way of life, provides a coda that portrays the perversion of that image into its modern representative, "Motorcyclist Blackfoot":

> whizzing faster than his ancestral steed past smokestacks bannershacks
> O the timid shade of Kiwago now! the mad roar exhaustpipe Indian
> like a fleeing oven clanking weeeeee weeeeeee no feathers in his oily

helmet . . . waiting, america, waiting the end, the last Indian, mad
Indian of no fish or foot or proud forest haunt, mad on his knees
ponytailing & rabbitfooting his motorcycle, his the final requiem the
final america READY THE FUNERAL STOMP goodluck charms
on, tires aired, spikes greased, morose goggles on, motor gas brakes
checked! 1958 Indians, heaps of leather—ZOOM down the wide
amber speedway of Death, Little Richard, tuba mirum, the vast black
jacket brays in the full forced fell.[5]

(*EF* 17; ellipsis added)

The attack here is scarcely subtle: in modern "america," where the Native Amer-
ican culture is considered primitive and uncivilized, the contemporary Native
American, torn between conflicting forces in the definition of his identity, is led
to irreverent and incognizant self-parody; the poem's earlier "heraldic henequen
tubas" (14) of tribal ritual give way to the "tuba mirum" of Berlioz's Requiem, here
mourning the death of an entire culture that honored the human relationship to
the natural world. In contrast, Corso complains that modern American culture
has destroyed its environmental connections, creating a "horrendous imbalance
of all things natural . . . elusive nature caught! like a bird in hand, harnessed and
engineered in the unevolutional ways of experiment and technique," until "we
breathe in stampedes of pollution" ("Elegiac," *EF* 5) and it is "[t]ime to return
from star trek / and scrub the earth" ("Clown," *HB* 53). Modern America has
fouled its own world, just as it has disfigured that of the Native Americans. Corso's
poem "Death of the American Indian's God" concludes with a passage whose
rhymes and bitter final word-play emphasize the critical question of responsibil-
ity for the dissolution of the way of the Native American:

They were the redmen
feathers-in-their-head men
now
down among the dead men
how.

(*LL* 18)

Attempting to provide an answer to the question of "how" this has happened,
Corso focuses on efforts (perhaps even with good intentions) to absorb Native
Americans into contemporary life—efforts that concentrate on assimilation rather
than enlightenment and on superficial advancements alien to the Native Ameri-
can spirit and culture, thus effectively distancing them from both societies:

Behold the Trickster seated before the bosomy social
    organizer

who's extolling the comforts of front porches
She taps her school stick upon the Shawnee prophet's
      nodding head
The gawky Blackfoot smiles all ears while she chirps
      the virtues of Mr. Crapper's outhouse in the house
Santana looks sad at the little window and envisions
      a prison hospital window from which he'll
      escape to his death
Miss Big Boobs warbles the 5 vowels
And Young Man Afraid of His Horses scratches his crotch
Little Wolf dreams to count glorious coups with Crazy Horse
      who's been hookey for the 82nd day.

                            ("Eleven," *EF* 36)

Corso's criticism is underscored ironically through specific allusions to Native American culture: Shawnee Prophet (Tenskwatawa), who was the brother of Tecumseh, received a revelation from the Native American master of life encouraging the renunciation of the acquired white ways and reaffirming Native American customs and values; in addition, one of the most celebrated rituals of the Blackfoot tribe was the vision quest, diminished in Corso's poem to a vision of a tawdry death. In the reservation schoolroom of the poem, the glory of the Native American culture is reduced to schoolchild escapist dreams for boys who are "Afraid," "Little," and "Crazy."

Corso also has little patience with pseudoliberal charity to Native Americans because it ignores the sources of their plight. In his brief play "In This Hung-Up Age," Mrs. Kindhead (significantly, not Kindheart), a *"Progressive Liberal House- wife do-gooder type"* (*New Directions* 149), tells the Native American named Apache, "If anyone's a true American, it is you, sir" (155), but earlier she claims, "I'm all for progress, any kind" (153), the very progress responsible for the destruction of the Native American way of life. She is apparently oblivious of the fact that the progress that has made her life comfortable has been a factor in the destruction of the culture and life style of the Native Americans and in the deaths of countless numbers of those "true" Americans. In the apocalyptic conclusion of the play, however, the typical Americans are killed in a stampede of rampaging buffalo. This ending reflects a common Native American belief, as Allen Ginsberg explains: "Old Indian prophecies believe Ghost Dance peace will Come restore prairie Buffalo or great White Father Honkie / be trampled to death in his dreams by returning herds' thundering reincarnation" ("'Have You Seen?'" 166–67). Thus, Corso allows the violated and dispossessed Native American culture its own revenge.

Corso also accuses modern Americans of destroying their own culture and traditions. Conventional religion has been devitalized by hucksters who have gutted it and served up the shell for mass consumption. His objections (articulated well before the indiscretions and unsavory business practices of Jim and Tammy Faye Bakker, Jimmy Swaggart, and Oral Roberts were revealed) direct themselves at the self-styled evangelists and Sunday morning television preachers who employ the hard-sell techniques of capitalism and contaminate spirituality with crass commercialism:

> I am telling you the American Way is a hideous monster
>   eating Christ making Him into Oreos and Dr. Pepper
> the sacrament of its foul mouth.
>
>   ("American," *EF* 70)

More importantly, Corso's objections stem from his basic antipathy to "mental-dictators" and to the destructive tactics they employ to gain control. He rejects the evangelists' projections of human guilt and a wrathful Christ, both of which they propagate to cow their congregations. Corso's attacks on specific personalities reflect his indignation in coarse, excoriating vulgarity:

> Without god
> the rev Jerry falwell
> could very well be putting onions on the hamburgers
> of the patrons of the White Swallow faggot bar
> . . . .
> when the caveman
> never Billy grahams god knew
> . . . .
> Prove to me there is a god
> stands between the wrinkled assholes
> of a Rex Roberts and an Oral Humbard.[6]
>
>   ("Hi," *WW* 8; ellipses added)

The interchange of the names of the last two preachers suggests the indistinctiveness of their personalities, of their techniques, and of their messages.

In Corso's poetry, the constant villains are those who abuse their power: "America's educators & preachers are the mental-dictators of false intelligence" ("American," *EF* 70). Furthermore, he suggests that, in America, success itself creates a vulnerability to subversion of the human spirit:

> The American Way that sad mad process
>   is not run by any one man or organization
> It is a monster born of itself existing of its self
> The men who are employed by this monster

> are employed unknowingly
> They reside in the higher echelons of intelligence
> They are the educators the psychiatrists the ministers
> the writers the politicians the communicators
> the rich the entertainment world.
>
> (72)

The result is a pervasive form of control and domination, very much like that detailed in the novels of William Burroughs, producing a stagnating loss of human individuality: employing Burroughs's terminology, Corso complains that "[r]eplica production make all the young think alike / dress alike believe alike do alike" (70). The processed products of this type of mental domination are not difficult to recognize in Corso's work. A typical representative speaks his narrow mind: "Boy, that [Walter] Winchell's sure got them Commies pegged right! Nothing but a bunch of Chinese opium eaters he calls them" ("In This," *New Directions* 151).[7] Such intolerant imbecility begins to permeate American society, from the level of the general public up through its leaders—or vice versa. As a result, Corso (showing no awareness of the flaws that he would later attribute to Franklin and Jefferson in "Elegiac Feelings American") claims, "Not Franklin not Jefferson who speaks for America today / but strange red-necked men of industry / and the goofs of show business" ("American," *EF* 73). This poem was originally published in 1961, almost twenty years before the ascendancy of Ronald Reagan to the presidency and five years before his election as governor of California.

Corso also suggests that America's culture is threatened by a similar nadir of quality: "America at the time was wallowed in a communicative consciousness that bespoke dopey advertisements, infernal patriotism, downright unsophisticated feelings of culture" ("Some of My Beginning," *Poets* 37). He cites specific examples: "this age that knows no Thoth condemning Set but Batman imprisoning the Joker" ("Detective" 69); "The PX newsstands are filled with comic books / The army movies are always Doris Day" ("American," *EF* 74).[8] The implication is that the flavors of this culture are bubble gum and vanilla. This dearth of variety and enlightenment is accompanied by the loss of genuine American exuberance and exhilaration, qualities Corso recalls from the past:

> glum days poor America bares—
> Old America could tell of laughter often as clowns tell—
> Ben Franklin, W. C. Fields, Chaplin, the fat of joy![9]
>
> ("Clown," *HB* 55)

Aside from the fact that Chaplin was born in London and did not arrive in America until he had gained his majority, the poet never clearly establishes his standards of comedic excellence, and his stance may seem to smack of aesthetic pretentiousness: are comic books by definition of inferior artistic quality? are they devoid of joy? how do W. C. Fields's roles differ from those of lesser comic performers? is Batman intrinsically less heroic than Thoth? does the presence of Doris Day in a movie deprive it of entertainment value or make it incapable of educing laughter? Although one could readily fashion a rationale for his preferences, Corso does not do so. Through extrapolation, one can recognize his rather classical/traditional values, and he attributes to them an emotional enrichment. In fact, Corso often reveals a conservatism that ennobles the past—personally, nationally, and historically. He can ironically recognize the fact that dissatisfaction with one's own place in time is itself traditional:

> Oh if she'd only cease complaining things have altered!
> "Nothing's the same!" she cries.
> What good my telling her the oldest existing piece of human writing
> Begins with this sentence: "Things are not what they used to be."
>
> ("Three Loves," *LL* 14)

However, his poem "P.S. 42" begins, "When I think back to grammar school / I am overcome with breathlessness and sweet feeling," and he goes on to recall his idealized lessons of American history, ranging from Columbus to Lincoln (*LL* 85–87). He also captures an urban American child's imagination as he walks the pavement,

> A trail that goes way back to a time of trees
> When trees were plentiful when birds and beasts
> When streams flowed and hills were visible
> When Redmen lightly strode
> And Dutchmen wore buckled hats and shoes.
>
> ("City Child's," *LL* 81)

The tenderness of this passage clearly identifies the past with a romanticism that characterizes Corso's poetic persona. His clown regrets that "there are no fields for me to dedragon / —impossible to kneel before ladies / and kiss their flowery gowns" ("Clown," *HB* 52). In his own voice, he celebrates

> the joy of all existence, the wonderment and realization that we are
> alive, man, the victory of life, here, now, on earth, breathing, that mad
> glorious mystery, with its love beauty sorrow laughter Agamemnon
> Goethe Shelley Christ Buddha fish cherries death—romance, this is
> what 1818 poetry had and what 1958 poetry lacks, not lacks really,
> because romance is here, is always here, it is just not enthusiasticly felt

and expressed, it is locked away like a throbbing purse of Raskolnikov rubles, always there, but untouched.[10] (Introduction 246)

Nationally, instead of the joyous tradition, America now only boasts moribund values, as Corso demonstrates in his mock-celebratory "Bomb." Furthermore, he sees America as pursuing deadly courses that also turn out to be self-destructive:

> The United States of america
> bombed itself 86 times
>   in the 40's, 50's and early 60's
> it bombed its Utah, its New Mexico, its Nevada
> and clouds took it to all surrounding states
>
>   All survived
>
>   It took two decades
> for the slow bullets of radiation
>   to strike;
>   two decades
> when the dead finally died.[11]
>
> ("All Survived," *WW* 3)

The image of America bombing itself on atomic and nuclear testing grounds works effectively as an emblem for the general criticisms Corso makes of his country's ruinous tendencies and programs.[12]

The possibility of reversing the self-destructive direction of the country is fraught with frustrations, for "The American Way" is amoebic in its power to co-opt, to absorb within it, even dissident elements: as Herbert Marcuse observes, "in this society everything can be co-opted, everything can be digested" (14). The rebellious Beats themselves were unable to avoid engulfment by this omnivorous entity:[13]

> And those who seek to get out of the Way
>   can not
> The Beats are good example of this
> They forsake the Way's habits
>   and acquire for themselves their own habits
> And they become as distinct and regimented and lost
>   as the main flow
>   because the Way has many outlets.[14]
>
> ("American," *EF* 74)

Gary Snyder has suggested that the importance of the Beat Generation lies in its alternative value system: "It is the first time in American history that a section of the population has freely chosen to disaffiliate itself from 'the American standard of living' and all that goes with it—in the name of freedom" (46). However, Corso recognizes that the rebellion and the rejection are hardly clear-cut, for "the fruits of America are irresistable" ("Literary" 194). Thus, although the popular image of the Beats involves the denial of conventional materialistic values, Corso reveals susceptibility to their attractions:

> MADE BY HAND if it's MADE BY HAND it's got to be good
> . . . .
> When I was a boy all the rich Italians wore MADE BY HAND
> In fact they used to keep the back side of their ties out
>   so that all could see their MADE BY HAND signs
> I even once sewed on a MADE BY HAND label
>   on a not MADE BY HAND tie, yes
> And I also sewed a CASHMERE SWEATER label on a
>   itchy cotton sweater.
>
>   ("Made," *Bedside Playboy*; ellipsis added)

The danger of succumbing to conventional values was especially clear when the most popular of the Beats found themselves vaulted into precarious prominence and adopted as role models by those who did not always understand them or their values. Thus, Kerouac, Ginsberg, and Corso found themselves prominently featured in such outlets as *Time*, *Newsweek*, and *Mademoiselle*. At the same time, one must acknowledge the fact that, though these media outlets scarcely celebrated the Beats, the attention they focused on the writers did much to popularize them and inadvertently to spread their ideas. In fact, Corso can marvel at the irony in their position as the pariahs have become protected spokespersons. As early as the first published version of "Police," appearing in *Big Table* in 1959, Corso records a similar irony in his own situation:

> Six patrol cars in all I've sat
> on my way to the Tombs
> Every contact with police I've had resulted in months, years—
> Yet now, last night, fifteen cops
> all guarding a poetry reading
> in which I was to read.
>
>   (152)

Thus, the rebel-poet finds his presentation of unconventional values safeguarded by the law-enforcement agents of the conventional society that he rejects. The embrace of the Beats by the establishment even turns profitable, as in an incident that Corso cites involving Ginsberg: "and the New York Times paid him 400 dollars / for a poem he wrote about being mugged for 60 dollars" ("Columbia U," *HA* 1).

In addition to self-criticism, Corso's complaints also refer to the distorted public image of the Beats projected by the popular press, and in 1962 he addressed this concern: "And I'm only down on the fact that the beat today—who came up as beat—are being Monsters of Frankenstein Replicas of the Mass Media—of the newspaper interpretation of Beat" ("From an Interview"). In an interview with Art Buchwald, Corso humorously fabricates the history of this development:

> Well, when we first started, the literary magazines tried to put us down. But they had no luck, so they asked Henry Luce to help them. They said: "Henry, we ain't got the circulation to stop them. It's up to you." So Mr. Luce put "Time," "Life," "Fortune," and "Sports Illustrated," at their disposal.
>
> Well, the elevators in the Time and Life Building went on a twenty-four-hour shift and everyone went to work. Pretty soon they were writing all about us. But instead of it becoming a drag, they were spreading the gospel faster than Western Union. People that never heard of beatniks suddenly became aware of us, and the little Frankenstein zoomed. (153)

The stereotyped image of the Beatnik that appeared in films, cartoons, and television programs would seem to support his charge,[15] but Corso's objection is more than mere personal self-defense—he feels that the literary mission of the Beats could be a crucial one for America.

In typical Beat fashion, Corso's patriotism encompasses extremes—love and hate, criticism and adulation. As he ambiguously exclaims, "I love America like a madness!" ("American," *EF* 69), and mad America hurt him into poetry. Corso's affection for America persists despite the flaws against which he inveighs. In his elegy for Kerouac, he portrays his fondness as characteristic of the Beat writers:

> And us ones, sweet friend, we've always brought America
> home with us—and never like dirty laundry, even
> with all the stains
> And through the front door, lovingly cushioned in our
> hearts; where we sat down and told it our
> dreams of beauty
> hopeful that it would leave our homes beautiful

> And what happened to our dream of beauteous
> America, Jack?

("Elegiac," EF 9)

Clearly the assumption here is that the dreams are righteous and that the fault lies with America. His disappointment notwithstanding, Corso does not believe that the task of cleansing America's Augean stables is an impossible one, and he directs himself to the Herculean effort. He argues that the role of the Beats becomes significant in the rejection of sterile, "deathic" American society: "And we will have our voice in changing and making the laws which govern so-called civilized countries today; laws which have covered the earth with secret police, concentration camps, oppression, slavery, wars, death" ("Variations," *Casebook* 94). The complaint is hardly new, and the resolution may scarcely seem revolutionary, despite Corso's characterization of the Beats as "Revolutionaries of the Spirit" ("Columbia U," *HA* 2). Gaiser pointed out in 1961 that "[t]hough poems may be written about the evils of 'The Bomb,' there are no prescriptions for altering the government or restructuring society. The three spokesmen for the Beat [Kerouac, Ginsberg, and Corso] are singularly disinterested in politics" (270).

Of course, to expect poets to provide solutions to problems that frustrate statesmen of the most powerful nations is unreasonable, as Corso himself notes, associating polemics with academic poets. In addition, surely Cassandra can play as important a role as Solomon. Corso demonstrates an awareness of both the limitation and the value of poetry as a vehicle for reform: "In America, yes, much civil social there, and poets are writing verses for its betterment, but they do it not as a duty but as a vast earthly joke, because these american poets lack a remedy; they can just show the condition, that is all" (Letter to Editor, *Cambridge*). The condition that Corso reveals is the result of oppressive laws and controls, and in opposition to them he suggests that the Beats provide the genuine spirit of American vitality and integrity: "Was not so much our finding America as it was America finding its voice in us" ("Elegiac," *EF* 4). The nationalistic impulse is significant:[16] asked in a 1974 interview, "Do you feel some kind of stress to express America?" Corso replied, "Oh yeah, I love America, I love America" (Interview with R. King 6). Despite their repeated avowals, the patriotic stance of the Beats toward America has been largely overlooked by their critics and their supporters alike, so much so that Corso feels compelled to point out, "I never did sneer nor snarl / at America" ("For Mary Rogers," *MF* 43). In an exquisite image with parallels to Corso's portrayal of affection for a stained America, Ginsberg limns an America "where we hug and kiss the United States under our bedsheets the United States that coughs all night and won't let us sleep" ("Howl" 20). Similarly, Corso can reveal his ambivalent feelings toward his country:

> I am not politic.
> I am not patriotic.
> I am nationalistic!
> I boast well the beauty of America to all the people in Europe.
> In me they do not see their vision of America.
> O whenever I pass an American Embassy I don't know what to feel!
> Sometimes I want to rush in and scream: "I'm American!"
> but instead go a few paces down to the American Bar
> get drunk and cry: "I'm no American!"
>
> ("America Politica," *EF* 95)

Even during the height of dissent during the late 1960s, many protestors found themselves cheering on American athletes and teams during the Olympic Games. Too often, those who dared to protest the policies of the United States were seen as traitors, even when they wore the colors and patterns of the American flag.[17]

The love and pride with which the Beats cherished America is genuine, if qualified, but too often only their criticisms received attention in the media. Their patriotism is of the brand that recognizes not only the right but also the responsibility to call attention to their country's failings. The usual reaction to them, however, is articulated by the Tourist in Corso's "In This Hung-Up Age": "if he doesn't like it here why doesn't he go to Russia. Go to Russia if you don't like it" (152). As Abbie Hoffman points out, the United States was founded because of precisely such attitudes: "America is a mythic land. Dreamed up by European beatniks, religious fanatics, draft dodgers, assorted hippie kooks, and runaways from servitude off to the New World of milk and honey. Europe said, 'If you don't like it here, why don't you leave'" (53). A typical response to the Beat critiques and to the protests of the Hippies, who donned many of the Beat mantles, reached the level of the ubiquitous 1960s bumper sticker, "America—Love It or Leave It," as though one could not object to deficiencies in something one loved. Rigidly endorsing such an either/or principle would result in few parents permitting their children to remain in their homes long enough to grow near adulthood. In fact, the Beat attitude toward America often resembles that of parents toward a stubborn, petulant child whom they nevertheless love; they feel that their role is to help guide that child toward the healthy, responsible behavior that they clearly expect of American diversity and democracy. Perhaps the issue can be illuminated by exploring a semantic distinction provided by George Orwell in his essay "Notes on Nationalism":

> Nationalism is not to be confused with patriotism. Both words are
> normally used in so vague a way that any definition is liable to be
> challenged, but one must draw a distinction between them, since two
> different and even opposing ideas are involved. By "patriotism" I mean

devotion to a particular place and a particular way of life, which one believes to be the best in the world but has no wish to force upon other people. Patriotism is of its nature defensive, both militarily and culturally. Nationalism, on the other hand, is inseparable from the desire for power. (362)

Obviously, in Orwell's terms, Corso's attitudes, as well as those of many of the other Beat writers and those who followed their lead during the 1960s, are patriotic rather than nationalistic.

Like a number of the other Beat writers, Corso envisions a youth rebellion and is ultimately optimistic regarding its success, because many of the young seem to him thoroughly disenchanted with the corrupted contemporary values and concerns of the American Way. Addressing Kerouac's spirit again, he proclaims, "Know that today there are millions of Americans seeking America," and assures his friend that he has been an influence on them: "And soon . . . behind thee / there came a-following / the children of flowers" ("Elegiac," *EF* 8, 12). Although America's young people may have heard the clarion of the Beats and attempted to transform the American dream into reality, he believes that interference and rejection have hampered their stripling efforts. An American tree of liberty supplies him with his image:

> And though the great redemptive tree blooms, not yet full,
>   not yet entirely sure, there be the darksters, sad
>   and old, would like to have it fall; they hack
>   and chop and saw away . . . that nothing full
>   and young and free for sure be left to stand at
>   all.[18]

> ("Elegiac," *EF* 6)

Despite this repression, Corso maintains his desire that the revolution initiated by the Beats will prevail:

> Americans are a great people
> I ask for some great and wondrous event
>   that will free them from the Way
>   and make them a glorious purposeful people once
>   again
> I do not know if that event is due   deserved
>   or even possible
> I can only hold that man is the victory of life
> And I hold firm to American man.

> ("American," *EF* 75)

Corso discovers the wellsprings of his confidence in an intense if idiosyncratic patriotism that sees Americans as essentially benevolent and well-intentioned, though admittedly easily misled and corrupted—errant youths (like himself) who can be rehabilitated to contribute to their own welfare and that of the total human community.

4
Modes of Rebellion,
Modes of Expression:
The American Express

The key to the puzzle lies in theater. We are theater in the streets: total and committed. We aim to involve people and use (unlike other movements locked in ideology) any weapon (prop) we can find. The aim is not to earn the respect, admiration, and love of everybody—it's to get people to do, to participate, whether positively or negatively. All is relevant, only "the play's the thing."

—Abbie Hoffman

America's emergence during the twentieth century as the dominant world power militarily, technologically, economically, and culturally resulted in a curious phenomenon: many Americans, blessed with formal educational training, with the promise of opportunity, and with an often naive faith in the rightness of the principles upon which their country was founded, grew up assured of their individual potential for greatness, though they were often confused about the direction toward which to apply their supposed talents. The world stretched before them as a frontier, and they stood confident of their ability to discover new territories that could prove meaningful to humanity. However, these new lands were unmapped, uncharted, multivalent: confidence (on occasion swelling to arrogance) sometimes induced a messianic impulse that frustration could easily warp into the extreme of ethical nihilism. The writers of the Beat generation provide virtual case studies of this scenario. Rebelling against what they saw as the staid, stale, and stable values of a comfortable society (which also allowed them the leisure for their travels and writings), they sought to reinvigorate and reenergize the arts, the

American people, and the people of the world. Their goal was nothing less than a reshaping of human values—a miracle to restore humanity to an Edenic existence. Gregory Corso's little-known 1961 novel, *The American Express*, portrays and critiques the ideals and tactics of exactly such a set of self-proclaimed saviors, providing parallels both to the dangers inherent in the approaches of the rebels and to the concerns of the Beats about how to use their talents to improve humanity.

The novel's plot is both surrealistic and morally committed. After a brief prologue about a sexual liaison initiated in an American Express building and the birth of the resultant child in the basement there, the novel introduces a cast of characters preparing to embark on the ship *Here They Come*. Arriving at "the land prophecy" (16), the travelers are preoccupied with accomplishing grand achievements. Although most of the characters are concerned with attaining a goal that will benefit humanity, their methods range from the distribution of bombs, through a plan to return Lucifer to heaven, to attempts to convince each human that he or she is God. Part 1 concludes with the eruption of war; part 2 includes the war and its aftermath, with the frustrated travelers finally departing on the ship *There They Go*, leaving behind Detective Horatio Frump, who had been investigating them, and the man born in the American Express.

The concern of many of the voyagers in *The American Express* is the failure of what they call "the human experiment" (28, 64, 147, 218). Their desperate and often preposterous attempts to deal with this failure function both as responses to the extremity of the situation and as evidence of its severity, which the outbreak of war later in the novel serves to underscore.[1]

The proposals of the voyagers span self-sacrifice and violence, but what seems to provide the foundation for many of their strategies is the emergence of the "new consciousness" (31, 32, 43, 44, and 45), which parallels Ginsberg's message "*Widen the area of consciousness*" ("Note" 100)[2] and Burroughs's claim that "I'm concerned with the precise manipulation of word and image to create an action, . . . to create an alteration in the reader's consciousness" (Interview with C. Knickerbocker 174). The extensiveness of the envisioned change is what Corso elsewhere calls "total alteration, personal work social political poetic, emotive—demanded by alteration of consciousness" ("Variations," *Casebook* 95). Most importantly, this alteration involves an adjustment of values: "We were expressing a change of consciousness in our generation—what was moral and what was not" (qtd. in "Bye"). Nevertheless, Corso recognizes how limited the awakening has been: "With the passing of the 50's it was not a decade that terminated but an Epoch, and a new consciousness has occurred but not many have experienced it" (Interview with A. Ginsberg 25). A year later, Corso is more positive, asserting that "a change in the Consciousness has happened." He elaborates on this claim, attributing social changes to an awareness of the Beat movement:

Now a beat person in the United States is not a person who has a beard—exactly. The consciousness is changed by the beat—it is entering the lives of people who go to college, who are married, who have children. . . . the Consciousness has altered there through everyone. ("From an Interview"; ellipsis added)

Ginsberg recalls the early focus of the founding Beat writers:

So we began talking about what in 1945 we called a New Consciousness, or New Vision. As most young people probably do, at the age of 15 to 19, whether it's punk or bohemia or grunge or whatever new vision adolescents have, there is always some kind of striving for understanding and transformation of the universe, according to one's own subjective, poetic generational inspiration. ("Vomit" 16)

For Corso the vision is not limited to adolescence: as recently as 1993, confronted with a question about America's future, he responds, "The United States is called a melting pot. A big mosaic of color. It's going to be a consciousness change" (Interview with D. O'Bryan). Although this new consciousness remains relatively vague, abstract, and mystical, Corso evidently associates it with the principles of American democracy, symbolically represented in the novel by the American Express offices; Hinderov, a character whose solution is the equal distribution of bombs, cites the connection: "The American Express will serve my purposes. It is a simple, admirably functional organization, extremely orderly, efficient, and, to an extent, benevolent—indeed it is just such a system that can appreciate whatever I deem to channel through it" (154). The proof of Hinderov's faith in the system can certainly be seen as reflected in the American response to the Beat Generation writers: not only did segments of American society "appreciate" the Beats; they often lionized them. The mass media reveled in the Beat escapades, and even when critical, the accounts are tinged with envy and enthralled by the often puckish Beat freedom and the absence of conventional restrictions on Beat attitudes and behavior.[3] Beat popularity (or notoriety) directly relates to the themes of Corso's novel: given such stature, the Beats began to take on messianic proportions and to assume the responsibility of providing direction to their disciples and audiences. They posed a question for themselves: "What lifestyles, goals, alternatives, and purposes are valuable and new?"

In Corso's novel the question becomes foreground, but the characters have such diverse interests and values—encompassing what Jim Philip sees in the Beat movement as "two rather contradictory tendencies, leading on the one hand towards spiritual leadership and regeneration, and on the other towards apocalyptic nihilism" (63)—that their ultimate goals and tactics are not concerted.

Hinderov's plan involves bombs (recalling Corso's 1958 poem "Bomb") "because everything is in a deadlock" and "bombs break deadlocks" (Corso, *American Express* 18); the aim of Rodger Wolfherald[4] is to burn the ship *Here They Come* "as an expression of enthusiasm" (80), "[a] pyre to nothingness" (81); Mr. D, who seems to be the uncrowned leader of the travelers, intends to buy the English language "to find a good language for the new consciousness" (43); the goal of Carrol Grilhiggen, the most mystical of the characters, is to "return Lucifer to heaven" (63); Harry, who finds the physical conditions of life's climates hostile, claims a "mission to triumph over the elements" (22); two other characters, Dad Deform and Angus Plow, the latter of whom began by desiring to prove that "[m]an can live without food" (133), are "determined to discover the lost city [*sic*] of Atlantis" (208). The novel explores diverse possibilities because the Beats themselves had no coherent program unifying them: their ideals and approaches encompass the gentle tenderness and compassion of Kerouac's writings and the brittle and crude cynicism of Burroughs's. Burroughs himself has called attention to such a difference when confronted by an interviewer who commented that "[t]he Beat/Hip axis, notably in such figures as Ginsberg, want to transform the world by love and nonviolence. Do you share this interest?" Burroughs responded,

> Most emphatically no. The people in power will not disappear voluntarily, giving flowers to the cops just isn't going to work. This thinking is fostered by the establishment; they like nothing better than love and nonviolence. The only way I like to see cops given flowers is in a flower pot from a high window. (Burroughs and Odier 74)

Burroughs certainly offers a curious alternative cultural revolution: let a hundred flowerpots fall.

Despite their obvious differences, the primary shared attitude of the Beats was a resistance to many of the conventionally accepted standards of American society. As Imamu Baraka (formerly LeRoi Jones) points out,

> Now the point of unity was the point of breakaway, that all those people loosely associated as Beat, and maybe Black Mountain and San Francisco and the other groups like that, they all could be linked together commonly only to the extent that it meant they were breaking away from the established, traditional norms. It's as if, say, a group of people were united by their being opposed to another idea but once you went in to investigate their commonality, you would see most of their commonality consisted of their opposition to something else, rather than them having a consistent or monolithic aesthetic themselves. (136–37)

Their lifestyles thrust them into the company of criminals and drug addicts, the disadvantaged and the dispossessed, the deviant and the *verboten*, the underbelly of American society; furthermore, their rebellion against academic creative writing led them to seek outré outlets as alternatives to the respectable university-dominated periodicals. In *The American Express*, Corso's travelers are identified as occupying similar positions. Detective Frump describes them to the manager of the American Express office as "determined creatures—they wish to push their objectives through American Express time— The system suits them— The difference will be in the transactions— You deal in money; they deal in human beings— They feel they can best deal in their 'commodity' through your firm's system" (26–27). His comments point to the contrast between the humanistic goals of the travelers and the economic motives of American capitalistic society.

In response to the question "where do they [the voyagers] operate from?" Frump answers, "From the underground" (16). Later, asked by the manager of the American Express if the travelers intend to use his offices, Frump says, "If not in your offices, under it" (27), and explains, "They're like moles—they build under their target and eventually incorporate themselves in the target" (28). This modus operandi parallels the "underground" activities and publications of the Beat Generation. Kerouac, who even called attention to such an alternative by titling one of his novels *The Subterraneans* (at the beginning of which the narrator credits the title term to Adam Moorad, a character based on Ginsberg), signals the emergence of this group, "rising from the underground, the sordid hipsters of America, a new beat generation" (*On* 54), and, in the early poem "In the Tunnel-Bone of Cambridge," Corso provides a narrator who refers to himself as "a subterranean" (*G/V* 66); in the later poem "Columbia U Poesy Reading—1975," he characterizes the Beat literary output as "a subterranean poesy of the streets" (*HA* 2). However, if the Beats did not exactly "incorporate themselves" into the American system, they certainly found themselves being engulfed by the system as *Time, Life, Newsweek*, and even *Mademoiselle* featured stories on them. The attractiveness of celebrity or notoriety provides a distraction from the idealistic goals of social change, and, as many rebels before the Beats had found, the spirit may be willing, but the enticements accompanying popularity can expose the weakness of the flesh. This is especially true when the primary spur of rebellion is dissatisfaction with the status quo, rather than a coherent, coordinated program of action. In Corso's novel no such coordination occurs: the travelers differ in their approaches and methods, when they have any at all. Questioned about the voyagers' plans, Detective Frump responds, "I don't know. Though I do know that their intentions, among themselves, differ" (16). The characters themselves often seem as confused as Frump (and the reader) about their goals.

Though the missions of the voyagers are ultimately unsuccessful, this lack of fruition does not disturb them. The very preposterousness of the voyagers' plans suggests that their ends are less important than the dissatisfactions that prompt them. Corso's character Simon offers an analogy to explain the importance of process rather than product when he lectures Albie regarding the latter's frustrated love for Molly, one of the three female travelers: "Love is not necessary after it has been found. To seek love is necessary, to find love is necessary, and to lose it immediately is necessary. Love is denial; you should be happy, Albie—without love you will always love" (135). Such Grecian Urn-like consolation offers a grand, "Cold" principle but little relief to the lovelorn character.

As countercultural dissidents, the travelers insist upon the need to change an ineffectual, inhumane society, to offer alternatives to conventional modes of thought, and to call attention to the failure of the controlling society's politics, religion, and conventions. Most importantly, the characters are imbued with a clear sense of purpose, even if the purposes themselves remain less than clear. The abstract altruism itself can be attractive, even (perhaps especially) when its program incorporates the rhetoric of mystical emptiness. Thus, Angus Plow asks Joel, who is making his first voyage, "Why are you going on this ship, Joel?" Joel replies, "Mr. Plow, I really do not know why. I just feel that something vast and beautiful will happen—and I want to be as near to it as possible" (11). Plow himself refers to the "one supreme fact—why are we here? It was understood, and agreed, that when we set out to come here, each of us, or groups of us, would achieve something. That is why we are here" (210–11). The radical quality of many of their programs reflects the intensity of their objections to the rigid indifference and irrelevance of contemporary institutions. The underground, collective nature of the voyagers' community supplies its energy and motivation.

In many ways the humanistic concerns expressed by the major characters are congruent with those articulated by the major Beat writers and with the literary strategies they employed. At times, the beliefs of the characters overlap, as frequently happens among acquaintances whose friendships and interchanges include the currency of ideas.[5] Thus, Simon, apparently modeled on Peter Orlovsky,[6] announces, "We are the God we always longed for" (44), and Carrol echoes, "You long for God and don't know that you're already God!" (45). In turn, this notion reflects the position taken in Kerouac's and Ginsberg's writings. In Kerouac's *The Dharma Bums*, Ray Smith, the narrator, persists in cajoling each of his friends with the illumination that "God is *you*, you fool" (111) and inculcating in himself the same Romantic insight: "I am God" (122). Kerouac also insists, "God is not outside us but is just us" (*Scripture* 22), and "every one of us is God" (*Desolation* 208). Similarly, Ginsberg finds himself "with no God to turn to / But what I Am" ("Journal Night" 13); speaking of the 1960 poem "Magic Psalm," which records his vision after drinking the Amazon spiritual potion Ayahuasca, Ginsberg explains,

> The point of that poem was that there was an abstract divinity out-side me that I was trying to summon to my aid or energy. The prob-lem was to integrate it into my own consciousness and to therefore become God, or to say I am God, or to say in the poem "I am God," or to imagine I am God—rather than that God be something exter-nal to me. (Interview with D. Ossman 89)

Ginsberg recognized that the frequent discussion of ideas among Beat writers made original attribution of the source of many ideas and sometimes even of language and phrasing problematical:

> Concerned that everyone receive proper credit for their original ideas, Allen worried about the cross-pollination of the group's creative ideas. "[M]y phantasies and phrases have gotten so lovingly mixed up in yours . . . I hardly know whose is which and who's used what," he wrote Jack. "I'm not haggling I just want to know if it's OK to use anything I want that creeps in." Much of his "Shroudy Stranger" poem, he pointed out, could be attributed to his and Jack's conver-sations. Allen and John Clellon Holmes were also concerned about the title of John's book: Was *Go* the title of one of Jack's unpublished earlier works? In his excitement over the group's success, Jack was inclined to be generous. "Don't worry about that at all," he advised Allen, admitting that some of Allen's ideas could be found in his prose. As for the title of Holmes's book, Kerouac noted that "'Go, Go, Go' was the title of a story I wrote about me n Neal in a jazzjoint, [but] it was Giroux [who] made up the title"; if *Go* worked as a title for Holmes's book, Jack said, then John should feel free to use it.[7] (Schumacher 141)

Furthermore, "Song: Fie My Fum" (excerpted from the poem "Pull My Daisy") was composed jointly by Kerouac, Ginsberg, and Neal Cassady in 1949; Kerouac and Burroughs coauthored a still unpublished novel, "And the Hippos Were Boiled in Their Tanks"; and Kerouac, Corso, and Ginsberg collaborated on a 1958 poem, "Nixon." The cut-up experiments in which Corso participated under the influence of Burroughs involved them in "collaboration" with each other's writings and with writers who were long dead. An interesting further variation on the interpenetra-tion of the Beat writers is the fact that Corso plays the Kerouac figure in the 1959 film *Pull My Daisy*.[8] They did not even seem compelled to demand credit for themselves: a letter to the *Wagner Literary Magazine* attributed to Corso, Ginsberg, and Orlovsky was actually, according to Robert Wilson, written entirely by Corso; two articles in *Holiday* with Kerouac's byline were written in collaboration with Corso, Ginsberg, and Orlovsky; and "The Literary Revolution in America" was written by Corso and Ginsberg but appeared under Corso's byline. This behavior of the Beats differs sharply from the selfish, ego-obsessed attitudes of the characters in Corso's novel, which instead focuses on the dangers lying in wait for the Beats. In this sense the novel can be seen as a warning that projects the possibilities of self-centered concerns. However, identifying the individual Beat writers with particular characters in Corso's novel can often be as difficult as trying to isolate their specific contributions of language and ideas. Instead, the characters often seem to be composites—soft-edged sketches whose outlines blur into each other.

The mission of the voyagers is spurred by a belief articulated by Carrol Gril-higgen, a principle that also reverberates in Beat writings: "Man is indeed the victory of life!" (45). This is a theme that appears repeatedly in much the same phrasing throughout Corso's writings in the 1960s: "we are alive, man, the victory of life" (Introduction 246); "Man is a select thing unto himself! He is the victory of life!" ("Moschops!" 66); "Man is the victory of life" ("Man," *LL* 10); "Because I find man indeed life's victory" ("Saint Francis," *LL* 39); "Man is the victory of life" ("Writ in Horace," *LL* 85); "The victory that is man" ("American," *EF* 71, 72); "I can only hold that man is the victory of life" ("American," *EF* 75). Especially poignant in Corso's novel is the fact that the mission's purpose is uttered by Carrol—a character with correspondences to (and even onomastic echoes of) Jack Kerouac, the most celebrated of the Beat writers. Finding himself "completely bereft of moral significance" (30), Carrol feels that religion, here specifically Catholicism, has failed him and that the church needs to be taken over by forces that have human concerns closer to the goals of a more idealistic program.[9] What he intends to do is to reinvent religion and to bribe God into accepting his accomplishment because he is certain that he can return Lucifer to God in Heaven.

The connection to Kerouac, who characterized himself as a "strange solitary crazy Catholic mystic" (*Lonesome* vi), is discernible on several levels: Kerouac was careful to point out that the very word *Beat* had religious connotations: "BEAT—the root, the soul of Beatific" (*On* 195). He claimed to have "had a vision of what I must have meant with 'Beat' anyhow when I heard the holy silence in the church . . . the vision of the word Beat as being to mean beatific" ("Origins" 42). Furthermore, throughout his novels, Kerouac uses religious terminology to redeem the behavior of what might ordinarily be considered aberrant characters. Thus, one of the most flagrant examples, Dean Moriarty of *On the Road*, becomes "a new kind of American saint" (39), "the holy con-man" (7, 213), "the Angel of Terror" (233), "a burning shuddering frightful Angel" (259), and ultimately "the

HOLY GOOF" (194). Similarly, in his cover blurb for Corso's *Gasoline*, Kerouac describes the author as "a tough young kid from the Lower East Side who rose like an angel over the rooftops." Thus, the wayward, fallen rebels become sanctified; the theme also becomes clear in the title *Desolation Angels*, a novel in which Kerouac's narrator avers, "I only know one thing: everybody in the world is an angel" (85), paralleling Corso's use of the character Angus Plow to assert "the fact that the human race is a race of angels" (Corso, *American Express* 133).

In his 1959 prose piece "Variations on a Generation," Corso himself referred to "glorious bands of angels that will be the human race when it has achieved its already many times glimpsed godhead, NOW AT HAND!" (96). John Tytell cites a pictorial illustration of Corso's application of this technique to his cohorts:

> In one of Gregory Corso's letters to Allen Ginsberg, there is a drawing of an angelic Virgin cradling William Burroughs in her arms while Ginsberg and Kerouac hover like desolate cherubim—the picture a brooding reminder of the messianic and reformist impulses of a movement that was steeped in sorrow while yearning for beatitude. (5)

Never mind that one can scarcely imagine Burroughs comfortable in such a distasteful position—the drawing demonstrates the Beat elevation of the rebels to spiritual, and here even messianic, status. Furthermore, the messianic role can be interchangeable: after reminding the late Kerouac that "[t]he ArcAngel Raphael was I to you" (in allusion to Corso's portrayal as Raphael Urso in *Desolation Angels* and *Book of Dreams*, graciously ignoring the less attractive nom de guerre of Yuri Gligoric in *The Subterraneans*), Corso characterizes Kerouac as "a Beat Christ-boy" ("Elegiac," *EF* 12). The same spirit infuses Ginsberg's depiction of "angelheaded hipsters," "saintly motorcyclists," and "those human seraphim" ("Howl" 9, 12); Ginsberg goes on to expand the sanctification of the mundane world in "Footnote to Howl," offering specific details of examples not ordinarily associated with holiness: "The world is holy! The soul is holy! The skin is holy! The nose is holy! The tongue and cock and hand and asshole holy! / Everything is holy! everybody's holy! everywhere is holy! everyday is in eternity! Everyman's an angel!" (21).

This celebration of life's holiness also corresponds to a passage from Kerouac's script for *Pull My Daisy* (in which Ginsberg, Corso, and Orlovsky have major performing roles) in which a visiting clergyman is bombarded by a series of rhetorical questions: "Is everything holy, is alligators holy, bishop? Is the world holy? Is the basketball holy? Is the organ of man holy?" (32). Kerouac would clearly answer affirmatively, for the sanctified characters of his novels roam across "old tumbledown holy America" (*On* 150) in a "[p]oor little angel world" (*Dharma* 218), with his heroes continually attaining "another pious frenzy" (*On* 245). His holy angels and saints have rebelled against convention, and the Beat portrayal of them corresponds to Carrol's attempt to reunite Lucifer with God. Corso and Kerouac were raised as Catholics—"the holy communion boys" (36), as Corso's character Thimble calls them—and Corso admits that "I always used to hail Lucifer in a silly romantic way, I saw him as a romantic figure, smart witty and wearer of cloaks, I used to call him the first free thinker, the first rebel, etc." ("Dear Fathers" 10). He continues, with a direct reference to his novel: "I had a young boy who wanted to bring Lucifer back to heaven so that everything would be all right again, bad brought back into the good graces of good." Elsewhere, Corso offers a celebration: "Lucifer is great, Lucifer is first free thinker, Lucifer is eternal rebel, hail Lucifer!" ("Variations," *Casebook* 90). The fallen angel's free thought and rebellious behavior were core principles for Beat writers.

The essence of Carrol's complaint is that conventional religion and its assumptions about God are outdated:

> I will find a better representation of Him! I will find a God fitting
> for me! A God of the new consciousness! The Catholic Church is
> done—your God has not changed. Man changes, therefore God must
> change.[10] (*American Express* 31)

Carrol's criticism reveals a symptom of a much larger problem, one that Kerouac was compelled to delineate:

> It is, face it, a mean heartless creation emanated by a God of Wrath,
> Jehovah, Yaweh, No-Name, who will pat you kindly on the head and
> say "Now you're being good" when you pray, but when you're beg-
> ging for mercy anyway say like a soldier hung by one leg from a tree
> trunk in today's Vietnam, when Yaweh's really got you out in back
> of the barn even in ordinary torture of fatal illness like my Pa's then,
> he wont listen, he will whack away at your lil behind with the long
> stick of what they called "Original Sin" in the Theological Christian
> dogmatic sects but what I call "Original Sacrifice." (*Vanity* 274)

Admittedly this is one of Kerouac's bleaker moments, but his theodicy frequently finds itself foundering in the dark night of the soul where submission has become subjugation.

Corso would seem to be able to relate to such bitterness: in a 1956 composition in which Corso and Ginsberg alternated lines, Ginsberg wrote, "But we'll meet, Yes! not Zeus, but God upwheres we wing," and Corso responded, "Wherewith twenty wideeyed lambs become certain of terrible yet pious sacrifice!" (Corso and Ginsberg, "ALGREINORSO" 314). However, Kerouac, childlike, clings tenaciously to his religious float, convinced by the very existence of fear, suffering, and loneliness that relief must exist, that peace and comfort, despite the odds against them, can finally be attained. Thus, in Kerouac's first published novel, Peter Martin finds himself aboard an endangered ship during World War II and undergoes a mystical conversion:

> The world was mad with war and history. It made great steel ships that could plow the sea, and then made greater torpedoes to sink the selfsame struggling ship. He suddenly believed in God somehow, in goodness and loneliness. (*Town* 308)

Later, Kerouac's God speaks to humanity about its suffering:

> my child, you find yourself in the world of mystery and pain not understandable—I know, angel—it is for your good, we shall save you, because we find your soul as important as the soul of the others in the world—but you must suffer for that, in effect my child, you must die, you must die in pain, with cries, frights, despairs. (*Maggie* 43)

Such promises of salvation are threatening, particularly to the sensitive soul unable to comprehend how a benevolent God could thrust the frail creatures of his love into a world of danger, where everything and everyone a person grows to cherish must break, depart, or die—and how this is all for one's own good. In *The American Express*, Harry, who always feels cold,[11] addresses this condition: "What kind of God is it that puts a thing in an alien climate, I ask?" (22). In *On the Road*, hope is forced to concede to reality: Kerouac's narrator, Sal Paradise, "prayed to God for a better break in life and a better chance to do something for the little people I loved. Nobody was paying any attention to me up there. I should have known better" (96–97). Knowing better, Corso's Carrol Grilhiggen determines to change God's edicts and attitudes.

Hope and belief often depend for their sustenance on a faith that is essentially childlike. In *The American Express*, Corso endows Carrol with such a characteristic: using a tactic familiar to many children and their parents, Carrol determines to hold his breath until God grants him an audience to discuss accepting Lucifer back in heaven. Such a strategy seems appropriate to a Kerouac whose Sal Paradise could ask in the conclusion of *On the Road*, "don't you know that God is Pooh Bear?" (309), equating the naive belief in both figures.

Recognizing that Kerouac serves as a model for Carrol can also help to explain one of the most puzzling episodes in Corso's novel: Carrol returns to his father's farm and, with an axe (Carrol-axe?), kills his father's prize-winning pig, a pig that is "like a child" (61) to the elder Grilhiggen. This brutal act appears so out of character for Carrol that its function in the novel can only be explained on a sym-

bolic level. Its significance seems to lie in its reflection of Kerouac's youthful ca-
reer as an athlete. Kerouac was a flashy football player at Lowell High School and
Horace Mann Preparatory School. During his last game at the latter school, he
returned a punt for a touchdown, made a sixty-five yard run, kicked a fifty-five
yard punt, and threw a pass for a first down; afterwards his "name was plastered
across sports sections from New York to Lowell" (Nicosia 61). His father, Leo,
actively supported his son's athletic career, attending games, pushing him to ex-
cel, and basking vicariously in the warmth of Jack's success, even visiting the locker
room and joking with Jack's teammates. Disappointed in the lack of publicity for
Jack's earlier high school athletics, "Leo would carp and grumble about the qual-
ity of press coverage for his boy" (McNally 27). Awarded an athletic scholarship
to Columbia College, Jack broke his leg in the second freshman game, after run-
ning the opening kickoff back ninety yards. The following season, miffed by his
coach's neglect, he quit college and suspended his football career, much to his
father's chagrin. Leo Kerouac's involvement was complicated even more by other
factors: in *Vanity of Duluoz*, Jack suggests that his father's employers promised
Leo a promotion if Jack went to Boston College and indicated that he would lose
his job if Jack went elsewhere, and Leo was fired; in addition, according to Nicosia,
acquaintances of Lou Little, Jack's coach at Columbia, had made promises, never
fulfilled, of a job for Leo. Leo often seemed to have tied his own aspirations to
the football career of his son, seeing Jack's success as a compensation for his own
professional failure and glorying in his son's athletic talent; "Become a football
star, Leo told him, it's your only chance" (Clark 49). Jack eventually returned to
Columbia, briefly dabbling in football practices before finally walking out after
he was not played during the first game of the season. This background from
Kerouac's life provides an explanation of Carrol Grilhiggen's violent act in Corso's
novel: the killing of his father's pig symbolizes Kerouac's slaughter of his father's
dreams of Jack's "pigskin" success.[12]

However, despite their apparent rebelliousness, Corso's characters seem to re-
tain concern for their parents' opinions. In a scene that seems to evoke Kerouac's
confrontations with his mother over his Beat companions, particularly Ginsberg
and Burroughs,[13] Joel's mother remonstrates with her son against meeting with the
travelers and warns him against associating with Mr. D: "He stands for danger!
disaster! death!" (56–57). In addition, Detective Frump poses a series of questions
to two characters identified as murderers: "Do you have families? . . . Are they
satisfied with you? . . . Do you believe in what you are doing?" (58; ellipses added).
Later, this table is turned on Frump; masquerading as a seal trainer, he is criticized
by Hinderov: "What kind of man are you? What about your poor mother and
father? Do you think they like what you are? What parent wants its child to be what

you are? Ha-ha-ha-ha-ha-ha! A seal trainer!" (116). Obviously, however, the characters feel the need to assert themselves, to follow their dream despite the objections of their families and despite the standards and values of their upbringing.

The novel's Mr. D sees language, not religion, as the medium for change: "'We'll triumph with this, for sure,' said Mr. D, weighing the heavy book ["a huge dictionary"] on a scale" (35). Corso has admitted that this character is based on William Burroughs: "Look, Mr. D. would be, except for the color, Burroughs" (Interview with M. Andre 132). In fact, the titular image of Corso's novel may arise, at least in part, from Burroughs's line "I am not American Express" (218) in *Naked Lunch*, which, like *The American Express*, was first published as part of the Traveller's Companion Series of Maurice Girodias's Olympia Press. However, even without Corso's acknowledgement, Mr. D's identity would be clear to anyone familiar with Burroughs's work: Corso's Mr. D, "tall and spectral" (17) like Burroughs's "spectral" Lee the Agent (*Naked* 218),[14] hopes to buy the English language, although his alternative plan is to go "to Egypt and buy some hieroglyphs" (43). Those acquainted with Burroughs's attacks on the word and with his interest in pictorial language can easily recognize the portrait:

> Admittedly, two model control systems, the Mayan and the Egyptian, were based on hieroglyphic writing. However, these control systems were predicated on the illiteracy of the controlled. Universal literacy with a concomitant control of word and image is now the instrument of control. An essential feature of the Western control machine is to make language as *non-pictorial* as possible, to separate words as far as possible from objects or observable processes. (Burroughs and Odier 103)

> A simplified pictorial script adapted to the typewriter would constitute a workable international means of communication. (*Book*)

Shiva,[15] another of Corso's three women voyagers, asserts that "Mr. D's plan depends upon the magic of words" (Corso, *American Express* 142). In a confused attempt to endorse different plans, she explains Mr. D's rationale:

> Words are not colorless. It is the word that makes all. In the beginning was the word. That means the word was there when the beginning began. It did not come to the beginning, the beginning came to it. It is Mr. D's intention to unspeak the word and so have done with the human *and* universal predicament. (141)

Similarly, Burroughs explains his beliefs:

Nothing basically wrong with the human beings themselves, but they certainly will have to take a very basic forward step in evolution. It's quite probable that at the real beginning point of what we call modern man was speech. In the beginning was the word. I think the next step will have to be beyond the word. The word is now an outmoded artifact. Any life form that gets stuck with an outmoded built-in artifact is doomed to destruction. (Burroughs and Odier 98)

Furthermore, Mr. D reads a statement that makes the parallel to Burroughs even more obvious: "In man's training tiger woman farm silk horses nibble on virus—cancer in a crusted Azoola stick. Man is raining Azoola a billion light years away. Cancer exists; therefore, cancer is God" (128). The statement captures the flavor of Burroughs's cut-ups (in which Corso participated, though with considerable reservations, for the 1960 collection *Minutes to Go*) and includes his major thematic concerns. In fact, a passage from *Minutes to Go* clearly reveals the influence:

> Words   Dealth   by   William Lee Dealer
> No   house percentage   CUT
> FUNCTION   WITH   BURROUGHS   EVERY MAN
> AN AGENT   CUT
> In THEE   beginning was THE word..   The word was a
> virus.. "Function always comes before form" L Ron Hubbard.
> Virus made man..   Man is virus..[16]
>
> (Beiles et al. 59)

The similar concerns of Burroughs and Mr. D are underlined in Corso's novel by another echo of this passage when Mr. D asserts that "whatever functions, functions with Mr. D" (211); in *Minutes to Go*, Corso quotes a phrase, "Function with Burroughs," from a letter written by Burroughs (58). In an interview of Burroughs by Corso and Ginsberg published in the same year as *The American Express*, Corso addresses an issue related to the concerns of the voyagers, asking, "Do you feel there has been a definite change in man's makeup? A new consciousness?" Burroughs responds,

> Yes, I can give you a precise answer to that. I feel that the change the mutation in consciousness will occur spontaneously once certain pressures now in operation are removed. I feel that the principal instrument of monopoly and control that prevents expansion of consciousness is the word lines controlling thought feeling and apparent sensory impressions of the human host. . . . The forward step must

be made in silence. We detach ourselves from word forms—this can
be accomplished by substituting for words, letters, verbal concepts,
other modes of expression. (80; ellipsis added)

Mr. D's interest in hieroglyphics supports Simon's assertion that "Mr. D is trying
to find a good language for the new consciousness" (43). However, Corso's novel
also includes an episode that highlights the importance of language and commu-
nication: Simon tells a fairy tale about a witch who cut out her own tongue; asked
twice by a woodcutter for directions to a town she does not know, she points to
her mouth to indicate that she cannot speak. Each time she does this, the wood-
cutter mistakes her pointing for an indication of direction; he finally returns an-
gry at being misdirected and chops off her head. The story becomes a parable about
the importance of language, even if only as a tool to communicate one's ignorance.

Burroughs's ideas are also reflected in Angus Plow's comments on food:

> Man can live without food. There are ways. But those ways are held
> back. There are certain forces, the restaurant industry in particular,
> that put all their effort into keeping these ways out of man's conscious-
> ness. Farmers, cattlemen, the entire scheme of eating, would crumple
> were the ways exposed. (133)

Burroughs articulates his own theories about such vested interests at length in
The Job:

> Vested interest of power and/or money is perhaps the most potent
> factor standing in the way of freedom for the individual. New discov-
> eries and products are suppressed because they threaten vested inter-
> ests. The medical profession is suppressing Reich's orgone
> accumulator and his discoveries relative to the use and dangers of
> orgonic energy. They are suppressing Dianetics and Scientology dis-
> covered by Mr L. Ron Hubbard. They are suppressing the use of
> massive doses of Vitamin E for the prevention of heart disease, the
> use of massive doses of Vitamin A for curing the common cold. . . .
> The medical profession is suppressing the use of apomorphine for the
> treatment of alcoholism and drug addiction and for the general regu-
> lation of disturbed metabolism. The medical profession has a *vested
> interest in illness*. . . . The real-estate lobby has a vested interest in the
> housing shortage. . . . The police have a vested interest in criminal-
> ity. The Narcotics Department has a vested interest in addiction. Poli-
> ticians have a vested interest in nations. Army officers have a vested
> interest in war. Vested interest, whether operating through private,
> capital or official agencies, suppresses any discovery, product or way

of thought that threatens its area of monopoly. (Burroughs and Odier 60–61)

In Kerouac's *On the Road*, Bull Lee, who is modeled on Burroughs, provides evidence that Burroughs's concerns have been long-standing:

> Why, Sal, do you realize the shelves they build these days crack under the weight of knickknacks after six months or generally collapse? Same with houses, same with clothes. These bastards have invented plastics by which they could make houses that last *forever*. And tires. Americans are killing themselves by the millions every year with defective rubber tires that get hot on the road and blow up. They could make tires that never blow up. Same with tooth powder. There's a certain gum they've invented and they won't show it to anybody that if you chew it as a kid you'll never get a cavity for the rest of your born days. Same with clothes. They can make clothes that last forever. They prefer making cheap goods so's everybody'll have to go on working and punching timeclocks and organizing themselves in sullen unions and floundering around while the big grab goes on in Washington and Moscow. (149)

Mr. D and Carrol are unsuccessful in their efforts to undermine religious conservatism, verbal control, and vested interests, but Corso incorporates the themes and techniques of his fellow Beat writers under the guise of the travelers and their obsessions. A sense of urgency informs the obsessive motives of the characters, an intensity that is underlined by the novel's repeated focus on a dual aspect of time and its effect on the voyagers: they are aging, though deathless. This apparent immortality calls attention to the fact that the novel itself is an artifact and to the likelihood that the solutions are symbolic rather than realistic.

By incorporating the artificiality of the work of art, the novel is able to provide its own contextual rules and to play games with its own literary status, as when Joel observes, "Albie ever since we arrived has been asking Where's Molly? What does that represent symbolically, Mr. Deform?" (108). In addition, character development can be indicated entirely through similes, as the novel reveals through Joel's wartime career:

> Joel raced into the muddy attack swinging swords and knives, shooting rifles and stens, flinging grenades and flares; and everybody dispersed in his path, and he skipped through the dispersion like a happy girl.

Tanks loomed before him; he threw tankbomb after tankbomb, and the tanks became all afire—

He shot the burning men teeming out of the burning tanks like a hard cold man.

The battle was over; he walked over the dead like an old market woman. (197–98)

Three similes carry him from innocent childhood through adulthood to old age. Furthermore, the relationship of the characters to mortality and time transcends reality. Characters can die and reappear later, as Carrol and Bronskier do. The novel is set in an unidentified transhistorical period—a world where the voyagers sail to tribal Britannia and where the combatants in the war employ swords, axes, and armor, but also have access to telephones, "a timeless composite of the middle ages and the present" (Stephenson, *Exiled* 78). Time can also be ignored or highlighted. Subjectivity becomes the ultimate control, as the pathetic fallacy accomplishes its own reality. Thus, Joel and Shiva find that their romantically heightened states can alter the dimensions of reality. Psychological time becomes chronological time as love controls and tempers duration:

If Shiva suggested they go and pick flowers it took them two days to do so. Everything said and done went slow. And in such rhythm did they stretch the beautiful feeling they felt for each other. It was their way, and it seemed to go with the motion of their habitat.

When the tempo went fast, when a buck dashed into their acre, they also went fast. They would run with equal speed and grace after it, and trap it in their fabulous snare which extended high and long across the trees. (233)

Once again a Kerouac parallel is appropriate: in *On the Road*, Sal Paradise claims that he reached "the point of ecstasy that I always wanted to reach, which was the complete step across chronological time into timeless shadows" (173), and Dean Moriarty asserts that "we know time—how to slow it up" (252). Neal Cassady, upon whom Dean was based, describes

an awareness that time in my head had gradually apexed to about triple its ordinary speed of passage, and as this thing happened, although I couldn't realize it then, it was just thought of as a circular flying object twirling through my mind for lack of a better way to think about this spinning sensation. But, actually, it was felt (nervously) only for what it was—a strange, pleasant quickening of my brain's action which was disturbing enough to frighten, yet resisted any rigorous attempt to throw it off and return to normal-headedness. This time-acceleration came and went of its own accord, making me thus dizzy-minded. . . . It was nearly a full score years later before I again had similar headspins (from different stimuli, such as marijuana) but which this time I tried to hold and analyze, and found by heavy concentration I could, for short moments, turn this time-quickening off and on at will once it had started. (112–13)

Corso's travelers, in similar fashion, recognize the subjective nature of time, but Detective Frump attempts to distinguish between the time of the creative artifact and the time of the real world. Speaking of the impending arrival of the voyagers on *Here They Come*, he explains, "A boat like that doesn't run on time, that is, not on time as we know it" (15). Nevertheless, he suggests the unreasonableness of the world of artifice:

Well, in a relative sense nothing starts and nothing ends. But for humankind things do start and end. Man, unlike the universe, is beginning with end. He is born into that which always was, and he dies from that which always is. The boat will come into what always was and what always will be. It is my firm belief that the passengers aboard are determined to disembark with the sole intent to change things somewhat. They do not like the idea that they depart and arrive. They too would like to be without beginning without end, just like the universe, gentlemen. (15–16)

The theme that Frump articulates here is one that Corso treats poetically in "The Leaky Lifeboat Boys":

Waiting for the world
not themselves to die
they scheme upon getting out of life alive
. . . .
These darling men ever getting older
are insufferably ass-bound
claiming the planet like the body
is a leaky lifeboat
and with a tinge of urgency, cry:
"It's bail out time, we gotta mutate!"

The desire to mutate mutates
'tis the fuel of evolution this desire

You see, it's not that they want to live forever
they believe they are forever
it's just the form they're in and on
that's deathable.[17]

(*HA* 15–16; ellipsis added)

For Corso, "the form they're in and on," the human body and the planet Earth, imposes restrictions on human potential, for it is "ephemeral / Time / . . . [that] leads me into conditional life" ("In the Fleeting," *G/V* 15; ellipsis added) and "[t]he clocked tower's scythed chime / bodes sorrow and the life of man equal time" ("Clown," *HB* 55). In two of Corso's contributions to a linked-verse poem that he wrote with Ginsberg, his preoccupation with mortality becomes manifest: "Ariseth from the pyre—phoenix-like—in search of Time, immortal"; "aware of mortal prey lashed upon Time's disembowered Granite" (Corso and Ginsberg, "ALGREINORSO" 313). The ideal is a transcendence of time and mortality: as characters in a work of fiction, Corso's travelers manage to achieve this, just as the Beat Generation writers hope to attain such an end through their creative achievements. Burroughs, who had attended lectures by Count Alfred Korzybski in 1939 and had been recommending the ideas of the Polish semanticist to Ginsberg and Kerouac since 1944, comments on the process available through writing:

> Animals communicate and convey information. But they do not write. They cannot make information available to future generations or to animals outside the range of their communication system. This is the crucial distinction between man and other animals. Korzybski has pointed out this human distinction and described man as "the time binding animal." He can make information available over any length of time to other men through writing. (*Book*)

Ginsberg also points to the connection between art and time:

> The thing I understood from Blake was that it was possible to transmit a message through time which could reach the enlightened, that poetry had a definite effect, it wasn't just pretty, or just beautiful, as I had understood pretty beauty before—it was something basic to human existence, or it reached something, it reached the bottom of human existence. But anyway the impression I got was that it was like a kind of time machine through which he could transmit, Blake could transmit, his basic consciousness and communicate it to somebody else after he was dead—in other words, build a time machine. (Interview with T. Clark 291)

Corso's characters repeatedly call attention to the special relationship between their existence and time.[18] "I know my time; I need nothing else," says Daphne (20), the third female traveler, who will later design the ship for the return trip, and Carrol echoes the sentiment: "More so, I know my time" (64); Hinderov too stakes his temporal claim: "I am in my time" (237). Their time is the *carpe diem* present moment, oblivious of past and future. Thus, when Dad Deform—who is a caricature of the writer Alan Ansen, with whom Corso had written collaboratively[19]—expresses his anxiety about being late for departure on *Here They Come*, Thimble reprimands him, noting that "you seem to ignore the time at hand—*at hand*, sir, the *Now!*" (10). This conventional theme is one that Corso reiterates in a later poem, "For Homer":

And there is no tomorrow
there's only right here and now
you and whomever you're with
alive as always
and ever ignorant of that death you'll never know.

(*HA* 14)

Corso's novel, however, recognizes limitations on personally determined temporality: Daphne's knowledge of time depends upon her "telling watch" (20), which is eventually stolen; Carrol's confident knowledge of time is qualified by his death (though this is not terminal); Hinderov, with appropriate confusion, asserts, "the motives of disorder differ with the succeeding periods and changes of my plans— what was not executed yesterday cannot be executed today—disorder demands immediacy" (154). Wolfherald expresses his doubts about human attitudes toward time while providing a grudging hope: "It is really curious how man insists on certainty. He can form no set idea of time, though I fully realize it is, after all, possible that he can" (65). Corso's "Eleven Times a Poem" recognizes these conflicting forces: "Miasma, I am able to enter the beautiful world / Stained as I am with the filth of human time" (*EF* 31). The characters in the novel seem intent on denying the "filth" of the aging process; asked, "What about old age?" Carrol declares, "I will never abandon myself to that authority" (64), despite the fact that just a page earlier "Carrol's young face tightened into an old man's face" (63); Shiva expostulates with Ephraim Freece: "But, Ephraim, please promise me you won't grow old. . . . No one who is beautiful should live to be old" (102–3; ellipsis added). Detective Frump recognizes that "I'm getting old, I guess" (122) and generalizes his own condition: "I say whatever grows grows old" (232).

On cue, immediately after Frump articulates this principle of mortality, Freece begins to detect signs of his own vulnerability to time's processes, as "he noticed hair on his young hands—he never saw hair there before" (235). Although Corso evidently empathizes with the travelers' cult of youth, he is realistic enough to recognize the likely frustrations of such a value system. Corso, the youngest of the major Beat writers (b. 1930; Burroughs, b. 1914; Kerouac, b. 1922; and Ginsberg, b. 1926), may have been witnessing the physical effects of time on his friends and projecting his own imminent aging onto their conditions: his poem "Hair," with a focus on the ravages of time on a man's head of hair, was published when Corso was only thirty years old. Few other poets have as regularly chronicled their age as Corso has, registering many of his birthdays and recording his "Feelings on Getting Older," on *Hitting the Big 5-0*, and on becoming "an old toothless messenger boy" ("I am rich"). In a relevantly penetrating moment during his 1961 interview with Ginsberg, Corso questions the very meaning of the Beat claims of a breakthrough of consciousness: "Could it be that there ain't no new consciousness, that perhaps all of it is us growing older and therefore consider it a miracle of Nature and not a familiar process which it could well be—I mean like we ain't ever experienced getting older before, ever, so how can we be certain" (29).

His novel, however, stops short of committing the travelers to death. In fact, Simon asserts, "But, Albie, you know very well none of us ever get *seriously* hurt . . . . It clearly stated to all those chosen to sail *Here They Come* that the practice of death was prohibited" (135–36; ellipsis added). As a result, the other characters, with the exception of Wolfherald, refuse to recognize Carrol Grilhiggen's "death." Mr. D tells Thimble, "You know we never die"; Thimble asks, "How come Carrol and Bronskier are always dying?" and Mr. D responds, "It's part of their plans" (36–37). When Wolfherald later exclaims that Carrol is dead, Thimble denies it: "None of us die" (116). What this indicates is that the voyagers have performed this ritual before and are aware that they are all involved in a creative performance. Wolfherald tries to explain this to himself by assuming that "Carrol possessed two lives—one life to die as he had, and the other to sit back and talk about it" (163); as a result, at the end of the novel, Carrol is accompanying Wolfherald as everybody congregates to depart on the ship *There They Go*.

This time- and death-consciousness may help to explain the urgency of the characters, even though they try to rationalize it away. Unfortunately, however, the humanistic concerns of the revolutionary voyagers are contaminated by another very human feature: vanity. Each of the characters has an ego-invested interest in being the one to provide the most stunning solution; efficacy takes a back seat. The characters are concerned to accomplish what they refer to as the "great act" or "grand achievement." The result is that, as Angus Plow describes it, "It's nothing but a contest, all of it. Now what part do we play—are they to succeed and we not?" (94), and Albie plaintively asks, "Why is everybody always trying to outdo everybody?" (137). Mr. D also questions the personal motivation of the voyagers: "Everybody wants to achieve something. Why? Do they seek the pageantry of social activities? The Nobel Prize? Movie contracts?" (209). Their ego-centricity, competition, and self-promotion seriously undermine the characters' integrity. Carrol Grilhiggen's religious disillusionment often seems heartfelt, but in announcing his goal, he reveals motives of self-aggrandizement: "If I can return Lucifer to heaven I would have accomplished the most humane and glorious feat ever performed by man!" (63). Asked by Rodger Wolfherald, "Is that why you are doing it, to achieve the greatest feat ever performed by man?" Carrol "proudly" responds, "I know no grander attitude," and exclaims, "All great acts will become insignificant to the one I shall perform!" (65). Corso's corrective lens for the characters' self-importance is provided by the method that Carrol chooses to gain an audience with God: "I will hold my breath until he takes me" (63), that clichéd threat of the misbehaving child.

However, Carrol is not alone in this contest of childish one-upmanship. Wolfherald, whose significant act is the burning of the ship *Here They Come*, relishes his own plan in comparison with the projects of the other voyagers, announcing, "Their acts would be insignificant to the one I perform" (80). Once again, however, the novel provides a judgment on the actions: Simon comments about Rodger's "[b]urning the ship, the claim of Carrol's death—this is the behavior of a schoolboy, not a heroic man" (136). Similarly, Hinderov plans to play a role that resembles that of Andrew Undershaft, George Bernard Shaw's armaments supplier in *Major Barbara*, by offering bombs to scoundrels and heroes alike: "The ruthless, the remorseless, the disillusioned, they will profit by me—kings, presidents, all leaders, they will profit by me" He imagines the superiority he will achieve: "I ask nothing because everything will be mine" (153). Hinderov wants to distribute the bombs so that "[o]nce everybody gets his own bomb then there will be no more demand for bombs. . . . It is all in the interest of man" (38; ellipsis added). However, Mr. D complains to Hinderov that such a "plan simply seemed paradoxically old hat and immature" (154), and Shiva believes that "Hinderov did not like women simply because he was afraid that they and not Hinderov . . . would achieve the grand achievement" (45; ellipsis added). Shiva has arrived without a plan, either constructive or destructive, but she is not to be denied her own ego-centered role: "I will do my utmost to destroy their plans" (45), she promises, like a child who has been denied and is determined that others will share her fate.

The roles of the three women voyagers reflect the confusion of the female roles in the society of the 1950s and 1960s. Molly, Shiva, and Daphne—their names seem designed to reflect cultural diversity—find themselves caught between the emergent forms of women's liberation and the traditional behavior of conventional society. On the one hand, they are courageous enough to sail to adventure with the men and to endorse in principle the belief that "[w]e are women," as Shiva proclaims, "therefore our objectives are boundless" (19). On the other hand, Daphne's response to Shiva's declaration is hesitant and apprehensive: "I feel something awful will happen to us because we're girls" (19), a sentiment with which Molly immediately agrees. They insist upon their equality with the male travelers, but when Frump's trained seal has been killed and cooked, "Daphne and Shiva began to set the table" (127). At another time, Daphne is able to demand a compromise between emancipation and tradition: when three of the men insist upon escorting her home, "Daphne, after many refusals, finally agreed, but on the condition that they walk five feet behind her" (176). In addition, despite her "little old Breughely parents" (33), Molly has the values of a child of the streets; shot in the arm by the two murderers in Hinderov's employ and asked by Detective Frump to identify her assailants, she responds in true (if inexplicable) subterranean fashion: "A policeman. Molly was brought up never to inform on anybody. As much as she despised Hinderov and his henchmen she wasn't talking" (34).

When the women disembark from the ship, reporters face them with a variant of Freud's famous question: "What do you ladies want?" (20). What they want is the same thing that the men want: to be treated with dignity, to be permitted the independence to do what they wish, and to be allowed to pursue adventure and achievement. Stephenson claims, "The female characters of the novel are more constructive in their pursuits, preserving and nurturing life, refusing to narrow their aims and potentials" (*Exiled* 80). However, Corso's portrayal is hardly so gender-simplistic. Stephenson cites Shiva's frustration of Hinderov's and Mr. D's plans (even though such activity hardly seems "constructive") as evidence of his view, but the novel suggests that her motives are not altruistic: having no plan, she ruthlessly devotes herself to the frustration of the plans of the others with the same kind of egocentricity as that of the men. She has a complexity appropriate to the positive and negative aspects of her namesake, but Hinderov sees her only as "the goddess of destruction" (89). Hinderov's misogyny turns her into a fearsome Everywoman: "she's your mother your sister your wife your child your master your entire womankind" (89). He and Bronskier complain that she "can repress her feelings" and that she has "too little compassion for man" (86), and she seems to corroborate this attribution of coldness when she tells Ephraim Freece, "I know nothing about love and cannot sympathize with you. There are some people love is wasted on, I am one of those ungrateful people" (91). In fact, she is so unfeeling that at one point she seems to try to manipulate Freece into committing suicide: "'Suicide is the noblest death,' said Shiva, caressing Freece's hair. 'Suicide is the great defiance—the gigantic diminish—how terrible it is for a proud man not to die of his own will'" (121). Her deviousness here scarcely fits Stephenson's claim of "preserving and nurturing life." To her credit, Shiva does finally succumb to the temptation of love, and this experience becomes transcendent for both her and

Freece. The only real triumph, however, belongs to Daphne, who designs the new ship for the travelers, a goal that for her was as calculated as the plans of the male travelers: "And so it was that Daphne, a girl, set out to achieve the 'great achievement'" (208). In this sense, the "girl" is as self-centeredly ambitious as the boys.

Finally, Detective Horatio Frump evaluates the voyagers, recognizing that "these characters want to be legendary" (146). If the ultimate goals of the voyagers truly involve the humanistic ideals they claim, those values are compromised by their selfish desires to be dominant. As Stephenson notes, Corso "distrusts the zealousness and insularity of self-proclaimed messiahs and other monomaniacs, whether their schemes for salvation are political, religious, dietary, meteorological or other" (*Exiled* 81). Corso's own statements around the time of the novel's publication underscore such feelings of distrust. In his 1961 interview with Ginsberg, Corso makes clear his concern about the dangers of egocentricity:

> Maybe the trouble then is that there are too many solutions and everybody wants to use their solution so that they could be the big hero of it all, like it's a kind of power grab in a way—so maybe then the solution is to do away with the solutions, what do you think? (23)

Later in the same interview, he returns to this topic with tactful qualifications:

> But just like everybody having solutions, everybody trying to help change the consciousness, people's minds, which I really believe to be a humane gesture, but what if folk are happy like they are and don't want no new consciousness—a real tricky business this, and kind of presumptuous in a way, too, because who is Subud or Burroughs or you or me to say people got to give up what they are and become what we feel they should be—like I'm sure it's got to do more than stopping them from destroying the globe—just where are we at really, why do you want to help change the consciousness? Beyond the benevolent, beneficial intent. I suspect something—.[20] (27)

Interrupted at this point by Ginsberg, Corso seems on the verge of specifically articulating the thematic concerns of his novel published in the same year as the interview. In *The American Express*, one of the ways in which the characters repeatedly reveal their attempts at presumptuous domination is by locking glances with others and overpowering them. Corso has cited his overuse of this technique of characterization, while at the same time identifying a historical precedent:

> The characters in *American Express* play too much of the eye game, you know, staring at each other like that. Hitler was doing that all

the time. When he had all the powerheads around him in this place up in Bercheesgaden [*sic*], he would stare to see who could eyedown who first. Speer wrote about that.[21] (Interview with M. Andre 147)

Corso's "powerheads" begin with noble ideals, but their competitive natures cause them to neglect their goal, so much so that they continually need to be reminded of it: interrupting a discussion, Thimble complains, "I say, are we not gathered here to consider and choose the plan best adaptable—what I mean to say is, have we forgotten our purpose?" (125); later he again asks, "Just where are we at? Do we want to achieve our purpose, achieve a noble path in which to wander in peace?" (130). Similarly, Freece is puzzled by the appearance of self-indulgence among the voyagers: "Well, we are men—we are man, and if our objective is man, then I think it's pretty strange to make what we are our objective" (223). Even more tellingly, Detective Frump comments, "I have watched and heard most all of you desiring not so much to aid man but to destroy him" (120). To the extent that the emergence of the new consciousness would require the destruction of previous human behavior and patterns, Frump's criticism is valid beyond what he can recognize.

At the end of the novel, the voyagers board the ship *There They Go* and depart, undoubtedly to return again, however: thus, Albie indicates that "if we're always leaving we must always return in order to leave" (136). Left behind are Frump and the young man born in the American Express, to which he returns: "Waiting there, perhaps on the very spot where the young man was delivered into the world, sat Detective Horatio Frump, glowing like a burning tree. The young man looked upon Death" (241). Stephenson interprets this as meaning that the young man discovers "the murdered body of Detective Horatio Frump" (*Exiled* 78), who is "killed before he can apprehend or disclose the name of the arch-malefactor" (83). Stephenson goes on to suggest that Mr. D is the most likely suspect, apparently because Dad Deform sings a ditty in the closing lines asserting that "*[t]hey can't find Mr. D*" (241) and because Frump had indicated "that the force he was after was not going to depart on that ship" (231). However, when Hinderov first announces that Daphne has designed a new ship for their departure, Mr. D is the first to respond: "'Well,' said Mr. D, gracefully moving to his closet, 'seems like time to be packing'" (212); in addition, after "[t]he clarion for departure *blew over the dreaming earth*" (235), Corso writes that Freece and "Mr. D headed toward the ship, laughing" (236). Although Mr. D is never actually shown aboard the ship, neither are most of the other characters. In addition, Wolfherald explains the ground rules of the travelers' participation when he tries to ease Freece's concerns about Shiva: "She *has* to return to the ship. . . . She has no other choice—none of us have" (216; ellipsis added). Later, when Carrol asks,

"Has anyone ever thought of staying behind?" Wolfherald explains, "It's impossible. To try to fight it and stay behind is folly—everyone must go" (239).

Thus, a more likely explanation involves the description of the clarion with Corso's italicized allusion to Shelley's spring wind, which brings rebirth and regeneration. Carrol Grilhiggen and Bronskier died earlier in the novel, but both return to the ship for departure; after all, they are playing roles that are part of the characters' cycles. The voyagers are saved by their literary status and their humanistic idealism. However, Frump, who, in his conversation with Carrol Grilhiggen's father, articulated his conventional but inhumane values as Duty, Law, and Justice, is left behind and is not so protected. After the discussion of plans at Mr. D's meeting, Frump concludes "that Mr. D, Hinderov, and the rest, were unreal and illogical builders in the spin. But it was not the builders he was after, no, it was the architect—the man unseen yet vividly present in the whole fabric" (148). That architect, that unseen but vividly present man, is the novelist himself, who is responsible for Frump's death. In fact, in the closing pages, Frump has retired, a concession to his age and mortality. A "burning tree" (rather than the unconsumed bush), he does not enter the Promised Land of immortality shared by the other characters, who at least aspired toward grand, if unachievable, goals.

5

The Deathmonger and
the Clown in the Tomb

Death is here and death is there
Death is busy everywhere,
All around, within, beneath,
Above is death—and we are death.

—Shelley, "Death"

The literature of Beat Generation writers provides a sharpened aware-
ness of the role of the individual and an attendant interest in the phenomenon of
death. In a "bomb culture," despite duck-and-cover drills, fallout shelters, and air
raid sirens, mass extinction was then, as it is now, a constant possibility, threaten-
ing to deprive even life's finale of its uniqueness. In addition, the accelerating pace
and complexity of modern society have resulted in what many Beat writers con-
sider a callous, mechanical attitude toward death. Articulating a surrealist posi-
tion, André Breton states that "[e]verything tends to make us believe that there
exists a certain point of the mind at which life and death, the real and the imag-
ined, past and future, the communicable and the incommunicable, high and low,
cease to be perceived as contradictions" (123). For Gregory Corso too, these dis-
tinctions begin to blur, but without easing human tensions toward death. He
suggests that our fears of death are introduced in childhood, citing the fairy tale
settings of "the woodcutter's" and "the gingerbread hag's" cottages ("Concourse,"
EF 100). In the same poem, he shows that those early intimations develop dur-
ing the course of life, accruing from school lessons on into adult experience:

the schoolroom of Death, classroom to first humor.
I pledge allegiance to death! Books on death!
Homework on death, tests and failures on death

graduation on death, citizen on death
banker on death, father on death, lost and senile on death.

(100)

However, despite this social inculcation, human anxiety prevents any meaning-ful discussion of death, leaving it mysterious and frightening. To compensate, Corso asserts, "I talk Death something we never talked" ("Spontaneous Poem," *HB* 25). His poetry reveals his belief that humanity need not fear death: though the body may decay, the eternal spirit of human energy cannot be extinguished.

In "Musée des Beaux Arts," W. H. Auden portrays a characteristic artistic de-piction of human responses to death:

> In Breughel's *Icarus*, for instance: how everything turns away
> Quite leisurely from the disaster; the ploughman may
> Have heard the splash, the forsaken cry,
> But for him it was not an important failure; the sun shone
> As it had to on the white legs disappearing into the green
> Water; and the expensive delicate ship that must have seen
> Something amazing, a boy falling out of the sky,
> Had somewhere to get to and sailed calmly on.
>
> (147)

In Corso's "St. Lukes, Service for Thomas," the narrator watches the action as it too "turns away" from the tragedy of death:

> A Ceylonese prince was first to leave.
> He waited by the church gate
> And little groups gathered, chattered.
>
> Across the street the school children
> Were playing tag-ball.
> The ball rolled in front of the innkeeper;
> He kicked it hard
> And strode back to his inn.
>
> (*G/V* 96)

Like one of Auden's "old masters," Corso offers a reportorial depiction of the scene and refuses to impose a moral statement, simply portraying the oblivious children and the rest of the mundane world as carelessly and naturally going about their business. The stature of both Icarus and Dylan Thomas heightens the irony of the dispassionate responses,[1] as both Auden and Corso recognize the "human position" toward suffering and death, neither condemning nor defending it. Elsewhere, Corso registers the unfeeling indifference to the death of individuals of lesser repute. In "Italian Extravaganza," the tone is cold and naive in its insensitivity:

> Mrs. Lombardi's month-old son is dead.
> I saw it in Rizzo's funeral parlor,
> A small purplish wrinkled head.
>
> They've just finished having high mass for it;
> They're coming out now
> . . . wow, such a small coffin!
> And ten black cadillacs to haul it in.
>
> (*G/V* 31)

This gossipy insouciance is also evoked in "Body Fished from the Seine," in which a tourist boat stops to allow the passengers to watch the recovery of a drowned man's body.

Corso traces his awareness of the human lack of compassion toward death to his childhood, when at eleven years old he read about the Esposito brothers on their way to the electric chair:

> I trembled on that landing and vowed I'd never be
> those Esposito brothers but came close
> and ran to my father and gave him his daily read
> and he read it like he read yesterday's
> I knew then nothing could save the Mad Dogs
> And I knew with certainty that nothing could save any man
> when I saw Rosalind Russell a female reporter
> record for the Chicago Chronicle the death of a gas-chamber man.[2]
>
> ("Police," *HB* 89)

The child learns that news of execution is cause for adult interest but not for concern, providing a "daily read" but no forgiveness of trespasses. Execution is also the subject of Corso's "That Little Black Door on the Left," a silent-film script featuring a gallows-humor scene in which the obesity of the condemned man prevents him from fitting into the electric chair, causing the officials technical problems that interrupt the usually smooth routine of execution. At another extreme, even the tortured and crucified figure of Christ in a painting by Theodoricus can be subjected to a clinical objectivity through which the poetic voice becomes that of an aficionado of torture: "The crown of thorns (a superb idea!) / and the sidewound (an atrocity!) / only penetrate the man" ("Ecce Homo," *G/V* 28).[3] The topic here is sensational, but Corso often employs anonymity to underscore a brittle response evidenced by brusque action: after a woman jumps to her death, "They take her away with a Daily News on her face / And a storekeeper throws hot water on the sidewalk" ("Greenwich Village," *G/V* 61). The objective tone of the poem makes the episode even more chilling to a sensitive reader.[4]

For some modern writers, suicide represents a gesture of heroic proportions. It is, with the possible exception of murder, the most dramatic action an individual can take—the ultimate gesture of defiant nay-saying. The apparent attitudes of the Beat writers toward suicide are markedly ambivalent. On the one hand, their ethos is generally exhilarative, life celebratory, and opposed in essence to the philosophical position that suggests that suicide is the honorable person's only possible act of freedom. On the other hand, the Beats are also undeniably attracted to those who have committed suicide: they idolize Hart Crane, as much for his life and death as for his poetry; Thomas Chatterton and Vladimir Mayakovsky they consider with similar affection. All three become representative of the artist-martyr. Their appeal, as well as that of Keats and Shelley and other artists who died at relatively young ages, suggests in the Beats not so much a death wish as a desire for mythopoeic glorification, as Corso recognizes when he confides, "I am nearing thirty / And have not died as I romantically wished" ("Saint Francis," *LL* 39). Corso indulges in an approximation of the death wish with frequency, but he usually strikes this stance from playful whimsy rather than from neurotic compulsion. He identifies with Alexander Hamilton, killed as a result of a duel, but with the exaggerated melodrama of youthful fantasy ("How Happy," *HB* 12). Similarly, Corso's death fantasy may be lightened by bawdy humor or surrealism, as when he imagines drowning:

> To breathe in Neptune's cup
> Nudge gale and tempest
> Feel the mermaid up
> To stay to pin my hair
> On the sea-horse's stirrup.

("Seaspin," *HB* 13)

The exuberant lightness suggests the sportive mood of the poet, and Corso even chastises those who indulge the death impulse:

> It were better to be alive in a world of death
> than to be dead in a world of life;
>
> they kill themselves because they fear death;
>
> only the lovers of life are fit to die.[5]

("For Those," *LL* 87)

As he repeatedly points out, "Only the living know death / not the dead" (♀ [*Ankh*]).[6] The choices and ironies in these poems may be somewhat oversimplified, but the poet's allegiance to life is eminently clear.

Throughout his poetry, Corso maintains an antagonistic attitude toward death, flinging disrespect at it and even revealing a propensity to challenge it. In an early poem, "The Game," he is willing to take on death as an opponent, assured that, even if he should suffer defeat, "[t]hen I shall lose this game / Of death to a pro" (*G/V* 81). In a subsequent poem, "Death," moving from a despair that drives him to cry, "Take me Death into your care" (*HB* 38), he rises to a derisive travesty that the poet and critic Richard Howard mistakenly characterizes as "necrophiliac nursery-rhyme" (79):

> Let's all die
> Let's practice a little
> Let's play dead for a couple of hours
> Let's everybody weave elegant everlasting cerements
> > build fantastic tombs
> > carve lifelong coffins
> > and devise great ways to die let's!
> Let's walk under ladders, cross the paths of black cats,
> > break mirrors, burn rabbit feet, snip the 4th petal,
> Yes! let's draw the ACE OF SPADES—
> Let's sleep with our doors unlocked.
>
> ("Death," *HB* 40)

Corso's attacks are sporadically hit-and-run, taunting insults hurled at the hulking bully just before the mocker scampers out of reach: "I screamed at Death I'm fed up with you! Stupid subject! Old button! / I unsalute you. On to greater things I go" ("Greece," *LL* 27). Despite such threats, death remains a topic that Corso confronts continually.

Like Shelley, Poe, and Dylan Thomas, Corso devotes considerable attention to the phenomenon of death, but though these poets rival him in the frequency of their preoccupation, none of them exhibits a corresponding attitude.[7] As Michael Horovitz notes, "[Corso's] work insistently probes the mystery of death, what lies behind that door . . . knowing that he can't *know*, preferring inspired guesses to logical deduction" (66). Corso's approach, like that of Woody Allen in his films, is disrespectful while still serious because he refuses to encounter death with solemnity. Virtually without exception, his tone is mocking and derisive. He may, in an early poem, establish a youthful, congenial relationship with Death:

> I was good to Death
> Took it with me everywhere
> Always spoke about it
> Introduce it to all my friends.

("It was")

By the end of the same poem, the narrator, older now, severs that relationship: "I drive Death from me / and have not asked for a map." Death at times seems obviously sinister to him. It becomes "reality's worm" or a presence "seated like a huge black stove" ("Ode to Coit," *G/V* 12, 13) or "the Inevitable Hook" ("Hello . . . ," *G/V* 40), "the Inevitable Door" (☥ [*Ankh*]), which can "[w]ith a bragged requiescat / spray blood Deathdrench the dash of life" ("Heave," *HB* 71). Even worse is death's pervasiveness: "Everything I see is Death" ("Death," *HB* 38). Nevertheless, he is reluctant to see it as more than an even odds bet against him.

More importantly, Corso offers himself as a symbol of life in a moribund world. Thus, in "For K. R. Who Killed Himself in Charles Street Jail," he assumes a vitalizing power: "By light follow, O child of dark, by light embrace! / Here / touch my electric hand" (*HB* 50). Corso sees Shelley's poet as the creator of "the image of life expressed in its eternal truth" ("A Defence of Poetry" 7: 115). As the generator of life-giving qualities, the poet is a fitting antagonist for the forces of death, and Corso exultingly exclaims,

> Hear my formulae!
> I have the way to bring back the dead
> I have I have and love me for it
> O I the KNOW of Death!
> I dark mad ah solace dreams grace miracle quack awful O!

("Death," *HB* 41)

The last line of this passage, with its jab of self-ridicule ("quack"), reveals Corso as the Trickster, intent upon employing any strategy, legitimate or mountebankish, to cajole humanity beyond the fear of death.

Humor is one of his most common tactics. Thus, he can paint a circus redemption scene: "Fifty shrouded clowns pile out / from a tiny tomb" ("Clown," *HB* 61); he can also inject grim comedy into the disaster of a bomb explosion in a composition that he has referred to as "a frolicy poem called BOMB" ("Many Have," *HA* 26):

> I do not know just how horrible Bombdeath is I can only imagine
> Yet no other death I know has so laughable a preview I scope
> a city New York City streaming starkeyed subway shelter
> Scores and scores A fumble of humanity High heels bend

> Hats whelming away   Youth forgetting their combs
> Ladies not knowing what to do   with their shopping bags
>   Unperturbed gum machines   Yet dangerous 3rd rail
> Ritz Brothers   from the Bronx   caught in the A train
>   The smiling Schenley poster will always smile
> Impish Death   Satyr Bomb   Bombdeath
>   Turtles exploding over Istanbul
>   The jaguar's flying foot
>   soon to sink in the arctic snow
>   Penguins plunged against the Sphinx
>   The top of the Empire State
>   arrowed in a broccoli field in Sicily.

("Bomb," HB)

The surrealistic landscape generated by the imaginary bomb disarms horror and softens tragedy through lyrical absurdity. Though the effects of the bomb may be spectacular, Corso's point is that physical death is inevitable and its vehicle is of no consequence, whether it be the bomb, "the jawbone of an ass," or any of the other alternatives cited in the opening lines of the poem. In an interview with Ginsberg, he explains:

> What I felt when I wrote *Bomb*, was that death is death after all, and isn't it kind of funny to want to march against heart attacks? . . . With that view of death and acceptance of it, how then can we be concerned with it, in any form, be it bomb or bicycle accidents? (22)

Corso elaborates in another interview:

> But it's not political at all. It's a death shot. You see, because people were worrying about dying by the Bomb in the Fifties. So I said, what about falling off the roof, what about heart attack. And I used the double old-age: old age I picked as being the heaviest—"old age, old age." (Interview with R. King 12)

What Corso ignores here is that bombs, unlike falls from the roof, heart attacks, old age, and bicycle accidents, involve the willful destruction of human lives. The Ban-the-Bomb protesters were objecting to a loss of lives that could be controlled. That those whose lives might be saved would die from other causes is beside the point, as Corso elsewhere seems to recognize:

> All know that it is man who operates the cannon, the viseboot, the electrode; everything imagined about hell is imagined by man; it was

man drove the tank, fired the bullet—men are killed more often by
men than by anything else. ("Some of My Beginning," *Poets* 181)

Whether such behavior is human nature and is as such incorrigible is an issue that
he does not confront.

Corso's impudence in the face of mortality stems from a belief that denies the
finality of Death. Death, he preaches, is simply a stage in the prevailing natural
order of existence: "Life. It was Life jabbed a spoon in their mouths. / Crow jackal
hyena vulture worm woke to necessity / —dipping into Death like a soup"
("Dreamed Realization," *HB* 49). The brutishness of the animals is not intended
to inspire fear or despair: the carrion-eaters can no more be blamed for their cui-
sine than the bomb can be blamed for the destruction humanity wreaks with it.
He believes that humans must be both willing and able to come to healthy terms
with death:

> I wipe the dead spider
> off the statue's lips
> Something there is is forgotten
> and what's remembered slips
> Butterfly and fly and other insectai
> wait themselves to die
>
> And so it's Spring again so what
> The leaves are leaves again no tree forgot
> > ("Reflection in a Green Arena," *LL* 29)

Such a conclusion offers a variant of Shelley's "If Winter comes, can Spring be far
behind?" ("Ode to the West Wind," 2: 297); and Corso's lines, "And these apples
whose certain death breeds more" ("Apples, *SP* 61) and "The cyclic apples blos-
som" ("Eden," *LL* 49) recall the death-rebirth cycle of the first stanza of Shelley's
poem, but with a specific tree that evokes the Fall, the mythical cause of human
mortality. Corso calls the awareness of this condition "[r]eality, that brick wall
which hits you after you open the last door of childhood." He goes on to describe
the impact of that realization:

> a man dies twice, he dies once in life, in that gap between childhood
> and manhood; and he dies lastly in that gap between time and eternity.
> > There is no set time that first death (the realization that there
> is such a thing as death). ("Between" 38)

For Corso, acceptance of the fact that death is a step in the natural order is crucial:

Yet if I leave this world
and weep that I must leave
then indeed I am laughable
and nothing to believe.

("To Die Laughing [?]," *LL* 58)

He suggests, however, that modern humanity has grown beyond awareness of its position within the continuing cycle of life.

Corso repeatedly rejects the notion of the finality of death: "Death is but is not lasting" ("Thought," *LL* 46), he promises, and he underscores the point with an ambiguously hopeful image: "A departed train is a train to arrive" ("Death," *HB* 38); "The countless dying prompts more than Death / —as in the distance / The little light's approach becomes a train" ("Beyond Delinquency," *LL* 17). The image aims for more than dismissal of the fear of death, as the poet attempts to convince humanity of the nonconclusiveness of death: "Over and over I repeat: / Outstep the circle acknowledge Death's good warrant / and do not die" ("Greece," *LL* 26).[8] The paradox is characteristic and the method of persuasion dependent on faith rather than empirical fact. The "good warrant" never does become lucid, nor does Corso believe it can: "Poetry is seeking the answer / Joy is in knowing there is an answer / Death is knowing the answer" ("Notes after," *HB* 11). Such abeyance appears to satisfy Corso, and he sometimes seems to subscribe to a belief in immortality as a defense against his own anxiety. Citing Corso's denigration of death, Rosanne Benedetto asks, "Is this attitude his approach to life or is it false bravado in the face of mortality?" (93). In "Thanatopsis," William Cullen Bryant's recommended response to such anxiety involved an acceptance of the patterns of Nature: "When thoughts / Of the last bitter hour come like a blight / Over thy spirit . . . / Go forth, under the open sky, and list / To Nature's teachings" (21; ellipsis added). In contrast, Corso's more contemporary response to the possibility of death is often unmistakably escapist. In a 1974 interview, he reveals this blatantly:

Now would you get scared if you felt your heart was feeling pattering and suddenly you turned pale? And you might just have a heart attack and drop dead here? I think I'd go to a movie theater. I would. If I felt that was happening I'd run into a movie house. . . . I thought I'd just get my mind off it or something. (Interview with R. King 21; ellipsis added)

He develops this ruse poetically in "How Not to Die," which Gavin Selerie refers to as "a typical piece of Corso drollery involving retreat to the logic of the cinema" (13):

> To the movies—to the movies
> that's where I hurry to
> when I feel I'm going to die
> So far it's worked.
>
> (*HA* 17)

The strategy recalls the joke about the man who, when asked why he is snapping his fingers, answers, "To keep the elephants away"; informed that no elephants are in the area, he replies, "See how well it works."

Even if Corso's poem is mere "drollery," it nevertheless involves several significant issues. First, Corso reveals the peculiarly modern relationship between the general public and figures of popular culture. Media attention inundates people with so much information about performers that a bond is formed, enabling the public to see them as special acquaintances; on the other hand, their prominence imposes a distance that keeps them at a privileged remove. Corso relates this ambiguous role to the topic of death: "as long as I live / matinee idols will keep on dying" ("Makers" 80); these lines provide a contrast between the matinee "idols" and the variety of god-related images that he cites earlier in the poem. The mere mention of the performers suggests their elevated social roles and the surprise involved in the recognition of their mortality. In a later poem, Corso elaborates on this situation:

> It's happening . . . As I age
> the celebrated unchanging faces of yesterday
>   are changing drastically
> Popes and Presidents come and go
>   Rock stars too
> So suddenly have matinee idols grown old
>   And those starlets
>   now grandmothering starlets
> And as long as I live
>   movie stars keep on dying.
>
> ("Feelings on Getting," *HA* 51)

Corso's point is that the mortality and death of these figures can be unimaginable in popular consciousness. They are, as the saying goes, larger than life and can appear invulnerable. Corso can even envision a special category of protected personnel: "And unthinkable deaths like Harpo Marx girls on Vogue covers my own" ("Bomb," *HB*).[9] Secondly, the performers *are* larger than life because of their projected images. Corso recalls a childhood incident:

Anyway my stepmother mentioned at dinner having read where the Lone Ranger was killed in an auto accident—I looked in the paper and sure enough, it said the Lone Ranger, who had another name, had indeed been killed. And yet that night and the nights after the Lone Ranger still came on the air. The same voice, the same everything, and no mention of his having been killed in an auto mishap. It was a mystery I found difficult to resolve.[10] ("When I Was Five" 85)

The value of such a memory to an adult is the recognition that through one's work one can live beyond death. For a writer then, the apparent immortality of art, provided in "How Not to Die" as cinematic projection, is both evasion and promise. In an early poem, Corso even attributes his own evasion to Death itself: "Death weeps because Death is human / spending all day in a movie when a child dies" ("Three," *G/V* 39). On the other hand, he identifies Death as "a rumor spread by life"[11] and resorts to truly preposterous rationalizations:

People are unreliable
and your parents your priest your guru are people
and it is they who tell you that you must die
to believe them is to die.[12]

("Window," *M* 225)

Corso prefers to reject the dominance of such authority figures, and he claims that he cannot "condemn fully any form of Power but that of Death" ("Power," *HB* 77). For the poet an escape from "unreliable" people is provided by fantasy. In "Uccello," he celebrates the painter's *Battle of San Romano* and yearns to share its eternity, a world of military splendor and battle glory without the threat of death:

how I dream to join such battle!
a silver man on a black horse with red standard and striped
   lance   never to die but to be endless
    a golden prince of pictorial war.

(*G/V* 29)

Such romantic whimsy, however, requires sustaining illusion. Discussing William Burroughs's idea that human beings are "all just bodies, just bags of water" (a phrase Corso later employs generally of people in "Feelings on Getting Older"), Corso demurs: "But myself, I question the idea that I'm just a bag of water. My body may be, but I'm not yet convinced that I am" (qtd. in Cook 145). Recognizing that physical mortality guarantees that the body must die, he chooses to place his trust in a deathless quality of the human spirit:

> The body is but a relay
> we are born of ourselves
> from incarnate dawn
> to disincarnate night
> to reincarnate dawn
> an endless connection
> the thread of which is spirit.

("Window," *M* 225)

The diurnal parallel reduces Death to what he calls "the solution of sunset" ("On the Death," *EF* 98). The energy that animates human life is eternal, though its bodily shell may be mortally fragile. The quality that persists is one that Corso associates with the traditional concept of the soul: "I can imagine a soul, the soul leaving the body, / The body feeding death, death simply a hygiene" ("Man," *LL* 9). In the end, however, apparently eschewing the religious connotations of that concept, he opts for a more secularized quality of life, which he celebrates as "Spiritus eterne" ("Feelings on Getting," *HA* 53), and he puts his trust in this spirit: "The spirit knows better than the body / To believe that life dies with the body / is to be spirit-sick" ("Window," *M* 225–26). Content with this intimation of immortality, he presumably finds no terror in the prospect of death:

> Spirit
> is Life
> It flows thru
> the death of me
> endlessly
> like a river
> unafraid
> of becoming
> the sea.

("Spirit," *HA* 41)

Corso's personal beliefs seem to closely parallel the Egyptian mythology that fascinates him so and that holds

> the creation infinitely
> reasserted; in which death is nothing real,
> And the next life a triumphant
>   continuation of this life.

("Geometric Poem," *EF* 48)

At times, his assertions seem to stem from a desire to believe rather than from a comfortable confidence: "I say not believing I believe / that after this world other worlds are" ("Earth Egg"). Nevertheless, in a later elegy he proclaims a regeneration that will conveniently obliterate human errors:

> When we all wake up again
> death will be undone
> nor the stain of killed & killer men
> remain in the wash of the sun.
>
> ("When We All . . . ," *HA* 50)

The last line of this passage echoes the vision of William Blake's Tom Dacre, the chimney sweeper in the *Songs of Innocence*, whose dream offers death as an escape from the tribulations of his young life. Similarly, Corso's eschatology seems to be a rationalized wishful thinking to absolve a misspent life, the kind of self-recognition that can lead him urgently to insist, "I swear to you there is in me yet time / to run back through life and expiate / all that's been sadly done . . . sadly neglected" ("Columbia U," *HA* 5).[13] Therein lies the glory of human existence and the foundation for Corso's motto, "Long live man," and for his casual valediction, "be seeing you on the rebound" ("Window," *M* 227).

6

"The Comedy Gone Mad": Corso's Surrealism and Humor

> He was born with a gift of laughter
> and a sense that the world was mad.
>
> —Rafael Sabatini, *Scaramouche*

One of the most critically overlooked aspects of the literature of the Beat Generation writers has been their use of humor. The Beats were outspoken in their objections to what they saw as the stagnant literature prevalent at the mid-twentieth-century mark, characterizing it as academic, as literature to be studied rather than enjoyed. In contrast, the Beat writers steered toward a populist response, attempting to provide serious literature that was also entertaining. Amusing word play and comic situations are significant elements in even their most compelling works, for, as Corso has pointed out, "Man is great and mad, he was born mad and wonder of wonders the sanity of evolution knoweth not what to do" (qtd. in Gaiser 271). Corso is among the most consistent and proficient of the Beat writers in the comedic mode. His poetic voice is often puckish, as he gives conventions ironic twists, situates images in alien environments, and spins language through unfamiliar contortions. The result is an uncomfortable system of conflicts and warps that disturb the conventions of language, imagery, and perceived reality. Corso's most effective strategies involve his peculiar strain of surrealism, with its unsettling combination of humor and threat.

More than many of the other Beat poets, Corso employs surrealist departures from rational patterns. Asked by an interviewer, "Did you read Philip Lamantia? Because you've got some images which really get into surrealism," Corso replied, "Yeah, yeah, him early, and Andre Breton" (Interview with R. King 24).[1] Bill Beyle has also noted the surrealist elements in Corso's work, but demurred in that Corso's technique "is less 'spontaneous' in the manner of Kerouac or Breton than 'rapid'"

(73). Breton himself, however, postulates that "I resolved to obtain from myself . . . a monologue spoken as *rapidly* as possible without any intervention on the part of the critical faculties, a monologue consequently unencumbered by the slightest inhibition and which was, as closely as possible, akin to *spoken thought*" (22–23; first emphasis added). In fact, Beyle's complaint calls to mind a humorous section from Kerouac's *The Subterraneans* in which Leo Percepied (based on Kerouac himself) confronts Yuri Gligoric (modeled on Corso) about the latter's poetic phrase "seldom nocturne": Leo complains, "I would say rather it was great if you'd written it suddenly on the spur of the moment"; Yuri protests that "it sounds like it's been planned but it wasn't, it was bang! just like you say, spontaneous vision"; and Leo concedes that "his saying 'seldom nocturne' came to him spontaneously made me suddenly respect it more" (114). In a similar vein, "Gregory said he once asked Jack if spontaneity forbade him from revising anything he wrote. According to Gregory, Jack replied, 'Well, if I want to change a word spontaneously, I do it'" (Jones 8). Both incidents wryly suggest that the quality of product is less important than the process, even though the process may not be readily identifiable in the product. On the other hand, one might also note that Corso describes his "Writ on the Eve of My 32nd Birthday" as "*a slow thoughtful spontaneous poem*" (*LL* 92). Nevertheless, whether "spontaneous" or "rapid," terms that Corso apparently does not find equivalent, Corso's approach affords significant parallels to the works of the surrealists. Radical juxtapositions of sheer unlikelihood abound, particularly in the early volumes: "Radio belly," "Apple deaf," "Penguin dust," "Telephone snow" ("Marriage," *HB* 30–31); "Corduroy eggs, owl cheese, pipe butter, / Firing squad milk" ("Food," *HB* 33); "Fried chairs, poached mattresses, stewed farms" ("Food," *HB* 35). These images all depend upon totally unconventional or nonrational objective derangement that Corso, in the original sense of the word, appropriates. Coming as they do in lists, series, and catalogs, some are bound to be more effective than others. The reader's response is likely to be very subjective: while "Corduroy eggs" may conjure a sense of comically textural innovation, "pipe butter" may seem to be merely arcane juxtaposition.

At other times, more dramatic in his imagery, Corso energizes fantastic activity: "May 1940 stevedores lead forth a platoon of leukemia" ("Vision of Rotterdam," *G/V* 16); "Four windmills, acquaintanceships, / were spied one morning eating tulips" ("2 Weird Happenings," *G/V* 18); "all the trees in the vicinity went insane" (*American Express* 186). Frequently these patterns occur in settings of violence, where Corso's wrenched situations reflect the dislocation of emotions. Thus, in the passages just cited, the first two examples occur in poems portraying the scars of the wartime era and evoke the apocalyptic terror faced by the populace, and the third example conveys the effects of war's violence on Nature. In fact, Corso often employs the surrealist image as a harshly disruptive force:

he can imagine the possibility that "planets kick dust in my eyes" ("Clown," *HB* 57), a frighteningly paranoiac vision with cosmic dimensions. He can also elaborate a conceit into disturbingly farcical but pregnant proportions:

> Together they ate a rose
> and together they dried their tongues
> upon the ashes and remaining bits of fur
>
> They loved and loved
> until their eyes fell within them
> and their faces fell away.
>
> ("The Crime," *G/V* 76)

The threat of love to individual identity becomes alarmingly clear. The type of malevolent, surrealistic violence that Lautréamont developed in *Maldoror* fascinates Corso and repeatedly controls the dramatic action of his poems. In a temporal vendetta, he exacts revenge for a distressed childhood: "Dirty Ears / aims a knife at me . . . / I pump him full of lost watches" ("Birthplace," *G/V* 31). In addition, he repeatedly employs a Rimbaudian symbolic violence against personifications:

> I ran to Kindness, broke into Her chamber,
> and profaned!
> with an unnamable knife I gave Her a thousand wounds,
> and inflicted them with filth.[2]
>
> ("But I Do Not," *G/V* 34)

In "Transformation & Escape," the narrator assaults Saint Peter in heaven after having dismembered himself. At an extreme, Corso can envision himself as a mad, transhistoric assassin:

> By the throat I smote the Age of the Reptile!
> So too the Age of the Mammal!
> So too O very much so the Ancestry of Man!
> Man descended from a walking ape!
> I awake the lazy greasy Neanderthal and spit in his big sad stupid eye!
> I pummel my Colt .38 into the iron skin of the Palaeolithic muralist!
>
> ("Lines Written," *EF* 28)

Antonin Artaud has ventured to explain the success of violence in art: "A violent and concentrated action is a kind of lyricism: it summons up supernatural images, a bloodstream of images, a bleeding spurt of images in the poet's head and in the spectator's as well" (82). The perverse thrill in violence leads Corso repeatedly to derive his materials from the world of the gangster, that ambiguous American hero, borrowing his language and employing him as an ominous symbol. Nonetheless, in his poetry he refrains from exploiting the sensationalism of violence: unlike Burroughs, Corso does not inflict on the reader the graphics of mutilated bodies, but instead portrays the actions as schoolboy bullying (which, of course, can have disturbing psychological effects), reduces the effects by blunting the casualties, or turns the recipients into generalizations. Corso's violence is that of the rebellious spirit, and its victims are distanced into abstractions. Thus, "The Whole Mess . . . Almost" catalogs the speaker's defenestration of Truth, Love, Faith, Hope, Charity, Beauty, and Death. Again, the surrealist manifestoes provide an explanatory model: Breton suggests that surrealism made

> for itself a tenet of total revolt, complete insubordination, of sabotage according to rule, and . . . expects nothing save from violence. The simplest Surrealist act consists of dashing down into the street, pistol in hand, and firing blindly, as fast as you can pull the trigger, into the crowd. (125)

In Corso's poetry, only the weapon has changed:

> Last night I drove a car
>   not knowing how to drive
>   not owning a car
> I drove and knocked down
>   people I loved
>   . . . went 120 through one town.
> I stopped at Hedgeville
>   and slept in the back seat
>   . . . excited about my new life.[3]

> ("Last Night I Drove," *G/V* 46)

Breton stops short of depicting specific violence and detailing the writhing pain and bloody gore, just as Corso's mayhem merely "knocked down" his victims. This is poetic violence, that of the page rather than that of the streets.

Devoid of gory details, Corso's surrealism is primarily of the humorous stamp. Seldom does a brutal image appear unrelieved by comedy, for

> I've new delight—and eternally toward delight
>   I've a possession to assume
>   to bestow.

> ("Greece," *LL* 27)

Corso's attitude toward humor is constantly ambivalent because of his perception that he is a clown straitjacketed by the inhumane brutality of the world:

> I know laughter! I know lots of laughter!
> Yet all I do is walk up and down hands behind back
> dreaming dungeons spikes and squeaking racks.

("Clown," HB 53)

Although he warns, "I can commemorate black laughter, too," he would that his situation were otherwise: "o there's that in me wishes each laugh / would knit an eternity of hilarity" ("Clown," *HB* 54, 56). As a realist, however, he admits with frustration that human conditions obviate the possibility that such an ideal could be imminently realized. Thus, his approach is similar to the laughter that convulses into a choking fit, "a charred humor and spidered smile" ("Written While Watching the Yankees," *HB* 47). Torn between the roles of jester and of indicter, a position most frequently occupied by the Juvenalian satirist, Corso's poetry usually lacks the bite associated with this satire, the complexity of which he shows himself aware: "A bee's both honey and sting" ("Logos," *LL* 79). However, without the satirist's sting, his normal tone mingles humor and sadness. He has a gentle openness that undermines violence; for example, when he encounters British fog for the first time, he conjures up a stereotypical Jack the Ripper in search of one of his victims, but with a comic deflation:

> So out into it I go
>   and ho the detective's hollow walk
> *Mary Dare? Art thou Mary Dare?*
> And banged straight into a tree
> and said: Excuse me.[4]

("Nature's," LL 49)

His good heart even compels him to entertain the position of devil's advocate: thus, he can turn atomic warfare into a delightful spectacle in "Bomb," write a poem celebrating "Power" that Ferlinghetti would refuse to publish because he saw it as "fascistic,"[5] decline to embrace the liberal position of so many of his compatriots in endorsing Fidel Castro's revolution in "Upon My Refusal to Herald Cuba," and even compose a poem whose title seems to challenge the conventional excoriation of racists—"In Honor of Those the Negroes Are Revolting Against." In fact, he often seems to adopt a contrary stance simply as a way of asserting his own independence, as though merely denying affiliation with contemporary avant-garde positions is a way of carving out an identity. The complexities of life impress him with both wonder and concern. He sees himself as what he calls "The Double Axe," "Ulcerated by clown turned phantom, / Dragging behind bright colors, profound melancholy" (*LL* 71), as in his "Harlequin death-trap" ("Paris," *G/V* 48) or in the funereal circus where "[f]ifty shrouded clowns pile out / from a tiny tomb," for the clown's "red nose / is antideath" ("Clown," *HB* 61, 59). His humor becomes a pointed jest, a weapon, or, as he has repeatedly called it, a "butcher," for "[a]nything destroyed has got to be with humor" (Interview with M. Andre 132).[6] Corso then is the clown of the apocalypse: "That hand-grenade humor dropped down the hatch / Of an armoured suit my proposed bit come doomsday Power!" ("Power," *HB* 80). He performs as a court clown, armed with a seltzer bottle of stagnant water, for his is an embittered jestership, leading Gordon Ball to suggest that Corso "may be our strongest poet who can say 'Nay!' in laughter." In "Clown," he compares himself to a jester, but a wise one who is completely aware both of his place in the social structure and of human vulnerability and mortality: "My joy could never wedge free / from sorrow's old crack" (*HB* 58). Nevertheless, he realizes the value of the clown's role in alleviating, if only momentarily, the havoc and the horror of the world. Corso sees this approach as characteristic of the Beat poets:

> The new American poet is not serious, he laughs at everything, the situation is hilarious, he laughs, his poetry is pained, one senses the pain, the poet especially senses his pain, sensing it, he laughs, what more can he do. ("Literary" 193)

Thus, he explains in "Bomb" that "I am able to laugh at all things / all that I know and do not know thus to conceal my pain" (*HB*),[7] echoing Lord Byron's sentiment: "And if I laugh at any mortal thing, / 'Tis that I may not weep" (*Don Juan*, 346). Humor becomes not merely a means of coping, but also a tactic for emotional survival, for, as his character Simon states in *The American Express*, "clowns know how to bring joy" (175). One of the most celebrated modern clowns, Emmett Kelly, has offered an explanation of the process involved:

> By laughing at me, they [the audiences] really laugh at themselves, and realizing that they have done this gives them a sort of spiritual second wind for going back into the battle. (126)

Thus, humor offers no tangible succor—only a fresh perspective that renews the spirit.

Corso's humanistic concerns ordinarily prevent him from indulging in meaningless frivolity, a common weakness of writers for whom humor is a frequent tool. He is careful to establish his serious intentions, despite the comedic hues of his poems: "I hoped and prayed and sought a meaning / It wasn't all frolic poesy";

on the other hand, the same poem goes on to show that the humorous elements are personally salutary: "I'd a humor save me from amateur philosophy" ("Writ on the Steps," *LL* 77). However, occasionally Corso's use of surrealism and humor does appear to be mere diversion, an imagistic counterpart of what the Beats called "goofing"—playful, if pointless, verbal recreation. Thus, in "Poets Hitchhiking on the Highway," he portrays a contest of surrealistic wits:

> Of course I tried to tell him
> but he cranked his head
>   without an excuse.
> I told him the sky chases
>   the sun
> And he smiled and said:
>   'What's the use.'
> I was feeling like a demon
>   again
> So I said: 'But the ocean chases
>   the fish.'
> This time he laughed
>   and said: 'Suppose the
>   strawberry were
>   pushed into a mountain.'
> After that I knew the
>   war was on—
> So we fought:
> He said: 'The apple-cart like a
>   broomstick-angel
>   snaps & splinters
>   old dutch shoes.'
> I said: 'Lightning will strike the old oak
>   and free the fumes!'
> He said: 'Mad street with no name.'
> I said: 'Bald killer! Bald killer! Bald killer!'
> He said, getting real mad,
>   'Firestoves! Gas! Couch!'
> I said, only smiling,
>   'I know God would turn back his head
>   if I sat quietly and thought.'
> We ended by melting away,
>   hating the air!

                                                        (*HB* 28)

The careless lack of variety in the repeated credit tags for the direct quotations, together with the purposeless imagistic stunting, can lead the reader to echo the speaker's companion: "What's the use?" Furthermore, Corso's dialectics suggests a complexity that can be disturbing: despite the companion's smile and laugh and the narrator's own eventual smile, the contest develops violent components independent of the actual discursive exchange. The narrator feels demonic and realizes that he is fighting in a war; his opponent gets "real mad," and the rivalry results in a displaced abstract hatred. What begins as a potential remedy for bored frustration turns into creative battle, with both combatants vying for imagistic one-upmanship in a nonrational exchange for which the surreal code seems to be mutually accepted. The status of the antagonists as poets is of little consequence: their behavior resembles children in a surreal game of king of the mountain. The struggle for dominance is as pointless as the final discontent with earthly—as opposed to verbal—existence, because the surrealistic currency has no established system of priorities, turning the contest into mutual cheating. The interchange itself is filled with threatening images and language: "chases," "pushed," "snaps," "splinters," "strike," "mad," and "killer." Dueling with words is no less aggressive than dueling with s(words), and the contest manages to climb only short rungs above the childish taunts that "your mother wears army boots" or "so is your old lady." In addition, Corso's humor sometimes gives the appearance of unintegrated jokes: "I predict Jeanne Dixon will die" ("Field Report," *M* 260).[8] "Describe freedom / I'm not at liberty" ("Verse," *HA* 25) seems to have the same throwaway quality, but, preceded as it is by the lines "I always believed freedom to be / a matter of individuality," this passage evokes the sociological dimensions of the tensions between individual freedom (no restraint) and political liberty (no unwarranted restraint); however, Corso does little to explore the conflict inherent here.

At other times, he can play games with language conventions: thus, toying with the cliché "fair and square" and the slang that equates a square with a member of the conventional or established world, he claims that a horse "won the race fair and hip" ("At"); similarly, reversing another cliché and playing with the physically bloated image of Kerouac late in his life, Corso indicates that his friend "poofed into fat air" ("Columbia U," *HA* 1). In addition, catalogs of surreal juxtapositions, as occur in, for example, "Food," smack of childish self-indulgence rather than creative disorder. One is reminded of W. H. Auden's advice to Frank O'Hara in a 1955 letter: "I think you . . . must watch what is always the great danger with any 'surrealistic' style, namely of confusing authentic non-logical relations which arouse wonder with accidental ones which arouse mere surprise and in the end fatigue" (qtd. in Perloff 62). The edge is a narrow one, and length is obviously a factor contributing to the level of exhaustion. Thus, the overstuffed "Food" turns into a belabored catalog resembling an out-of-control response to a writer's work-

shop exercise; the occasionally witty and surprising images are not enough to res-
cue the poem from its self-indulgent courses.

On the other hand, "Bomb," from the same volume, switches its focus and
perspective before the point of tedium is reached: imagining the explosion as a
"Zeusian pandemonium," Corso creates a futuristic and time-levelling Olympic
scene with transhistoric figures competing in a baseball game: "the spitball of
Buddha / Christ striking out / Luther stealing third." However, rather than offering
the reader Joseph Smith being walked, Mohammed getting picked off first base,
the pope committing an error, and a bench full of evangelical pinch-hitters, Corso
moves on erratically, refusing to go into melodramatic extra innings. The triplet
of baseball lines, however, illustrates one of Corso's favorite surreal techniques: he
establishes a dislocation by conflating temporal periods and then populates that
new setting with similarly displaced figures. Thus, in the poem "At the Big A," he
imagines the Freak Stakes, a race at Aqueduct track in which the entries include
Centaur, Nightmare, Winged Horse, Unicorn, Sea Horse, the Lone Ranger's Sil-
ver, and Hippo (River Horse)—and the race is won by Corso's longtime favorite
"horse," heroin, "the only horse that wasn't running." Although the poem could
hardly be classified among Corso's major works (it remains as of this moment
uncollected in any of his volumes), it does effectively illustrate his control of the
catalog technique: he keeps the field limited, declining to include Alexander the
Great's Bucephalus, Robert E. Lee's Traveller, Black Beauty, Flicka, Hopalong
Cassidy's Topper, Roy Rogers's Trigger, Gene Autry's Champion, *de combat*, and
d'oeuvre, among numerous other possibilities. What he has done then is to em-
ploy poetic economy, including only as many examples as are necessary to provide
variety and to provoke wonder, without indulging in the exhaustive and exhaust-
ing comprehensiveness that sometimes mars his explorations of narrowed topics,
too much like the exasperating, monomaniacal enthusiasm of children.

Much of Corso's humor depends upon a childlike sense of wonder and incon-
gruity, and as Breton asserts, "The mind which plunges into Surrealism relives with
glowing excitement the best part of its childhood" (39), when transgression against
adult standards and restrictions is less inexcusable. Perhaps for Corso, whose or-
phaned childhood was less than idyllic, surrealism offers an opportunity not only
to experience that period again, but also to create a new childhood. Corso was
the youngest of the prominent Beat writers, and his reckless behavior and liter-
ary eclecticism sometimes resemble the precocious teenager's exasperating testing
of his family's love, with the Beats serving as a family substitute. In Corso's po-
etry, childhood, children, zoos, and animals offer recurrent subjects as he uses
innocence of vision as both topic and technique to portray "the best part" and
the worst part in disturbing surrealistic detail:

I turned to my father
    and he ate my birthday
I drank my milk and saw trees outrun themselves
    valleys outdo themselves
    and no mountain stood a chance of not walking

Dessert came in the spindly hands of stepmother
I wanted to drop fire-engines from my mouth!
But in ran the moonlight and grabbed the prunes.[9]

                          ("This Was," *G/V* 43)

Here the child's dismal experience is rescued from the spoiled birthday and from the unpleasant climax of prunes by a pilfering manifestation of Nature. Even the loveless, oppressive conditions cannot stifle the imaginative exuberance of youthful humor. The childlike perspective also results in occasional moments of "off-color" humor, particularly in the taboo areas of sexuality and excretion.[10] Thus, in "Open the Gate," his narrator, warned not to curse, "let out a big dirty word" (57); in "Marriage" he envisions a honeymoon night on which everyone, including hotel clerks, elevator operators, and bellboys, knows "what was going to happen" (*HB* 30), where the reader becomes complicit in imagining the wedding night copulation that is never specified; the death-wish of "Seaspin" is relieved by the narrator's "sea-ghost" as he pauses to "[f]eel the mermaid up" (*HB* 13), an adolescent male vision of sexuality that, when imposed on an imaginary figure, takes on the irrepressible satyriasis of Harpo Marx; he can imagine himself in unmarried old age, "all alone in a furnished room with pee stains on my underwear" ("Marriage," *HB* 32); in a small Greek village, Corso's narrator and fellow drinkers in a tavern without a toilet go out in back and "all did wondrously pee" ("Some Greek Writings," *LL* 69). Liberated from social conventions by death, projected old age, and provincial setting, he can indulge, as in dreams, childish licentiousness and unpunished violation of adult expectations.

At other times, the childlike naiveté offers a wide-eyed perception of reality, while humanity provides its own absurdity:

The Berlin Zoo
has two pay entrances.
One for the West
and one for the East.
But after the tickets are bought
they both join at the gate
and stream toward the monkeys.

                          ("Berlin Zoo," *M* 215)

Visitors converge to watch simian antics that are hardly less ludicrous than the human behavior that splits a city and country in two or that arbitrarily separates people into geographical divisions and political factions. Similarly, a found poem creates unlikely neighbors in a "Direction Sign in London Zoo":

Giant Panda
Lions
Humming Birds
Ladies.

(*SP* 51)

No reasonable person could suspect that the zoo includes women on exhibit, but the humorist's eye catches an absurdity conjuring such a comical possibility (nor is the observation sexist; the poem would work equally well if the last line were "Gentlemen").

At his best, Corso's wit and precise sense of timing function to provide materials that satisfy the classical criteria of *utile et dulce*. Focusing on his poetic role, he characterizes himself as

> devoted to Mercurio
> the greatest messenger of them all
> in Greece they know him as Hermes
> in India as Ganesha
> in Egypt as Toth
> in Israel as Moses
> in Scandia as Loki
>   in the Northern reaches as the Bellosurian arrow
> in America as CBS.[11]

("Field Report," *M* 244)

Thus, he humorously caps the catalog with a telling observation on the loss of mythic mystery and of wonder in modern times.

In "The Whole Mess . . . Almost," Corso provides a model for his approach. The speaker throws out the window Truth, God, Love, and a series of other "things most important in life." Finally, he finds himself facing the last occupant of the room—Humor: "All I could do with Humor was to say: / 'Out the window with the window!'" (*HA* 48–49). The jesting twist reveals Corso's belief that human beings, even when deprived of most of life's values and verities, still have a significant alternative to which to turn. The poem portrays and embodies this message, providing both illumination and delight. It also illustrates Corso's poetic technique. Once asked, "Why write poetry rather than prose?" he answered, "There's nothing more to say, man, now you've gotta play" and went on to explain "his preference . . . for the play theory of art" (Scully 245). The combination of the words *play* and *theory* offers clues to the strategy that he uses in his writings—and to the problems that he recognizes in his approach. He even seems to realize that some of his early work may be vulnerable to charges of comedic posturing and that maturity (a quality seldom applied to Corso by his critics) has taught him the need to make his humor pointed:

> I don't act silly any more.
> And because of it I have to hear from so-called friends:
> "You've changed. You used to be so crazy so great."
> They are not comfortable with me when I'm serious.
> Let them go to the Radio City Music Hall.
>
> ("Writ on the Eve," *LL* 92)

Clearly, Corso believes that his humor has outgrown mere entertainment and must have a point to satisfy his poetic goals.

In a world that often seems disintegrating and destructive, Corso employs humor and surrealism in his works as ways of reducing or relieving the tensions of an oppressive age: "'It takes humor to get you through this life,' he [Corso] stated with a knowing smile" (Dossey). In such conditions, these techniques encounter the danger of becoming tainted by the very disorders they might alleviate: "The comedy gone mad! / Poor clown, the weather of sorrow" ("Clown," *HB* 60). Corso, however, indicates that humor can serve to enhance the treatment of sociopolitical problems: "And if one must by one's need see civic social how much grander it'd be if one worked that see into a wild mad illuminating humour" (Letter to Editor, *Cambridge*). Whether challenging conventional positions (liberal or conservative), discarding accepted ideals and values, or even rejecting the gods, Corso is game for the action—a three-card monte dealer in life, a hustler with such élan that even his victims are entertained. Corso's ultimate effect is the enhancement of the values of life. He celebrates his own poetic power in terms of comedic potential: "Alive with a joy a sparkle a laugh / That drops my woe and all woe to the floor / Like a shot spy" ("Power," *HB* 80). Breton has pointed out that true Surrealism is not an end, but a means—its aim is *the creation of a collective myth* through the medium of art (232). For Corso, both the myth and the medium must be allowed to frolic in their natural, humorous dimensions.

7

"The Poesy That Cannot Be Destroyed": Corso's Prosody

O I dont know
You can get it out of a book
If the right words are
    important

—Jack Kerouac, *Mexico City Blues*

Corso has suggested that the Beat Generation made its strongest impact on the form and content of contemporary poetry:

> The most outstanding of all the great services the Beat Generation has thus far rendered is in connection with the use of 'measure' in poetry. When the Beat Generation came into existence, poets, with prophetic insight, were already insisting upon the overwhelming importance of supplementing their supplies of old iambics by the use of mixtures containing spontaneity 'bop prosody' surreal-real images jumps beats cool measures long rapidic vowels, long long lines, and, the main content, soul. ("Variations," *Casebook* 88)

Crediting the Beats alone with these changes would be myopic, but one can scarcely deny the influence of the Beat experiments and innovations in prosody. The popular success of the Beat writers ensured the promulgation of their literary strategies, even when the mass appeal of those techniques would seem unlikely. Corso's works show that he has drifted in his creative career, suffering the influence of his fellow Beat writers, pursuing (sometimes halfheartedly) their experimental directions, diligently trying to keep pace with their theoretical explorations while still maintaining his own focus and voice. Though a number of his efforts have resulted in stilted productions, his intense individuality has managed to lift a substantial number of his works to a level of creativity and innovation that have afforded him a considerable cult status—and more importantly have allowed him to create a body of visionary poems that possess the qualities of greatness. As a product of a lower-class world, more limited in formal education and less confined by conventional social skills than most of the other Beat writers, he creates poems with an authentic quality of the streets, and he articulates a significant perspective on the common world, even when his work may be marred by undeniable limitations. Corso's contributions to the Beat canon offer idiosyncratic efforts of varying success in the areas of metrics and rhyme, form, and, most significantly, diction.

The assault on traditional metrical systems permeates Corso's work. His impatience with conventional iambic patterns informs the poems as they thunder along or dawdle, bending and curling, flowing from quiescent pools into treacherous rapids like willful and dangerous mountain streams. Searching for "a new prosody to fit the ecstatic rhythm of the new American tongue" ("Variations," *Casebook* 91), he challenges the dominant rhythms with the charge that they are outmoded and useless to the modern age: "Where is your music, lost in the dusty iambic attic of the 19th century? . . . Who dare talk of tradition when the ear is dead when invention is forgotten when the riot of 20th Century truth is lisped in the melancholy of Oxford pentameter?" ("Variations," *Casebook* 91; ellipsis added).[1] In creating his own music, Corso can provide harmonic variations on the iambic pattern, reinforcing them with such standard devices as alliteration and assonance to generate mellifluous rhythms, even in his earliest works: "breaking into little bits broken men call broken ships" ("Coney Island," *G/V* 60). On the other hand, attempting to escape what he sees as stultifying rhythms, Corso sometimes errs on the dark side of felicity. In the poem "For Black Mountain," he asserts, "The idea / not the *line* / must be measured." At times, however, his ideas and his lines are flat, and, straining at the limits of poetry, he occasionally slips into cheap truisms or bald declamation, as prosaic didacticism replaces poetic expression:

> Cemeteries are just like parks. Even better.
> Of course the cemetery in Paris (the big one)
>   is not as pleasant as the one in Charleston,
>   not as quiet, and not as many trees.

> ("Park," *HB* 65)

Such flatness is a natural, though not inevitable, danger when poets attempt to reflect the patterns of normal spoken language. William Carlos Williams, whose influence on the Beats was powerful, both defined the program and pointed to the possible potholes in this experimental road:

> We must go forward—uncertainly it may be, but courageously as we may. Be assured that measure in mathematics as in verse is inescapable; so in reply to the fixed foot of the ancient line, including the Elizabethans, we must have a reply: it is the variable foot which we are beginning to discover after Whitman's advent. (251)

Corso's reference to the "variable poet of humankind" in "Lines Between Past & Future" seems to echo Williams's projection. If Corso himself goes "forward uncertainly," that movement involves an element of apparent carelessness. Specifically, a peculiarity occurs in Corso's use of the apostrophe to indicate the absence of "paragoge," the artificially appended pronounced syllable of traditional poetry (as in *wingèd*). Conventionally, a poet would use the apostrophe to signal the reader that an *-ed* ending did not constitute a pronounced syllable. This usage establishes a signal system for the reader, and the absence of the apostrophe indicates that the regular past-tense marker is to be pronounced. Such clues can be crucial in comprehending the poet's intended rhythms in a passage. Thus, in Blake's "The Garden of Love," the system of signals reveals the regularity of anapestic trimeter:

Sŏ Ĭ túrn'd ■ tŏ thĕ Gár ■ dĕn ŏf Lóve
. . . .
Ănd Ĭ sáw ■ ĭt wăs fíll ■ ĕd wĭth gráves.

In Keats's "Ode to a Nightingale," the same pattern of signs indicates the rhythms and reading within a single line: "Cáll'd hĭm ■ sóft námes ■ ĭn mán ■ ў ă mú ■ sĕd rhýme." However, the successful transaction between writer and reader depends on the consistent and rational deployment of the system of cues, as is true of any pattern of exchange.

Unfortunately, too often Corso seems to use the apostrophe as mere decoration, to sprinkle it haphazardly on his poems without recognizing its effect, apparently simply inserting it on occasion to give a poetic appearance. Thus, when a single line describes "Ox-flushings, scour'd malady, suffused sulphur" ("Death," *HB* 41) or when a pair of lines states, "Soft-voiced Velveteer! with buttons snow pronounc'd— / When your wings closed" ("Errol Flynn," *EF* 86), a reader is likely to assume either that "suffused" is intended to be a three-syllable word and that "voiced" and "closed" are each to be pronounced as two-syllable words or that Corso is not applying his typographical indicators according to any meaningful pattern. For a later poem, "Dear Villon," with its "laundr'd," "unsoiled," and "claimed," the reader tends to support the latter possibility, as opposed to attempting pointlessly to pronounce "unsoiled" as three syllables and "claimed" as a two-syllable word, especially in view of the fact that in the same volume Corso uses his typography to indicate clear instances of paragoge: "depresséd"; "Blesséd," "blesséd"; "fleshéd." Because this problem affects the rhythms of Corso's poetry, it can scarcely be dismissed as inconsequential. For example, the brief poem "When a Boy . . ." begins, "When a boy / I monitored the stairs / altar'd the mass" (*HA* 33); the pattern suggested by the apostrophe yields attempts to pronounce "monitored" as four syllables, and the result is a decidedly unappetizing line. In a later poem, "the blue-drap'd mountains" suggests an equally distasteful reading of the line "solsticed my brain" ("Noted for Having," *M* 232). A more complex situation occurs in the poem "Artemis": "she took aim / and arrow'd him / between his branched horns" (*Grègorian RANT*). The expected paragoge of the last line of this passage provides smoothly iambic trimeter, but consistency would then require paragogic readings in other lines of the same poem ("The deersman, antlered tall," "she tried but failed to grab her father's beard / He laughed and agreed") that would be virtually emetic. The only conclusion one can reasonably arrive at is that Corso's use of the apostrophe in his past tense verbs has no recognizable system or pattern at all; it serves only as a spotty cosmetic to give the appearance of a traditionally poetic complexion—contemporary poems in Romantic drag.

Ordinarily, however, Corso's experimental range in measure is impressive, from the Whitmanesque long line of "Elegiac Feelings American" to the clipped, fragmentary short lines of "Proximity"; from the dithyrambic chants of the conclusion of "Army" to the rhapsodic formality of "Mutation of the Spirit"; from the trimeters and dimeters of the early "Vision Epizootic" to the appropriately harsh discord of "Train Wreck." He moves from one rhythm to another, refusing to be confined by any single metrical mode, despite the fact that such variety might open him to charges of artistic dilletantism or of the inability to discover the rhythms of his own voice. Sometimes, as in "Field Report," Corso will shift measure even within a single poem, wandering in and out of rhyme, giving free turns to the kaleidoscope of mood and feelings as they drift with the erratic tempo of human nature, reflecting what he calls "my sporadic measure and rhyme" (Letter to Editor, *Genesis*).

Corso's idiosyncratic use of rhyme is also especially notable. In his earliest collection, *The Vestal Lady on Brattle and Other Poems*, such poems as "The Horse Was Milked" employ conventional and unimaginative rhyme schemes. This volume, however, already shows evidence of his impatience with these forms. "Vision Epizootic" follows a conventional quatrain structure with alternating lines rhyming, but the second line of each quatrain is dimeter in contrast to the trimeter of the other three lines. "Dementia in an African Apartment House" provides casual variety by offering varying line and stanza forms, as well as shifting rhyme schemes. Nevertheless, the distortions and inversions of normal phrasing typical of apprentice verse or doggerel become disturbingly noticeable in this poem: "The wife ran up to it, and on her knees fell: / 'Lion, lion,' she said, 'my mind is not well'" (*G/V* 58). The "uncomfortable inversions of syntax" (139) that Schwartz identifies persist in later poems as well:

> O youth, you who were born in my youth of woe,
>   of lonely mothers and killing fathers,
>   ye babies of war who now to war go
>
> Though your father the same helmet wore
>   . . . his head never thought to picket
>   and hoist placards of anti-war
>   . . . .
> Thus bullets flying, war-babies crying,
>   and rebels in smoking napalm lying;
>
> ("War-Babies" 15; line ellipsis added)

> I would a tinkler of dreams be
> deluded in zodiacal pretence
> than have to wonder such reality
> as human violence
>
> ("Eleven," *EF* 32)

> True, I boast an encyclopedian mind
> and in the Encyclopedia
> my name you'll find
>
> . . . .
> Had I never been born
> would Shakespeare a reality be?
> And when I cease this sojourn
> what then were he to me?
>
> ("Field Report," *M* 240, 251)

At times, Corso's formal concerns result in structures more uncomfortable than mere inversions. The four-syllable rhymed lines that conclude "I Dream in the Daytime" result in wrenched elliptical syntax:

> I cringe my sink
>   I gloom my stove
>
> They leave me pink
>   I dip my glove.
>
> (*EF* 111)

"Body Fished from the Seine" illustrates Corso's rhyming strengths and the poetic perils of his inversions. The poem's opening and closing couplets reveal a clever awareness and control of language's sounds, perhaps developed through an American ear for the French and English pronunciation Corso encountered during his travels:

> He floats down the Seine
> The last victim of the FLN
>
> . . . .
>
> They fresh from Eiffel and Notre-Dame
> —A break of camera calm.[2]
>
> (*EF* 109)

Lines in the body of the poem, however, are considerably weaker than its head and tail: "He's Arab, he's soft, he's green / 'He's a long time in the water been.'" Here, the artificial grammatical structure, coupled with the bouncy rhythms and the forced rhymes, creates a callous insouciance. Gregory Stephenson sees the narrator— in contrast to the tourist boat's gawking passengers who are taking photographs of the victim—as "appalled and full of pity" (*Exiled* 61). However, even though the narrator refers to "the sad victim," the dispassionate images, casual language, and couplet rhymes combine to create effects that undermine the possibility of narrative sensitivity: "Like a wet sponge he bounces and squirts / Somehow you feel though dead it hurts." In "The Game," another early poem, Corso's weak, facile rhymes are compromised even further by varieties of internal rhymes:

> I am too effete to compete
> With you, sir;
> You are a master and I, an amateur.
> Pray sit, do not stir—
> It would please, if not appease, me
> No end if you were to spend
> Some time with me
> And I, the game, comprehend.
>
> (*G/V* 81)

At times, the shackles of the rhyme scheme impose forced or imprecise word choice:

> He strapped the belt across his arm;
> wiped the needle so it'd not harm
>
> and tightened, tightened the belt for a vein.
> He pulled and his arm began to pain.
>
> ("The Horse," *G/V* 75)

At the end of each of these couplets, the final word functions for reasons of rhyme rather than for appropriate, idiomatic usage. In a rather remarkable moment during an interview with Michael Andre, Corso picked up the interviewer's copy of *Long Live Man* and found the notation "[u]sual cheap commonplace rhymes"; after an uncomfortable moment for both men, Andre asked, "Do you ever think you use easy rhymes?" and Corso responded, "This is too easy, you're right. But, what the Hell, if I use some hard ones, why can't I use the easy ones?" (156). In the same interview, Corso goes on to note that the poet Hayden Carruth convinced him to change the word *pain* to *joy* in "Sura," resulting in the only unrhymed lines in the first three stanzas of that poem.[3] In "Sea Chanty," the first stanza employs couplet rhymes, but the second retains only traces of rhyme, almost as though Corso may have revised the latter stanza and forgotten that he had been working with rhymes—a possibility that seems applicable to many of his later rhyming excursions as well. The process can apparently occur in both directions: the lines "I take back all I took / The spirit is a charitable thief" ("Earth Egg") revised into rhyme become "I take back all I took / the spirit is a charitable crook" ("Honor"), and later still the second line is dropped altogether in the conclusion of "Ancestry."

Gavin Selerie complains about "Corso's fondness for the neat, polished or clever rhyme" (17). Such a judgment is likely to be subjective, but Corso's clever rhymes frequently shape his structures and often reveal delightful sensitivity to spoken language:

> And in the world the world at large
> there is talk soft talk of bombs
> Carter talks like a monk whispering psalms
> of bombing Russian bombs
> of bombing the Russians in charge
> even Brezhnev and the cars in his garage
> And Russia threatens to bomb the U.S.
> plus Carter, congress, the MX, the whole mess.[4]
>
> ("Bombed Train," *HA* 27)

The ironic rhyme of *bombs* and *psalms* adds poignancy to the poem's theme, and that of *U.S.* and *mess* reveals his use of acronyms and abbreviations for rhymes (as in the link of *Seine* and *FLN* in "Body Fished from the Seine," cited earlier). Rhyming contrast becomes humorous in the April Fool's joke "Was Papa Haydn Born April 1st?" with its rhymes of *Mozart* with *Humphrey Bogart* and *adagio* with the slang *roscoe*; similarly, at the end of "Lines Between Past & Future," the rhyme of a scientific term and of the word for the trophy for popular films offers a humorous play on the various meanings of *star* and provides comic closure, much as a punch line does in a joke:

In some distant age
long after here there'll be another stage
I'll portray a dying star in a universal flick
and hear light years tick
while the producer from Tibetan Jerusalem
will say my role of a pulsar
shall win me an Oscar.

Rhymes can also underscore Corso's irony, as can be seen in the growth of a single section through various stages of development. A passage from the 1958 poem "A Spontaneous Requiem for the American Indian," "whaa whaa dead men red men feathers-in-their-head-men night" (*Yūgen* 2; repeated in the revised poem in *Elegiac* 13), is revised in "Detective Frump's Spontaneous & Reflective Testament," a prose piece that Corso freely plundered for several poems in *Long Live Man*; he concludes a section celebrating "the American Indian" with the sentence "O they are the redmen feathers-in-their-head-men down among the deadmen, pow wow!" (72).[5] Returning to this passage for an early version of "Death of the American Indian's God," Corso skillfully enhances the assonance and the rhyme structure:

Everyone is dressed in crow
Oh

    they were the redmen
    feathers-in-their-head men
    now
    down among the dead men
    how.

(SP 59)

A slightly later printing eliminates the word "Oh"; reducing the sound rhymes emphasizes the ironic chanting dirge:

Everyone is dressed in crow
    They were the redmen
    feathers-in-their-head men
    now
    down among the dead men
    how.[6]

("Death of the American," *LL* 18)

Although Corso's rhymes often lack subtlety, an important exception is "'Let Us Inspect the Lyre,'" which, despite its title's allusion to Keats's "On the Sonnet," employs not a sonnet form but primarily a quatrain structure in which the opening line of each stanza after the first rhymes with the concluding line of the previous stanza. In the powerful conclusion of "Reflection in a Green Arena," one might object to his coinage of *insectai*, but it offers an effective internal rhyme and end rhyme, and the concluding couplet's slant rhyme provides epigrammatic closure:

> I wipe the dead spider
> off the statue's lips
> Something there is is forgotten
> and what's remembered slips
> Butterfly and fly and other insectai
> wait themselves to die
>
> And so it's Spring again so what
> The leaves are leaves again no tree forgot.

(LL 29)

The thematically metaphoric rhyme of "Inter & Outer Rhyme" is echoed in the *abab* rhyme scheme and the internal eye rhyme of the brief poem's last line:

> Last night was the nightest
> The moon full-mooned a starless space
> Sure as snow beneath snow is whitest
> Shall the god surface the human face.[7]

(HA 21)

Generally, Corso's rhymes are most effective when used to achieve a playful sing-song effect: "Leap Bomb bound Bomb frolic zig and zag / The stars a swarm of bees in thy binging bag" ("Bomb," *HB*);

> Children children don't you know
> Mozart has no where to go
> This is so
> Though graves be many
> He hasn't any.

("Writ When," LL 32)

Corso asserts, "I like to rhyme when I want to rhyme. When I don't want to rhyme I don't rhyme" (Interview with R. King 7). In fact, one of his later poems even playfully incorporates his self-conscious awareness of rhyme and its demands into the fabric of his work:

> Then again
> when was it when
> Sumer? We're not talkin' Sumer

Ah, for the purpose of rhyme
Kelly, it's a tumor.[8]

("Field Report," *M* 240)

Corso explains, "there are only two kinds of poesy I hold to, one is real, usually lyric form, the other is happy funny, usually scattered form, the two combined together is where I'm at" ("Dear Fathers" 11). Such artistic capriciousness is scarcely reprehensible in itself and can offer qualities of organic structural development, but pointless patchwork must nevertheless stand upon its own demerits.

Corso's poems frequently have a modular structure that contributes to their anarchic appearance. In the late 1950s, he participated in William Burroughs's cut-up experiments, contributing to the collection *Minutes to Go*. Essentially these experiments involved cutting up pages from various sources and rearranging them into a composite text. Corso's participation was characterized, it must be admitted, by faint heart and less success. In self-defense, Corso issued a statement at the end of the collection that deserves to be quoted at length:

> Poetry that can be destroyed should be destroyed, even if it means destroying one's own poetry—if it be destroyed. I join this venture unwillingly *and* willingly. Unwillingly because the poetry I have written was from the soul and not from the dictionary; willingly because if it can be destroyed *or* bettered by the 'cut-up' method, then it is poetry I care not for, and so should be cut-up. Word poetry is for everyman, but soul poetry—alas, is not heavily distributed. . . .
>
> Unwillingly because my poetry is a natural cut-up, and need not be created by a pair of scissors; willingly because I have no other choice. I have agreed to join Mr Gysin, Mr Beiles, and Mr Burroughs in this venture, and so to the muse I say: 'Thank you for the poesy that cannot be destroyed that is in me'—for this I have learned after such a short venture in uninspired machine-poetry.[9] ("Post-script"; ellipsis added)

One reason Corso might feel that his poetry is "a natural cut-up" is that many of his longer poems are loosely constructed, particularly those that focus on a single topic. "Marriage" follows a chronological development from courtship to parenthood, and "Army" maintains, through the experiential growth of its narrator, a rough structure; but "Sun," "Hair," "Bomb," "Food," "Death," "Clown," "Park," "Power," "Police," "Friend," "Elegiac Feelings American," and "Triptych: Friend, Work, World" are much more ruminative collections of reveries, observations, familiar associations, and projective musings, with little observable rationale for the order of the materials. Corso has specifically addressed his approach:

> How I love to probe life. . . . That's what poetry is to me, a wondrous prober. . . . It's not the metre or measure of a line, a breath; not "law" music; but the assembly of great eye sounds placed into an inspired measured idea. (*HB* back cover; first ellipsis added)

Keying on this principle, Ginsberg elaborates on Corso's process:

> I'm taking the word "probe" for poetry—poetry as a probe into one subject or another—from the poet Gregory Corso. He speaks of poetry as a probe into Marriage, Hair, Mind, Death, Army, Police, which are the titles of some of his earlier poems. He uses poetry to take an individual word and probe all its possible variants. He'll take a concept like death, for instance, and pour every archetypal thought he's ever thought or could recollect having thought about death and lay them out in poetic form—making a whole mandala of thoughts about it.[10] ("Meditation" 147)

The seeming randomness within these poems lends them the appearance of spontaneity, even those that have gone through considerable revision, although they sometimes suffer from weaknesses in transition and coherence. Ginsberg refers to Corso's "Elegiac Feelings American" as a "poem cluster" ("On Corso's" xiv), and the term seems appropriate for many of his other poems as well. Corso exploits his structural looseness in "Mutation of the Spirit," a nine-page poem that he prefaces with an explanatory statement: "These poems all bear the same theme, yet each page is a separate poem, and yet again each joins up to make a whole poem . . . and the poems can be shuffled up and read as chance would have it. . . . No one poem comes first or last" (*EF* 18).[11] The influence of Burroughs is evident in the form and strategy of this poem, which is a remarkable achievement that explores the indomitability of the human spirit, viewing it from different heights and in varying lights, refusing to settle for a facile solution, weaving instead into and out of avenues of thought, offering suggestions and intimations rather than glib explanations. Unfortunately, however, the modular structure begins to seem pointless. Aside from the fact that Corso's shuffle option carries little literal weight once the poem appears in a bound volume, reading the leaves of the book in arbitrary order provides no new surprises, insights, dimensions, or perspectives, unlike, for example, Julio Cortázar's novel *Hopscotch*, which also affords alternative reading opportunities. Corso's structure reveals no purposive meanings to the reader; it grants the poem an autonomy of shape and design, a freedom of which bound publication subsequently deprives it.

The scheme of "Mutation of the Spirit" is especially instructive in that it illustrates a way in which Corso's poems are natural cut-ups, though not entirely in

Burroughs's sense. Frequently Corso seems to compose in blocks and then to build a poem by arrangement of those blocks. As a result, passages are often discrete units—so much so that they can be dislodged, sometimes to stand by themselves and at other times to be used in other constructions. Thus, the lines "When I sleep the sleep I sleep / is not at will / And when I dream I dream children waving goodbye" ("Hair," *HB* 14) reappear in the poem, "Death," in the very same volume of poems. The phrase "protect of Death" occurs in "Spontaneous Poem After Having Seen the Metropolitan Museum" and "Clown," again in the same volume. The third section of "Three Loves" later appears in "Reflection in a Green Arena," still again in the very same collection of poems. He recounts an episode in which Dwight D. Eisenhower flew in a helicopter over Athens and states that the American president gazed down at the Acropolis "like only Zeus could," in both "Some Greek Writings" and "America Politica Historia, in Spontaneity." Corso's assertion that man is the victory of life appears in *The American Express*, "Man," Saint Francis," "Writ in Horace Greeley Square," and three times in "The American Way." A passage about the "blessed knockout" of "stars of kayo" concludes the third section of "Eleven Times a Poem," is echoed in a page of working papers of "The Geometric Poem," and is adapted to provide the conclusion of "Return," which then also concludes a version of another poem, "Getting to the Poem". Developed from the fifth entry in "A Small Notebook," the first three lines of the ninth poem in "Eleven Times a Poem" become, with minor changes, the opening lines of "Daydream";[12] the other six lines of "Daydream" are variations of passages from "Reading about Nicaraguan & Mid East Wars," and Corso is creating still another version of this poem in an interview with Andre. Similarly, the brief doggerel poem "Writ When I Found Out His Was an Unmarked Grave" reappears with minor revisions in *Way Out* and as the conclusion of "German Visitations of Music Men."[13] Lines from "Bath,"

> The finest arcana is seldom told
> The Magus
>   is a dazzling boy when old
> Tap an Arab on the shoulder
>   and a Babylonian will turn
>   and smile

(MF 27)

reappear in essentially the same form at the beginning of "From Rome to Boulder," still again within the same collection of poems. Furthermore, the poems "Bath" and "On Gregory Being Double the Age of Shelley" later appear with only minimal changes as passages in the poem "Field Report." "Hedgeville" originally appears in the periodical *Combustion* in 1957, is revised as "Last Night I Drove a

Car" for the collection *Gasoline*, but then reappears in its original form in *Elegiac Feelings American*.[14] A section on wealth and commerce from the middle poem of "Triptych: Friend, Work, World," originally published in *The Hasty Papers* in 1960, is revised as part of "Mr. Moneybag's Lament" before reappearing in its original form in *Elegiac Feelings American*, and the "Friend" section of the triptych is a slight revision of a poem appearing in his previous volume, a point that Corso himself mentions in his interview with Andre. Ginsberg has commented that for Corso, "As engineer of ideas, certain concepts recur retailored for nuance" ("On Corso's" xiii),[15] but too often his repetitions constitute a curious phenomenon of self-plagiarism. In "The Geometrician of Milano," Corso asserts that "[t]he blank page of the poet / is like the slow broom of a janitor / sweeping the same floor for 25 years" (*HA* 29). At times, Corso seems to be sweeping the same leavings over and over again, and sometimes they are strangely recycled. A poem that begins as "Ode to Myself" is revised as "Ode to Myself & Her," which is then reprinted as "Ode to Sura"; the depersonalization is further evidenced by the fact that lines from these poems are revised for "Rembrandt—Self-Portrait." Similarly, "Piffle" is a self-examination:

> I'll starthrow no more
> when tomorrow
> I close a door
> like an act of Jesus
> It'll be neither day nor night
> when my hair gone white
> shall become blonder than gold
> I'll walk the vast
> > savannahs
> beside your resurrection
> and with silver legs of spiritus
> I'll wade in the hosannas
> > of new water.

Selerie cites a modified version of this poem that Corso read as "Metaphor" in London in 1980. The major changes involve the opening of the door in line 3 and the addition of four lines to the end of the poem. The next alteration of the poem is truly startling: the self-focused poem is converted into an elegy for John Lennon, with the shift of the pronouns from first and second person singular to second and first person plural ("For John Lennon," *HA* 28).[16] The faint smell of imposture revealed here creates a distant form of ventriloquism. Such interchangeability supports Richard Howard's assertion that Corso "does not write poems, he writes poetry" (79).[17]

In addition to his formal vagaries, Corso also allows himself grammatical, syn-
tactical, and verbal liberties. André Breton provides an explanation for an impe-
tus in this direction: "People pretend not to pay too much attention to the fact
that the logical mechanism of the sentence alone reveals itself to be increasingly
powerless to provoke the emotive shock in man which really makes his life mean-
ingful" (152). Corso's poetry attempts to regenerate that power, rejecting conven-
tional language and grammatical patterns as he truncates, distorts, and reconstructs
syntax and language in a process that provides verbal reinvigoration. Thus, he
scrambles the normal order of parts of speech within clauses, even when he is not
attempting to serve the demands of self-imposed rhyme schemes: "It is better man
a word elongate" ("No Word," *G/V* 41); "Luck is of chance made" ("Hunch," *HA*
57). Neeli Cherkovski refers to this technique in Corso's poems as "a deliberate
transposition, giving to the phrase an oracular tone" (186). Further structural obli-
quity is created by what Ginsberg refers to as Corso's "elliptical phraseology" ("Ab-
straction" 74), particularly of verbs—"While he eats let's a magic so the prisonyard
pivot / dull lifers from solitary" ("1953," *HB* 23); "He'd me carry his sword and
shield" ("Ares Comes," *LL* 70); "I would out I would putter in the garden" ("Mu-
tation," *EF* 21); "Now I would less knowledge than more" ("Dear Villon," *HA*
24)—and of prepositions: "I decided sunset to dine" ("This Was," *G/V* 43); "No
chance his beautiful bullets hitting us" ("1953," *HB* 23); "beg Zeus Polyphemus
a new eye" ("A Difference," *LL* 62);[18] "And now man yearns death no more"
("Eleven," *EF* 35); "What thinkest thou the poppy?" ("Columbia U," *HA* 4).
Corso is especially fond of trimming the idiomatic prepositional structure *out of*
by eliminating *of*: "from out parlors and cellars" ("Cambridge, First," *G/V* 98);
"and not once did I catch from out the dark" ("Cambridge, First," *G/V* 99);
"Thank God it did not run out the room" ("For Black Mountain—2"); "from
out torturous vulvas" ("In Praise," *HA* 43); "From out an apse" ("Field Report,"
M 251). He also takes the conversational omission of the relative pronoun—
"breaking into little bits broken men call broken ships" ("Coney Island," *G/V* 60);
"the rhythms I walk to hear" ("Cambridge, First," *G/V* 97); "There's that in me
knows the proximity" ("At")—to extremes that go beyond familiar usage:

It is life has flawed my gentle song

("Clown," 56)

Something there is can imagine gold with closed eyes
. . . .
Something there is can put itself in its eyes
. . . .
Something there is can open its eyes

. . . .
Something there is can sufficiently drench

("Something," *SP* 56–57)

There's a truth limits man

("Writ on the Steps," *LL* 77)

Quite often it is night blends them

("City Child's" *LL* 81)

And the coming of days
           have already gone by.

("Eyes," *HA* 37)

Revisions perhaps best reveal how calculatedly Corso designs his ellipses: "That curious warm is all too familiar" from "Man About to Enter Sea" is altered by the elimination of the copulative verb in "Man Entering the Sea, Tangier"; in a holographic work-paper, the line "and wait for the stars to appear" undergoes the cancellation of the preposition "for" ("Geometric Poem," *EF* 57). The effect of the ellipses is not to obliterate meaning, but to distance the reader from familiar constructions so that the dynamics of the sentences is freshened and renewed.

Corso's experiments with diction achieve a similar effect. An early poem expresses his impatience with conventional language and reveals his revolutionary poetic purpose and process:

I know no word that is mine
and I am tired of his
It is better to sew his mouth
dynamite his ears hearless
drown his vocabulary

It is better
his eyes speak and listen as well as see.

("No Word," *G/V* 41)

One tactic Corso employs to achieve this end is to force words to function as parts of speech other than those to which they are accustomed. He favors using proper nouns, especially names, to serve as verbals: "Life! St. Francis all police!" ("Police," *HB* 87); "Bitter remnant Agora St. Pauled" ("Greece," *LL* 24); "the America you Johnnyappleseeded" ("Elegiac," *EF* 9); "O just and brave King of Kish Virgil me" ("Eleven," *EF* 32); "One day while Peter-Panning the sky" ("One Day . . . ," *EF*

88); "Albion I'll Mercury thee! Apollo thee! Jupiter Minerva Mars thee!" (*American Express* 41); "when Dionysianing in the cockpit" ("Lines Between").[19] Corso explains his verbal adventurousness: "I also like changing words around, or adding things to words that you won't find in the dictionary, like miracling" (Interview with M. Andre 127; Corso's example occurs in "After Reading 'In the Clearing'": "miracling all that is lovely old lovely bard" [*LL* 89]). As a result, parts of speech alter their normal syntactical functions: "You were never too vitamin" ("You Came," *G/V* 57); "An hour in an hour you cease your slow" ("Giant Turtle," *HB* 49); "Now against his own for" ("History," *EF* 82); "when I poem'd it so" ("The Day Before," *HA* 35); "'Hold on there!' tidaled the seas" ("I Gave Away . . . ," *HA* 41). Corso also coins nonce words, frequently by following principles of analogy: to conventionally acceptable words or roots he appends suffixes characteristic of nouns, adjectives, or adverbs in order to modify the meanings of the original words or to change their function as parts of speech. The following table of recurrent forms illustrates Corso's variety:

Suffix	*Examples*	*Sources*
-ian	pyramidian, voidian,	*EF* 41, 45,
	flowerian	77
	cosmosian	*HA* 38
	glyphian	*M* 241
-ic	vegetic	*G/V* 37
	zombic	*HB* 23
	spectric	*SP* 60
	catacombic	*EF* 23
	tattooic, wolfic	58, 77
-ry	minstrelry	*HB* 13, 80
	searchry	*EF* 98
	chemicry	*HA* 4
	oraclry	*HA* 4
-y	cheruby	*HB* 70
	fooly	*LL* 16
	hosty, bendy	*EF* 16, 81
	atomy	*M* 266

Interestingly, Corso refuses to allow his own coinages to limit his language, for he employs optional forms: "deathical" ("Paris," *G/V* 48) and "deathonic" ("Spontaneous Requiem for," *EF* 13); "Chronicleleer" ("Power," *HB* 79) and "chronicleers" ("The 5th Estate," *MF* 54). Sometimes the alternatives occur within the same volume of poems: "voidical" and "voidian" (*EF* 20, 45); "chasmic" and "chasmal" (*EF* 52, 79). In at least one instance, the options appear within a single poem:

"Indianic" and "Indianical" ("Spontaneous Requiem for," *EF* 13, 15). Corso is also not deterred by the existence of perfectly legitimate words of long-standing currency, which offer standardized alternatives to his verbal creations (*pyramidic, flowery, glyphic, spectral, cherubic, foolish*).

Ginsberg has characterized Corso as "a great word-slinger" (Introduction 7), but sometimes he appears to have an itchy trigger-finger, to be too quick to draw. Certainly an artist should not be restricted to familiar, and sometimes shopworn, tools, but occasionally Corso's coinages seem downright silly, campy, or self-in-dulgent. In addition, his phrases can become purposelessly redundant, as in "Getting to the Poem": "And on the wall / I write thereon" (*HA* 34); "O my heart! finally / at long last / I am at peace" (35). Emphasis is here supplied by reiteration, not by prosody. At other times, his careless word choice (perhaps born of the "rapidity" of his process) is clearly erroneous. In "Coney Island," an infelicitous choice of verb, perhaps for *deadens* or *muffles*, can destroy literal meaning, even if the intended paradoxical thrust remains: "The mass silence deafens the last echo of a happy child" (*G/V* 60); in "Ares Comes and Goes," a verb again is misused: "and yet it does imbibe us drive on" (*LL* 70) (*imbibe* should perhaps be *impel*); the faulty subject-verb agreement of "[s]ometimes I scream Friends is bondage!" in "Triptych: Friend, Work, World" (*Hasty Papers*) is corrected to "[s]ometimes I scream Friends are bondage!" in a later revision as "Friend" in *Long Live Man*, but returns again to the original form and title in a still later volume (*EF* 91); in an inexact allusion to Emily Dickinson's poem "I taste a liquor never brewed," Corso claims that she "tested a liquor never brewed" ("Columbia U," *HA* 4);[20] in "Window" he uses *whereby* when he apparently means *whereas*:

> The cancer victim of healthy spirit
> is nothing terminal
> whereby the body of health
> dim of spirit, is.

> (*M* 226)

In "Bath" he orders, "Fill the tub up / at the knees" (*MF* 27), a nonidiomatic phrasing that is corrected when the lines reappear in "Field Report": "Fill the tub up . . . / to the knees" (*M* 264). Corso at times seems to recognize his verbal deficiencies, and in a remarkably engaging instance, he even incorporates his uncertainty into his poetry as he cannot determine whether to use the subjective or the objective case of the relative pronoun: "Who/whom do I report to, you wanna know?" ("Field Report," *M* 238). In rather cavalier fashion, Ginsberg comments on Corso, "But what is he *saying*? Who cares?! It's said" (Introduction 7).[21] However, when meaning is compromised by negligence or incompetence, surely the poet is culpable.[22] Corso frequently uses words to function in ways that might lead his contemporary readers to believe that he has altered their parts of speech, but research proves that archaic usage predates Corso's manipulation of them: *noosy*, which Corso spells as "noosey" (*HB* 23), is a rare form extending back to the seventeenth century; *seldom* as an adjective (*G/V* 98, *HA* 3) is also a rare, archaic form, this time dating back to the fifteenth century. The question of whether Corso was aware of those archaic uses is problematical. He has pointed out in interviews that as a teenager he read a 1905 standard dictionary in a library and that this book stimulated his interest in reviving archaic and obsolete diction. Whether such precociousness extends to reviving archaic grammar is uncertain.

Another significant area of Corso's word-coinage system involves the conjoining of two words by running them together as one. He explains his process as though he feels words are chemical elements:

> I love putting words together like "wheels of rainlight," "treelight."
> . . . Oh, yeah, that's compound, that is like chemistry. You put iron and another element together and you get a third. So that gives the birth, right? And when you put the heavies like "sexdeath" together, what do you get? You put two together, you do get a third. One and one does make three. (Interview with R. King 24)

The purpose then is to yoke together two units, retaining properties of both units, but forming a new unit with properties distinct from the constituents. Such verbal chemistry is rare, especially when the process is mere contiguity. Nevertheless, Corso does provide some genuinely creative compounds, as when he coins the word "deathmuch" to serve analogously as a contrast to the word "tuneless" used later in the same line: "Of deathmuch sequence the tuneless moon the apes of kill" ("On the Death," *EF* 98). He has explained the thought behind his creation of the word "virgina" for the poem "Of One Month's Reading of English Newspapers" (*EF* 77): "There is no word appropriate enough, the outer part, that mass of hair, that *mound*, that's not the womb, I couldn't say womb—and vagina is so ugly a word. I once spelled it 'virgina' but only because it happened to fit, poetically—it had to do with a virgin's vagina" ("When I Was Five" 30). At times, elision of letters effectively binds words into a unit much more closely approximating his ideal, much like what Lewis Carroll's Humpty Dumpty explains as "portmanteau" words, in which "there are two meanings packed up into one word" (271): "deatheme," "of Indianever again to be," "the Indianlessadly desert" ("Spontaneous Requiem for," *EF* 13, 15, 16). However, once again inconsistency of technique becomes apparent: a passage that employs elided compounding of "belfry" and "yell"—"Bat-searchyell beamhits from churchyardyell / To Belfryell"—follows only seven lines after the coinage "[d]eathhymn," in which such elision could also have occurred ("Mutation," *EF* 26), and, as a matter of fact, the combined word was spelled with only one "h" in the original publication of the poem by Death Press, as well as in the excerpts from the poem published in the periodical *C: A Journal of Poetry*. When effective, however, the device affords just enough distortion to give the reader pause, but not enough to prevent comprehension, and provides the poetic magic of what is at once strange and familiar.

Corso creates a similar effect through a peculiar pattern of verbal repetition in which a specific word is repeated consecutively to function grammatically in separate clauses: "all doors if they close close like Chinese bells" ("Ode to Coit," *G/V* 12); "What dies dies in beauty" ("On Pont Neuf," *HB* 24); "And I trembling what to say say Pie Glue" ("Marriage," *HB* 29); "Something there is is forgotten" ("Reflection in a Green Arena," *LL* 29); "Something there is is not elsewhere" ("Senile Genius," *LL* 53); "In this direction what grows grows old" ("American," *EF* 71); "I say to you you can separate / the yolk from the white of the egg" ("In Praise," *HA* 44); "All that is is finite" ("Haiku," ["All"] *MF* 18). When initially encountered, the device forces the reader to backtrack in order to solve an initially puzzling structure, and disentangling the confusion can provide delightful recognition.

In a related technique, variants of a base form function as different parts of speech within a single line: "When I sleep the sleep I sleep / is not at will" ("Hair," *HB* 14; "Death," *HB* 39); "The judge judges" ("Written While Watching Lenny Bruce" 56); "what means this dream dreamt long ago" ("A Dreamed Poem"); "A natural rot rots everything" ("The Prognosticator," *HA* 19). More conventionally, Corso uses verbal and structural repetition as reiteration, primarily to intensify (and sometimes sentimentalize) an emotional effect—"and kneeling beside Her, I wept. I wept" ("But I Do Not," *G/V* 34); in a catalog of possible scenarios of death, he lists "[f]alling off a roof electric-chair heart-attack old age old age O Bomb" ("Bomb," *HB*); "Our son, our son," "A daughter, a daughter" ("For My"); "And you, Jack, poor Jack, watched your father die, your America die, your God die, your body die, die die die" ("Elegiac," *EF* 10); "To die to die to die to die to die . . . america, requiem" ("Spontaneous Requiem for," *EF* 17); "old so old and far from the child I used to be" ("Columbia U," *HA* 4)—or to mimic action—"I kiss kiss kiss O not so bad life" ("Mutation," *EF* 23). The repetitions are especially used to underscore the difficulty of finding answers to perplexing questions: "what to choose? what to choose?" ("In the Fleeting," *G/V* 14); "now where? now where?" ("Army," *HB* 82); "where came where came that skinless light" ("Greece," *LL* 25); "When was it when was it" ("Greece," *LL* 26); "What's seen What's seen" ("Mutation," *EF* 25).

On occasion the repetitions are incremental, developed through elaboration: a child being born encounters "[l]ight winged light O the wonder of light" ("In the Fleeting," *G/V* 14); "You rise from the sea an agony of sea" ("Giant Turtle," *HB* 49); "The day is changing the day is always changing" ("City Child's," *LL*

83); "By the wings I yank by the wings the wings the lovely wings" ("Lines Written," *EF* 28); "And in the world the world at large / there is talk soft talk of bombs" ("Bombed Train," *HA* 27). Once again Corso's revisions are instructive about his tactical deployment of poetic techniques: lines from "The Turning Tide," "And I wondered there on the steps of the cradle / If my country were its grave" (10), are revised as "and I wondered, wondered if my country were its grave" ("Eleven," *EF* 33); in the opposite direction, the passage "the same when comes the crash, and it's crashing, aye crashing" ("Spontaneous Requiem" 25) is restrained in revision by elimination of the phrase "aye crashing" ("Elegiac," *EF* 11). Occasionally, repetition is used emblematically to embody meaning in form, much like Allen Ginsberg's "boxcars boxcars boxcars" in "Howl": in Corso's "The Horse Was Milked," a junkie "tightened, tightened the belt for a vein" (*G/V* 75); in "Vision of Rotterdam," bombs detonate in "[e]xplosion explosion explosion" (*G/V* 16); in "Giant Turtle," he illustrates the production of

> Eggs eggs eggs eggs eggs eggs eggs eggs eggs
> Eggs   eggs   eggs   eggs   egg   egg   egg
>
> (*HB* 49)

In a later poem, "Children attend their spirits the old knit knit knit knit" ("Mutation," *EF* 18). Corso also effectively employs repetition for rhetorical purposes. Antonin Artaud has said that the modern artist must learn "to consider language as the form of *Incantation*" (46). Corso provides chants to contribute just such an incantatory effect:

> Army's sacred prayer
> Holy be to Papa Patton who leads us
> into the poolrooms and brothels of War!
> Holy be to Papa Patton, he'd not fight Nebuchadnezzar!
> He leads us fatherly martherly gartherly into
> Death! Death! Death! Death! Death!
> Bullets in our blue eyes, holy be to Patton!
> Grenades in our bellies, Patton!
> Tanks over our bright blond hair!
> O Harpo Death and thy clanking harp, hear!
> Holy be to Patton he gives hills to Death!
> Army! Army! Army! Army![23]
>
> ("Army," *HB* 85)

This mock litany, with its structural and verbal repetitions, provides the shock and innovation for which Artaud called, as well as accentuating the bitter, satirical thrusts.

Another technique Corso employs to disturb the sensibilities of the reader is his idiosyncratic diction, including the vocabulary culled from the turn-of-the-century dictionary previously mentioned: "I downed a 22-inch 1905 standard dictionary / like a pill each word, / especially the obsolete and archaic" ("Lines Between"). He prides himself on the use of "philosoph," "brool," "scry," and other recondite words that he sees himself as rescuing from oblivion: "See, I know words—beautiful words from the past that people don't know, and it really saves the words" (Interview with R. King 23). In addition, such archaic contractions as "e'en," "e'er," "ne'er," "o'er," "'tis," and "whate'er," forms that in the second half of the twentieth century appear almost exclusively in crossword puzzles, make their way into Corso's poems, together with archaic verb forms, such as "spake," "hath," "sayeth," "mayest," and "doth," as well as the biblical pronouns "ye" and "thy." Corso even reworks his materials to incorporate archaic structures, often imposing subjunctive mood forms: "It is the condition of our minds" ("American," *Outsider* 14) is revised as "[f]or it be the condition of our minds" (*EF* 75); the line "it be the living not the dead" ("Leaky Lifeboat," *HA* 15) appears as "it's the living not the dead" in a previous version published as "The Wise Fuckers."

On the other hand, his revisions sometimes eliminate archaisms: "Thou art / double the age of him" ("On Gregory," *MF* 11) later becomes "I am double the age of him" ("Field Report," *M* 259). Corso explains that one of the functions of archaism is the creation of tone: "I use it in 'Bomb' but only because it has something apocalyptical and biblical, like 'ye BANG ye BONG ye BING'" (Interview with M. Andre 151). Most often, the obsolete forms occur in poems characterized by what Selerie calls Corso's "bardic" tone (17), and Geoffrey Thurley argues that "Corso had always shown great sophistication in his use of archaism" (208). On the other hand, Geoffrey H. Hartman complains that Corso's "high or didactic style is more easily recognized now as a debased version of what the Romantics stole from religious effusion, but then it was a Promethean act" (375). The most surprising aspect of Corso's use of archaisms, however, is their appearance together with contemporary slang and structures. Selerie notes a critical weakness in such a mixture: "There is in much of Corso's verse a curious oscillation between gothic imagery and diction and a modern colloquial street-talk. This can be remarkably effective, but it sometimes leads to a deflation of the magic which has been conjured forth" (15). Corso makes clear that such a combination is intentional, rather than careless or accidental: "I would use a word like 'thee' but I'd make sure I use 'you' in it, you know" (Interview with M. Andre 150).[24] The result is a system of tensions within a poem, sometimes within very brief passages:

Garnishment mayest ravish the vile.
Festooning mayest shanghai the accursed

may seize the nauseating the foul the beastly
may rape the unspeakable.

"Mutation," *EF* 18)

The archaic "mayest" is balanced by the current usage, "may," each form appearing twice; furthermore, the archaism works in counterpoint to the adjacent slang of "shanghai." Similarly, a later poem combines traditional poetic contraction and nonstandard grammatical usage: "—o'erhead bullets whiz by / they're not real, them's poetry bullets" ("Field Report," *M* 238). Just as he revises his poems to incorporate archaisms, Corso also returns to his poems to insert slang: the passage, "And I claim to know all there is to know / in that there isn't that much to know" ("Dear Villon," *HA* 24), later becomes "I claim to know all there is to know / because there ain't that much to know" ("Dear Villon," *M* 181). Corso's farrago of discourse, a quality that Schwartz calls "clashing levels of diction" (121), provides the double function of evoking poetic tradition and articulating an unmistakably modern voice. In "Cambridge, First Impressions," Corso recounts an experience that could serve as a symbol of his own technique: "Walking, I catch Cambridge in a seldom jubilee:— / Vivaldi, Getz, Bach and Dizzy, / in a melody all together contained" (*G/V* 98).[25] The combination of baroque and jazz, classical and modern, captures effectively the mixture of elements in Corso's own poems.

Though the collision of these levels of discourse may not interfere with comprehension, Corso's errors of orthography can cause significant problems: the strange "paradiscal" of "In the Fleeting Hand of Time" (*G* 16) remained throughout twelve printings until 1976, when City Lights Books issued a combined volume, *Gasoline & Vestal Lady*, at which point the word is changed to "paradisical" (15).[26] In addition, the two misspelled words in the line "May 1940 stevedors lead forth a platoon of lukemia" ("Vision of Rotterdam," *G* 17) are also finally corrected in the combined volume; and the obviously incorrect and miscommunicating "Desert" of "This Was My Meal" (*G* 43) is emended to "Dessert" (43). Similar errors persist, however, throughout Corso's published work: "exhult" for "exult" (*G/V* 25); "dramaticly" for "dramatically" (*HB* 27); "portentuous" for "portentous" (*EF* 33); "proto-Cassiday" for "proto-Cassady" (*HA* 20); "illicit" for "elicit" (*M* 266). The arcane "oracalry" ("Satyr's Chant," *Grecourt Review*) is revised into the jaw-breaking coinage "oraclry" (*HB* 73), a form that he repeats in "Columbia U Poesy Reading—1975" (*HA* 4) and that can appear pages later in "Sunrise" as a slightly more mellifluous but still inaccurate "oralcry" (*HA* 6).[27] The holographic worksheets of "The Geometric Poem" provide clear evidence of Corso's orthographic weaknesses. This is not, of course, to deny the creative personalization that misspelling can offer. Thus, Abbie Hoffman recalls his discovery of the word "Yippie! It pops right out. It's misspelled. Good. Misspelling can be a creative act" (51). Roland Barthes provides provocative insight into this artistic function:

> The first effect of spelling is discriminatory; but it also has secondary effects of a psychological order. If orthography were free—free to be simplified or not, according to the subject's desire—it might constitute a very positive practice of expression; the written physiognomy of the word might acquire a properly poetic value, insofar as it emerged from the *scriptor's* phantasmatics, and not from a uniform and reductive law; just think of the kind of intoxication, of baroque jubilation which explodes in the orthographic "aberrations" of old manuscripts, of texts by children and the letters of foreigners: might one not say that in such efflorescences as these, the subject seeks his freedom: to trace, to dream, to remember, to understand? Are there not occasions when we encounter particularly "happy" spelling mistakes—as if the *scriptor* were obeying not academic law but a mysterious commandment that comes to him from his own history—perhaps even from his own body? (44–45)

Thus, the "oralcry" cited above could also be evoking an oral-cry, although this possibility would still not explain Corso's inconsistency in its usage. More damaging are the instances in which Corso's spelling errors obscure his meaning. The unrecognizable usage in the passage "a didiam for American life upon which the twinship of private property and God could be established" ("Spontaneous Requiem" 23) is confused and confusing until revision corrects the spelling to "diadem" ("Elegiac," *EF* 7). The significant problem is that, in the shadow of frequent carelessness of vocabulary and spelling, the poet's coinages might be attributed to ineptitude rather than to feverish spontaneity or creativity. As a result, Corso's innovations and talent can be dismissed by readers who would patronize him as a mere curiosity, a phenomenon despite (and paradoxically because of) his literary and educational primitivism.

Corso's weaknesses are compounded when he alters his own direction. The line "one is the same unlike the rest" ("Detective" 71) recurs in "History Is Ended" (*Nomad*), is reversed as "one is the same like the rest" ("Air Is," *LL* 67), and then returns to the original in a later version ("History," *EF* 82). In the original publication of "The American Way," Corso asks, "Do I say the Declaration of Independence is old?" and answers, "No. I do say what was good for 1780 is not good for 1960" (*Outsider* 11), but the revised version of the poem responds, "Yes I say what was good for 1789 is not good for 1960" (*EF* 71). "War / is hard to deplore / when peace generates hate," the opening of the eighth poem of *10 Times a Poem*, later becomes "War / is to deplore / when peace generates hate" in "Eleven Times a Poem" (*EF* 34). In "Clone 3⁶¹," Corso's "trees" illogically scream, "Birds are ours when in transit"; in later revisions, the insertion of a negative in the line makes more sense, but a singular pronoun used for the plural "trees" produces an error in agreement: "Birds are mine when not in transit" ("I Gave the Sky Away," *Bombay Gin*); finally, he arrives at a more polished and logically reasonable result: "Birds are ours when not in transit" ("I Gave Away . . . ," *HA* 41). Such reversals are not isolated: the perplexing line "I will not untruth lies" ("Who I Am," *Renegade* 28; *Bombay Gin* 37) is revised into the more coherent "I will not entruth lies" (*M* 222); "Earliest Record of Hell" cites "such hell as Dante ever knew" (*10 Times*), which later becomes "such Hell / as Dante would never know" ("Eleven," *EF* 32); the passage, "Waiting for the world and themselves / to die" ("Wise"), later becomes "Waiting for the world / not themselves to die" ("Leaky Lifeboat," *HA* 15); "For Miranda" concludes with the line "—there are no white horses in Manhattan" in one version (*WW* 34) and "—there are white horses in Manhattan" in another (*HA* 14);²⁸ the passage, "It's with how wide a third eye be / tells what you may or mayn't see" ("Bath," *MF* 27), later in the same collection of poems reverses itself:

> It's not how wide
>   a third eye be
> allows what you may
>   or mayn't see.

("From Rome," MF 45)

Readers might be tempted to truncate Ginsberg's earlier cited appraisal to a more fundamental response, "But what is he *saying*? Who cares?!" since Corso himself seems so uncertain. Particularly in view of the brief time lapse between the published reversals, changes such as those cited seem to violate Corso's own stated principles: "I was struck by the young romantic thing, that you should never retract. The changing of poems is not retraction unless you change your feeling, your idea" (Interview with M. Andre 139). Corso's revisions of substance can often lead one to suspect that the poet has not carefully thought through his statements or that he disregards the meaning of his poetry. Finally, such reversals seem to provide supportive evidence of Corso's assertion that "I speak certainties / and entertain doubts" (☥ [*Ankh*]). The danger here is that the poet may mistake inconsistency for complexity.

On the other hand, Corso's revisions and elaborations can also offer instructive insights about the strengths in his poetic process. What might appear to be a pointless surreal collocation, "werewolf bathtubs" ("Marriage," *HB* 29), is clarified in a poem later in the same collection: "Werewolf hair from Transylvanian bathtubs" ("Death," *HB* 41). Marilyn Schwartz has addressed the significance of

Corso's textual variations: "Often publishing poems in variants and in what he calls 'mutations,' Corso views his work as ceaseless because experience itself is fluid, and as a consequence the imagination must constantly rediscover values in new conditions" (120).[29] The poetic stance here reflects Tolstoy's principle that writers never finish a work; they only abandon it.

Corso's variations frequently reveal the dimensions of his values and imagination. "Immutable Moods" opens with a description that is stark and dismal:

> The rain
> How it rings
>> the chopped streets
>> the umbrellad bicycles
>> the tires of cars.
>
> (*EF* 116)

However, neither the mood nor the form is immutable. In an earlier poem in the same collection, Corso elaborates the setting in a more detailed, expansive presentation:

> but rain to walk—How it rings the Washington streets!
> The umbrella'd congressmen; the rapping tires
> of big black cars, the shoulders of lobbyists
> caught under canopies and in doorways.
>
> ("America Politica," *EF* 94)

"Seed Journey," a poem whose conclusion was published in four different forms, is even more instructive about Corso's struggle with meaning and form:

> For some seeds bread
> is the end of the journey
>
> (*SP* 53)

> For some seeds
> meal is the end of the journey
>
> (*LL* 59)

> For some seeds
> bread is death
>
> (*Beat Journey* 175)

For some seeds
bread is the end of the journey.

(*M* 110)

The variants clearly encompass the curtailed emotional extremes of depression and hope, with a possible glance at Christ's parable about the sower and seed (Luke 8: 5–8). In all four instances, the conclusion is limiting: some seeds will never reach the stage of regeneration. Their destiny is death, meal, or bread, the latter two of which at least suggest a serviceable function—the last with especially significant Biblical correspondences to Isaiah's "seed to the sower, and bread to the eater" (55: 10); this perhaps explains its preferential usage as a form of symbolism, as opposed to "meal" with its more mundane connotations. The lineation is crucially important here too, with the final version positionally emphasizing "bread" not "end."

A later poem that Corso published in a variety of stages indicates similar development: his narrator gives away the sky, the trees, the seas, and the gods; in protest, the trees "screamed," the seas "tidaled," and the gods "thundered" ("Clone 3⁶¹"). However, in three later revisions, Corso, evidently aiming for consistency of response, changes the verbs so that the trees, seas, and gods all "screamed" ("I Gave the Sky Away"). When the poem was finally collected in *Herald of the Autochthonic Spirit* as "I Gave Away . . . ," Corso returned to the variety of verbs, but he found an alternative method of supplying parallelism, providing a process of gradual growth that is instructive. In the "Clone3⁶¹" version, the narrator's actions are loosely structured:

I gave the sky away
. . . .
So I gave the trees away
. . . .
And thus I gave away the seas
. . . .
I give the gods away.

The next two early versions, published in the periodicals *Renegade* and *Bombay Gin*, move closer to structural parallelism, by substituting "so" for "thus" in the line about the seas; the next version illustrates Corso's continuing structural concern: he retains the "so" substitution and reshapes the last line as "[s]o I gave the gods away" (*Birthstone*), thus employing the past tense in all four lines and utilizing "so" in all these lines after the first; the final version incorporates the changes noted, but it sculpts the assertions in a more logically progressive syntactical pattern:

I gave away the sky

. . . .

So I gave away the trees

. . . .

So I gave away the seas

. . . .

And so I gave the gods away.

(*HA* 41)

In addition, in all four early versions, the third line in this sequence is the only one in which the adverb precedes the direct object; in the final version, he uses this word order in the first three lines, employing the structure in which the adverb follows the direct object only in the concluding line. Furthermore, in the first three versions of the poem, Corso had spatially isolated the last line by separating it from the rest of the poem. In the final printing, however, he integrates the line graphically with the rest of the poem, refusing artificial separational emphasis and relying instead on language itself through the culminating "And" and the dramatic shift of the adverb to the end of the line. These are only a few of the changes that this single poem underwent, but they illustrate structural and verbal concerns that are too often ignored in treatments of Corso's poetry.

Corso's poetic vision is unique, and his manipulation of structure and of language revitalizes his poetry by adjusting its conventional qualities to his own inclination. He compares his technique to improvisational jazz:

> When Bird Parker or Miles Davis blows a standard piece of music, they break off into other own-self little unstandard sounds—well, that's my way with poetry—X Y & Z, call it automatic—I call it a standard flow (because at the offset words are standard) that is intentionally distracted diversed into my own sound. Of course many will say a poem written on that order is unpolished, etc.—that's just what I want them to be—because I have made them truly my own—which is inevitably something NEW—like all good spontaneous jazz, newness is acceptable and expected—by hip people who listen.[30] (qtd. by Ginsberg, Introduction 9–10)

Such a conclusion seems designed to hamstring potential criticism (a rather frequent Beat self-defense) by suggesting that anyone who recognizes Corso's flaws simply is not "hip" enough to recognize his strengths. In fact, in defense of his irregularities, Corso says, "My poetry is mostly spirit, some of it wild, haphazard, and some of it controlled and straight—but spirit it is" (Letter to Editor, *Genesis*). Nevertheless, all published poetry is susceptible to conventional rather than idiosyncratic criteria. Burroughs has noted Corso's weaknesses, but also asserts that his poetic spirit still deserves attention: "Gregory is a gambler. He suffers reverses, like every man who takes chances. But his vitality and resilience always shine through, with a light that is more than human: the immortal light of his Muse" ("Introductory" xix). Though Corso sometimes blows rather jarring notes, he often achieves the jazz-like uniqueness for which he strives. His language, hardly standard, refuses to settle into fixed forms or structures, defining its own patterns as it grows, remaining always plastic as it drifts erratically, restricted only by his own anarchic poetic imagination.

8
Conclusion

Deciding just which writers constitute the major Beats is a contentious game among current aficionados of the movement. In the mid to late 1950s and into the early 1960s, however, their identities were more obvious, and Corso was clearly prominent among them. His fellow Beat writers offered extravagant praise of him, as might be expected among a closely knit social group, with Kerouac even calling him "[a] fabulous young American poet of the very first magnitude in the history of English" (*Good* 146). Ginsberg and Corso highlighted a marathon benefit reading in January 1959 for *Big Table*, a periodical that was founded to publish the Beat materials responsible for the suppression of an issue of *Chicago Review* by the University of Chicago for alleged obscenity; that first issue of *Big Table* included works by Kerouac and Burroughs and fifteen pages of poetry by Corso. *Time* and *Newsweek* seemed to be especially enamored of Corso. The former published an article on the North Beach and Venice West "beatniks," in which about one-third of the article consisted of a passage from Corso's "Bomb," and a photograph accompanying the article, titled "Bang Bong Bing," showed just one member of the group—Corso. The *Newsweek* article, "Every Man a Beatnik?" reviewed a 1959 New York symposium on the Beats with responses by Ginsberg, Corso, and Orlovsky and included a photograph of one of the three—Corso again. When *Mademoiselle* featured the Beats in a 1959 article by Michael Grieg on "The Lively Arts in San Francisco," one literary work accompanied the article: "The Shakedown," a poem by Corso. In 1960, G. S. Fraser could assert that "Corso's verse seems to me to show more talent than Ginsberg's" (746), and John Fuller too asserted "Corso's superiority" over Ginsberg (74). In Thomas Parkinson's 1961 collection *A Casebook on the Beat*, the full-length essays with titles indicating a primary focus on a single Beat figure focused on just two writers: Kerouac and Corso. In 1963, *Newsweek* devoted more than two columns to Corso's first marriage as a "symbol of the Beats' eclipse" ("Bye"). Hayden Carruth, in 1963, called him "an exceedingly talented poet who has written perhaps two dozen really good poems" (356). Kenneth Rexroth wrote, "In my opinion Gregory Corso is one of the best poets of his generation" (*American* 170).

Since those glory days, Corso's stature has shrunken considerably. Part of the reason for this can be traced to Corso's background and behavior: without formal education and with a penchant for disruptive activity and illegal pursuits, to many observers he resembles Thomas Hardy's "blast-beruffled" darkling thrush (187–88), an unlikely source for the song and inspiration he produces. In addition, his self-admitted drug addiction since the middle 1960s, which has resulted in the fact that his "output has been of late / seldom and chance" ("Columbia U," *HA* 3), has affected his reputation and esteem. He has also declined to assume the politically *engagé* stances of Ginsberg and Ferlinghetti and devote himself to the politically correct ecological focus of Gary Snyder, positions that have helped to vault these poets into popularity and allow them to remain there. Furthermore, in an age in which Beavis and Butthead and Bart Simpson have become virtual role models of youthful rebellion and unconventionality, Corso's version of the renegade figure can seem less startling. The decrease in Corso's status as a *cause célèbre* provides the opportunity for an objective examination of his output, and, removed from the colorful hues of his erratic behavior, analysis of his work reveals that the strengths of his most powerful work deserve to survive and to find a receptive audience once again.

Corso's earliest volume, *The Vestal Lady on Brattle and Other Poems*, published in 1955, is marred by most of the weaknesses of young poets, a number of which persist throughout his career: sentimentality, brashness, self-consciousness, derivative rhythms, didacticism, and uncertainty of imagery. Only about one-third of these poems are included in his compilation *Mindfield: New and Selected Poems*. "Greenwich Village Suicide," "Sea Chanty," "St. Lukes, Service for Thomas," and "The Crime" possess the toughness of tone that Corso would go on to further explore, poised between tears and stoicism; the latter poem, unfortunately excluded from *Mindfield*, anticipates the theme and technique of Ted Hughes's "Lovesong." In addition, "Requiem for 'Bird' Parker" and "Cambridge, First Impressions" are important experimental works, as Corso, sorting through his cultural influences, searches for his voice—and the search itself makes the poems effective.

Gasoline, published in 1958, is Corso's second book and is much more surehanded in its control, even though it still wanders in its forms, and Corso has included two-thirds of these poems in *Mindfield*. Some, such as "Ode to Coit Tower" and "Sun," are pretentious, random, and forced, but even these reveal moments of poetic brilliance. Most of the successful poems in *Gasoline* are brief ones, one to two pages apiece, packed with wit, conceits, humor, and irony. The short compositions "Italian Extravaganza," "Birthplace Revisited," "The Last Gangster," "The Mad Yak," "This Was My Meal," and "Last Night I Drove a Car" are classics in regard to tone and timing, and they signal the emergence of a major poetic talent.

Published in 1960, *The Happy Birthday of Death* is perhaps Corso's best-known collection. What is most impressive in this volume is the sudden strength of the long poems, the extended "probes" into particular topics. "Hair," "Marriage," "Bomb," "Clown," "Power," and "Army" reveal a confident voice in poems that explore the complexities of social issues, personal integrity, and societal values. "Marriage" and "Bomb" in particular are powerful treatments—controlled yet expansive, humorous yet serious, much like the films of Charlie Chaplin and Woody Allen—revealing substantial growth over his earlier works in the form of the long poem. In addition, a number of the shorter poems—"How Happy I Used to Be," "Poets Hitchhiking on the Highway," "A Dreamed Realization," "The Sacré Coeur Café," and "Mortal Infliction" especially come to mind—are minor gems. *Happy Birthday* goes a long way toward fulfilling the promise suggested by Corso's previous works.

Corso's 1961 novel, *The American Express*, is a charming fable too long out of print that affectionately explores the methods and motives of the underground rebels during the 1950s and early 1960s. With metafictive license, it toys with conventional notions of character development, plot, chronology, and structure. Typically idiosyncratic, this neglected novel images and questions the tactical goals of protagonists representing Beat values, offering significant criticisms but stopping short of condemnation; it serves as a qualified endorsement of the need for societal change. *The American Express* reveals Corso's thoughtful individuality within the larger scheme of countercultural rebellion.

Long Live Man, published in 1962, strikes me as the most strained of Corso's volumes. Many of the poems have an occasional quality, providing notations on his travels that are too often uninspired and uninspiring. The poems are frequently repetitious and prosaic; in fact, a number of passages from poems in this collection are plundered from Corso's 1960 prose piece "Detective Frump's Spontaneous & Reflective Testament." The poetry also seems didactic, intent upon imposing his points rather than revealing them, and even the poems that had been published earlier and then revised for this collection often seem to lack a sense of direction. Several of the poems, particularly "Reflection in a Green Arena," "I Where I Stand," "Seed Journey," and "A Difference of Zoos," possess the strengths of his previous poems, but of these four only the latter two are included in *Mindfield*.

Elegiac Feelings American is a considerably stronger collection, perhaps in large part because, even though the volume appeared in 1970, almost all of the poems were originally published in periodicals between 1956 and 1963. Especially noteworthy are the long poems, particularly those in which his heart seems most engaged. "The Geometric Poem," a holographic poem of work-papers including the poet's revisions, offers illuminating glimpses into Corso's poetic processes. "The American Way," unfortunately, is a preachy diatribe, exposing the poet's mixed feelings about his native land, perhaps his self-conscious attempt to create his own version of Ginsberg's ambivalence in "America." In fact, Corso even seems to be invoking Ginsberg's poem at one point: his "This is serious!" (74) appears designed to recall Ginsberg's "America this is quite serious" in "America" (34). "Lines Written Nov. 22, 23—1963—in Discord," Corso's elegy on the assassination of John F. Kennedy, is a truly unusual hybrid; on the one hand, its references to the captain and his ship clearly call up one of Whitman's elegies on Abraham Lincoln, another slain president; on the other hand, the narrator's adoption of the role of a transhistoric assassin seems intended to do for assassins what "Bomb" did for bombs—to deny the agents of destruction both credit and responsibility. The collision of the two forms of discourse reflects the discord of the title, but ultimately prevents the poem from being completely effective. The title poem of the volume, Corso's moving elegy for Kerouac, "Elegiac Feelings American," provides a blend of Shelley's elegy for Keats, "Adonais," with Whitman's elegies for Lincoln, "When Lilacs Last in the Dooryard Bloom'd" and "O Captain, My Captain." Corso's poem is generally dismissed as sentimental, though such a complaint is seldom lodged against Shelley's poem or Whitman's poems, in part perhaps because Kerouac has not earned the esteem of the other two subjects. However, even those readers who are moved by Corso's lament for his friend (and I number myself among them)—and for the America that Corso sees him as representing—must be embarrassed by the poem's hyperbolic final section, in which Corso portrays Kerouac as "a Beat Christ-boy" (12).

More than a decade passed before Corso's next collection was published in 1981, *Herald of the Autochthonic Spirit*. The first poem, "Columbia U Poesy Reading—1975," the only long poem in the volume, is a curious combination of self-accusation for the waste of the author's talents through drug abuse and of rationalization of his drug use based on the fact that respected nineteenth-century writers had also partaken of opiates: his narrator screams "I'm not ashamed!" but shortly afterwards feels the need to "expiate / all that's been sadly done" (5). The poem fails to arrive at a solution, and the poet does not honestly seem to want one. On the other hand, the collection is filled with a wide variety of short poems that reinforce Corso's mastery of this form. His language returns to the conversational, forsaking the heavily arcane diction of his middle volumes, and his images recapture the irony and humor of his best earlier works. "Proximity," "Many Have Fallen," "I Gave Away . . . ," and "The Whole Mess . . . Almost" especially are lapidary compositions with the poet back in full control of his creative powers.

Mindfield: New & Selected Poems, published in 1989, includes excerpts from the earlier volumes, together with "Previously Unpublished Poems" (most of which, more accurately, are previously uncollected poems). The major new work, "Field Report," is the collection's last poem—a disjointed and disappointing poem that seems to have been assembled by simply stringing together disparate stanzas with little sense of coherence or integrity. The poem has a quality of valediction to it, even concluding with the word "STOP" (268).

Corso's place in the canon of American literature is considerably difficult to characterize. His voice is usually recognizable (one could not easily mistake a poem by Corso for one by Ginsberg, Kerouac, Ferlinghetti, or Snyder, for example), but his poetic forms are so diverse that he tends to be neglected by literary critics, who too often tend to dismiss him as a curious form of artistic primitive despite his multicultural classical allusions and concerns.

What Corso has to offer us as individuals and as a civilization, however, is extremely important. He projects a utopian future when the healthy exercise of imagination will triumph:

> The seer will continue seeing
> and the blind will remain wanting
> 'til that day when what's seen
> fades out and what's imagined
> comes into view.
>
> ("Shots" 8)

In the midst of a society seemingly bent upon death, destruction, and despair, the visionary poet offers life, creativity, and hope, for "[o]nly a poet can renew hope!" ("In This," *New Directions* 158). In realistic recognition of the inevitability of death, Corso can only express astonishment at the shape and organization of life:

> How perfect the entire system of things
> The human body
> all in proportion to its form
> Nothing useless
> Truly as though a god had indeed warranted it so
> And the sun for day the moon for night
> And the grass the cow the milk
> That we all in time die
> You'd think there would be chaos
> the futility of it all.
>
> ("For Homer," *HA* 13)

Whether or not one agrees with Corso's thanatopsis, one of the reasons for his continuing appeal to young Americans in the second half of the twentieth century becomes clear: abandoned by his mother at an early age, sent to live with foster parents, entangled in crime in his mid-teens, confronting serious drug problems throughout much of his life, resistant to the conformity that the age demanded, Corso emerges with a salubrious and life-affirming resilience. In an age in which the cult idols of the young seem cut down in their prime, and in a nation in which by 1993 annual suicides outnumbered the victims of criminal homicide and in which children are raised in a society whose divorce rate approximates fifty per cent, Corso offers a positive and healthful perspective, celebrating the complex wonders of life and affirming the possibility of the apparently endless vitality of human energy and spirit.

In the aptly named poem "The Double Axe," Corso sees "[l]ife's miseries many times frayed by joy" (*LL* 71), and the surprising inversion of life's offerings effectively conveys his sense of life's proportions; nevertheless, in the poem's conclusion, "The inhabitants, all covered with black moss, / Enkindle hopes with butterflies." The hopeful symbol parallels that of Kerouac's Ray Smith in his epiphany near the end of *The Dharma Bums*: "The chipmunk ran into the rocks and a butterfly came out. It was as simple as that" (243). The illusion of metamorphosis suggests the triumph of hopeful imagination over the mundane busyness of reality. Corso suggests, "Something there is can sufficiently drench / All man in its gold vision splendour" ("Something" *SP* 57). This magnificence can only be attained by recapturing the visionary capacity, "in order that consciousness grow ever more perfect, and man ever more human, and life ever more total" ("Some of My Beginning," *Poets* 181). The bleakness and traumas of Corso's own childhood (and of many periods of his adulthood) could hardly allow him to dismiss the tribulations and tragic circumstances of life or to don rose-colored glasses to tint his perception of human existence. Instead, with Shelleyan wisdom, he recognizes that we all incur the responsibility to maintain hope and to trust in visionary possibilities, because the opposites—despair, distrust, and denial—are self-fulfilling. It is as simple as that.

Notes

■

Works Cited

■

Criticism, Reviews, and Commentary
on Gregory Corso

■

Bibliography of Works by Gregory Corso

■

Index

Notes

1. Introduction

1. The Department of Special Collections of the Kenneth Spencer Research Library at the University of Kansas houses a truly amazing document, a twenty-one-page, 14,000-word typed letter from Corso to Jack Kerouac from the fall of 1958. Corso wrote the letter in response to Kerouac's portrayal of him in *The Subterraneans*, and by way of explanation, Corso provides a moving and detailed history of his childhood.

2. Breton attributes the internal quotation to Baudelaire.

3. See especially Henry Nash Smith's *Virgin Land*, R. W. B. Lewis's *The American Adam*, and Daniel Hoffman's *Form and Fable in American Fiction* for treatments of this motif in American literature.

2. The Uses of Imagination

1. Marilyn Schwartz points out, "Thus expanding the imagination's power, poetry prepares one for the act of self-transcendence and identification with the good that for Shelley is the basis of morality" (121).

2. John Garfield (Jacob Julius Garfinkle, 1913–52) was an American stage and film actor who spent his belligerent childhood on New York's Lower East Side, Brooklyn's Brownsville, and the Bronx; his early films established his screen persona as a rebellious, smoldering, street-wise youth.

3. The French primitive painter Henri Rousseau (1844–1910) was self-taught (as is Corso, with only six years of formal schooling) and was referred to as *Le Douanier* because he had worked in the Paris customs service. Artaud (1896–1948), the French actor, director, and writer, was officially determined to be insane in 1936 and thereafter spent much of his life in mental institutions; he espoused a "theatre of cruelty" and recommended violence as a theatrical tactic. Tzara (1896–1963), the Rumanian-born Dadaist writer, anticipated aspects of the cut-up techniques of William S. Burroughs; Corso participated in the cut-up experiments with Burroughs in *Minutes to Go*.

4. Bremser (b. 1939), best known for *Poems of Madness*, spent two months in Jersey County Jail (1951), six and a half years in Bordentown Reformatory (1952–58), six months in Trenton State Prison (1959–60), one month in Webb County Jail in Laredo (1960), and four years in the state prison in Rahway, New Jersey (1961–65) for charges of armed robbery and violation of parole. See Moodnik and Horowitz 36–38 for more. Underlining the connection between delinquency and art is the fact that Allen Ginsberg printed an excerpt of a letter to him from Bremser as "A Listing of Ray Bremser's Poetry Readings & Treatments for Alcoholism since 1974" in *Friction* 5/6. See Bremser listing in works cited.

5. Veronica Lake (Constance Ockleman, 1919–73), a popular Hollywood actress of the 1940s, was known for a puff of hair that swept down, partially covering her right eye and seductively conveying a sultry peekaboo effect; Lake's hair style become so fashionable that in 1943 the War Manpower Commission requested that she wear her hair up because the more than twenty thousand women working in munitions plants faced dangers from obscured vision and from hair caught in machinery. Readers familiar with Truman Capote (1924–84), the American author of *Breakfast at Tiffany's* and *In Cold Blood*, from his appearance during his later years as a squat, balding gnome on late night television talk shows might be surprised to find his name in this list; perhaps Corso has in mind the Capote whose photograph appeared on the dust jacket of his first novel, *Other Voices, Other Rooms*: this controversial large photograph showed the boyish Capote stretched out in sulky, tousle-haired languor. Ishka Bibble (also spelled Ishkabibble and Ish Kabibble) was the stage name of Merwyn Bogue (1908–94), a trumpeter with the Kay Kyser band, who sported a haircut with long bangs curtaining his forehead: "Pulling my comb from my pocket, I combed my hair straight down in front of my face. It was so long that it blocked my vision—I couldn't see where I was going. So I reached for a pair of scissors that were handy and cut my hair just above my eyes—not to get bangs but just so I could find my way onto the stage" (Bogue 64). Responding to prejudice against hirsute "beatniks," Corso once suggested, "They should shave all their statues of Jesus and cut His hair if they feel so strongly about grooming, then they wouldn't be so hypocritical" (qtd. by Schroeder). Nicolo Paganini (1782–1840), Italian violinist and composer, is probably used here as archetype of the "longhair"—the classical musician.

6. Arthur Rimbaud (1854–91), the influential French poet, is often seen as the embodiment of the rebel, an unlikely wielder of a lawnmower. Tannu Tuva was actually a republic on the Siberia-Mongolia border: controlled by Mongolia from the thirteenth to the eighteenth centuries, it became part of the Chinese Empire from the mid-eighteenth century until 1911, was annexed by the USSR in 1944, and was granted autonomy in 1961; philatelists—and Corso in his youth was a stamp collector (see "Notes from" 86 for more on this)—would find Tannu

Tuva particularly memorable for its colorful and unusual triangular and diamond-shaped postage stamps from the 1930s (for reproductions of some of the stamps and a unique perspective on the republic, see Leighton's *Tuva or Bust!*); in Corso's *The American Express*, the seventeen-year-old character Ephraim Freece is an avid stamp collector and "preferred the stamps of small countries to all else, especially tiny unknown countries" (134).

7. The references here are to Tacitus (c. 55–117), the ancient Roman historian; Johann Sebastian Bach (1685–1750), the great German organist and composer; Piero della Francesca (c. 1420–92), the important Italian Renaissance painter; the Parthenon (built in the fifth century B.C.E.), the temple on the Acropolis at Athens, often seen as the culmination of Greek architecture.

8. The 1887 novel by Haggard (1856–1925) was made into a silent film at least seven times; a black-and-white sound version was released in 1935.

9. Corso echoes this "contradiction" in a later poem, seeing himself as "a realist in dreams / a dreamer in reality" ("Gregorian RANT," *Gregorian*). In an early letter, Corso made the same point: "I may be a dreamer in life, but in dreams I'm a sanguine realist" ("Dear Fathers" 8); in a later interview, he states, "Mostly a dreamer I am" (Interview with D. O'Bryan).

10. In 1973, Corso indicated that this response has folk roots: "And it's an old Italian expression, but I don't know it in Italian but I know it in English. If you have a choice between two things, and you can't decide, take both" (Symposium 59).

11. Corso's focus here involves an area that has recently received considerable attention from psychologists, particularly in the areas of childhood recollection and eyewitness testimony. See Loftus; Loftus and Doyle; Yarney. Swiss psychologist Jean Piaget has provided an illustration of the interplay between memory, imagination, and reality:

> I can still see, most clearly, the following scene, in which I believed until I was about fifteen. I was sitting in my pram, which my nurse was pushing in the Champs Elysées, when a man tried to kidnap me. I was held in by the strap fastened round me while my nurse bravely tried to stand between me and the thief. She received various scratches, and I can still see vaguely those on her face. Then a crowd gathered, a policeman with a short cloak and a white baton came up, and the man took to his heels. I can still see the whole scene, and can even place it near the tube station. When I was about fifteen, my parents received a letter from my former nurse saying that she had been converted to the Salvation Army. She wanted to confess her past faults, and in particular to return the watch she had been given as a reward on this occasion. She had

made up the whole story, faking the scratches. I therefore must have heard, as a child, the account of this story, which my parents believed, and projected it into the past in the form of a visual memory, which was a memory of a memory, but false. (188)

12. [Walter] Liberace (1919–87), an American pianist, was a flashy popular entertainer and facile performer of Romantic and semiclassical arrangements.

13. Louella Parsons (Louella Oettinger, 1881?–1972) was one of the most powerful gossip columnists during Hollywood's golden age. Alice Faye (Alice Leppert, 1915?–98), once a singer with Rudy Vallee's band, was a bubbly, bouncy, blonde leading lady in nostalgic films of the 1930s and 1940s.

14. In the 1959 film *Pull My Daisy*, based on a play by Jack Kerouac, Kerouac's voice-over reading provides a line for the character Gregory (played in the film by Corso) using the word "goofing," which he then goes on to explain as "playing around with words."

15. "Bomb," originally published as a broadside in 1958, is reprinted as an unpaged, folded leaf bound between pages 32 and 33 in *The Happy Birthday of Death*.

16. Alexander Hamilton (1755–1804), American statesman, was mortally wounded in a duel with Aaron Burr. The duel took place on the banks of the Hudson River at Weehawken, New Jersey, on 11 July 1804, and Hamilton, who did not fire at Burr, died the next day. The likelihood of Hamilton lying in the snow in July is small and serves as a further romantic embellishment on the part of Corso's narrator. In addition, Hamilton was shot in the abdomen, a less glamorous area than the brow.

17. Paolo Uccello (c. 1396–1475), the Florentine painter, is probably best known for the three-panel *Battle of San Romano* (National Gallery, London; Uffizi Gallery, Florence; Louvre, Paris); in 1987, Mirall de Glaç published a pamphlet with a color reproduction of a scene from the Uffizi panel together with Corso's poem in English, Catalan, and Spanish.

18. Corso is apparently fond of this color process, for it recurs in several poems: "Yellow-eternity and blue mystery / Clash to allow me a green secret" ("I Am Colors"); "The blind of blue and yellow, / Birth + death = green" ("Eden," *LL* 49); "there where no blue yellow knew / where the Spring-born child froze / and no green grew" ("Return," *HA* 8).

19. Errol Flynn (1909–59), born in Tasmania, Australia, was a Hollywood actor who starred as a swashbuckling hero in such adventure films as *Captain Blood* (1935), *The Charge of the Light Brigade* (1936), *The Adventures of Robin Hood* (1938), and *The Sea Hawk* (1940). Humphrey Bogart (1899–1957), American film actor, is known for his roles as gangsters and hard-boiled detectives. Franz Joseph Haydn (1732–1809) was an Austrian classical composer, as was his younger brother Michael (1737–1806).

20. Cook recalls Corso's parallel personal assertion: "'The thing that hit me hard when I was starting out to learn was where you go to look for wisdom. And then the answer, who can a poet go to but another poet?' He [Corso] broke off, laughing, then added almost as an afterthought, 'not to that Catholic God anymore!'" (144).

21. Corso makes a similar allusion elsewhere, citing "Hölderlin's wondrous paradox 'man is nearer to God in His absence than he is in His presence'" ("Life, Death" 35). In his *Journals* from the mid-1950s, Ginsberg cites a similar statement from Corso: "Lead us to a paradise far from God" (365). [Johann Christian] Friedrich Hölderlin (1770–1843), German lyric poet, shared Corso's interest in classical Greece and blended classical and Christian themes. Perhaps Corso has in mind a passage from Hölderlin's poem "Abschied" ["Farewell"]:

> Aber weiß ich es nicht? Wehe! du liebender
> Schutzgeist! ferne von dir spielen zerreißend bald
> Auf den Saiten des Herzens
> Alle Geister des Todes mir.
> [But don't I know it? Alas my loving guardian spirit, when I am far from you, soon all the spirits of death, tearing them, will play on the strings of my heart.]

(28)

22. Corso retells this dream in "Poetry and Religion: An Open Letter" (121) and in poetic form in "30th Year Dream" (*M* 220); in both cases he changes the address from that of God to that of Christ. Despite his renunciation of religion, Corso seems to retain a Christian perspective: viewing a crucifixion painting by Theodoricus (Theodoric of Prague, fourteenth-century painter), he claims, "the nails went thru the man to God" ("Ecce Homo," *G/V* 28); he also asserts his belief that "Christ be the victory of man" ("Man," *LL* 10) and that "I know within my soul that Christ will always be. . . . Christ is the victory of man" ("Saint Francis," *LL* 37); in *The American Express*, Bronskier approvingly attributes the latter assertion to his son, Albie.

23. See also Corso's essay "When I Was Five I Saw a Dying Indian," passim.

3. Elegiac Feelings American

1. Corso cites lesser known rebels, in contrast to the conventional heroes of schoolchildren's history textbooks: Nathaniel Bacon (1647–76) led what has come to be known as Bacon's Rebellion in colonial Virginia in 1676, protesting high taxes, low tobacco prices, and privileges for those close to the English-appointed governor; Samuel Adams (1722–1803) was a political leader during the American Revolution and helped organize the revolutionary Sons of Liberty, but after

America gained independence was considered a radical agitator; Thomas Paine (1737–1809) wrote the pamphlet *Common Sense* and a series of pamphlets called *The Crisis*, all of which were enormously influential during the American Revolution, but his deistic work *The Age of Reason* offended adherents of the Bible, and his written attack on George Washington further ostracized him.

2. While not a major focus of this study, the Beat attitudes toward women should not be ignored. The male chauvinism and sexism of the Beat writers simply cannot be denied. Their extremes include Kerouac's woman-on-a-pedestal stance, the virgin/whore complex, and Burroughs's misogyny. To his credit, Corso has occasionally articulated a position that shows some sensitivity to the issue; at a symposium discussion of Kerouac in 1973, he introduced the topic:

> On this panel you don't see any female, but female was in it at that time. And I'll lay it on you. They were put into places, when they were changing like the men were. They were put into . . $50 a day at that time . . . into places like *Stockbridge*, you know, head shots. The families thought if they were paying $50 a day, their kids would be alright. They didn't want the two cars anymore. They didn't want to marry. The girls started reading Rimbaud. They started loving life and beauty. And they got fucked. Really. They were the victims of the beats. See, the men were tough babies. They took it and they got out of it. . . .
>
> Well, the females, you see, Hope, my first girl friend, what a name, "Hope," and the last name Savage. Right. Hope Savage. Right. This girl, when she was 15 years old, read Rimbaud, the Marquis de Sade. The whole shot. When was that? 1947. And she wrote beautiful poetry at nine years old. They sent her to a place where you get, you know, your shock treatment. What a sad shot. Well that's America for you. They did that. (Symposium 18–19; last ellipsis added)

Corso also reinforces these sentiments and elaborates on the specific details regarding Hope Savage in his 1993 interview with Danny O'Bryan. However, in an interview published the same year that the symposium took place, Corso says of the same woman that "[s]he was the only chick around the time of that beat thing" and goes on to add, "She loved me because I liked Shelley and she liked Shelley, so I used to call her my Shelley with a cunt" (Interview with M. Andre 141, 142). Furthermore, in the aforementioned symposium, Corso discusses his sexual relations with one of Kerouac's lovers (fictionalized as Mardou Fox in Kerouac's *The Subterraneans*):

> I fucked her. Jack thought I was . . . He put me as a sharp man and thought I did a bad turn by balling his chick. What happens is, years

later, all the girls I have, I offer to Jack, and they don't want him. They
want me. So it never worked out. See? So it was all fucked up all the
way. But I offered it. How dare a man offer a woman to another man?
See that's where I put myself on the spot. And why shouldn't I ball
anybody that wants to ball me? He was too moralistic. (78)

Even if we suspend moral judgment temporarily with regard to Corso's word
choice and phrasing, the offer of a lover as a gift or possession to bestow upon
another betrays what might otherwise have seemed an enlightened attitude on the
part of Corso. Thus, Corso seems more like the speaker in his early poem "This
Is America," a poem whose title suggests that the narrator represents the coun-
try: "and I love a woman / and hate the rest and I'll make it / with anything fe-
male ten to fifty" (*G/V* 79). The crass depersonalization signaled by the word "any-
thing" compounds the offense of the perception of women (and even girls) as mere
sex objects.

Corso has moments of projected sensitivity:

And oh and now I know
having had enough of her
how women suffer
And that hate which men bash against men
suffers less and is with end
but a woman's loss endless

("Reflection in a Green Arena," *LL* 28)

Honor if you can
   the vertical woman
though we value none
   but the horizontal one.

("Honor")

Unfortunately these seem to be moments of posturing rather than heartfelt be-
lief; the coldness of the phrasing in "having had enough of her" in the first poem
and the shift from the second person pronoun to the first person plural in the sec-
ond poem underscore this suspicion.

What must be recognized is that, despite the recent celebration of the Beat and
Hippie eras, the "significant" position women assumed during these times was
most often supine. For some realistic perspectives on the role of women during
this period, see Bonnie Bremser, Carolyn Cassady, Diane di Prima, Joyce Johnson,
Brenda Knight, and Catherine Stimpson. Although we do not want to impose,
in the interests of political correctness, ex post facto standards on a man whose
gender values did not differ considerably from those of his contemporaries, Corso's

own criticism of "the declarers of independence" who "declare it only for part of the whole" seems relevant: if Jefferson is guilty for retaining black slaves, then Corso's sexist attitudes (as well as those of his generation) toward women are equally culpable.

3. In a later interview with Michael Andre, Corso has admitted an error in this passage:

> It wasn't Pitt, it must have been Penn. The Indians told him he could have as much land as he could walk over in a day. So this guy gets three guys who look like him, and they ran like mad. One guy drowned in a stream. And so the Indian says, "They no stopping to eat 'em, they no stopping to shit 'em, they no stopping to smoke 'em, all they do is lun, lun, lun." And that's how they got the city of brotherly love. But I don't think it was Pitt Junior. It must have been Penn Junior or something, you know. (131)

In fact, the event to which Corso is referring, known as the Walking Purchase, occurred in 1737 (Penn died in 1718) and involved the Delaware Indians and agents of Penn's son Thomas; the area acquired is north of Philadelphia, and apparently no one drowned during the episode. Otherwise, Corso's brief sketch is roughly correct. For more elaborate, and accurate, accounts of the "deception," see Buck 53–202, Jennings 28–31, Wallace 25–30, and Weslager 188–89.

Further, in an essay about his adolescence, Corso says, "At thirteen I thought Ben Franklin to be maybe one of the greatest people that ever lived" ("Notes from" 86). Regarding Corso's charge that Benjamin Franklin paid bounty money for Indian scalps, I have been unable to unearth any supporting evidence whatsoever. In fact, such behavior would seem completely out of character for Franklin, who was a vocal and sympathetic admirer of the Native Americans. Furthermore, Franklin published a moving attack on the Paxton Boys' murder of Conestoga Indians in 1763. His *Narrative of the Late Massacres in Lancaster County* is an impassioned plea for justice and civilized treatment of Native Americans. Perhaps Corso has again gotten confused about one of William Penn's offspring: his grandson John Penn, then governor, offered a bounty for male or female Indian scalps. See Van Doren 311.

Thomas McClanahan has addressed Corso's treatment of Jefferson: "His [Corso's] failure to mention Jefferson's efforts to free his own slaves coupled with his praise of a man like Samuel Adams, who was famed for his brutal raids on Indian villages, reflects the rather shallow understanding of history supporting Corso's polemics" (146).

4. George Smith Patton Jr. (1885–1945), American World War II general, commanded the 3rd Army in its dramatic charge from Normandy, through Brittany, across the Rhine, and through southern Germany into Czechoslovakia;

known as "Old Blood and Guts," Patton was impetuous and unpredictable as a military leader. Alexander the Great (Alexander III, 356–323 B.C.E.), king of Macedonia, was a brilliant military leader and conquered much of Asia; but Corso's classical idealism ignores the resentment among Alexander's soldiers caused by his harsh despotism, by his execution of Parmenion and Callisthenes, and by his demand that he be treated as a god. Douglas MacArthur (1880–1964), flamboyant commander of the U.S. armed forces in the Far East in World War II and five-star general of the army, accepted the surrender of Japan; he was commander of United Nations military forces in South Korea during the Korean War; "Shades" would refer to his penchant for wearing sunglasses.

5. In his interview with Michael Andre, Corso explains one of his allusions here, together with others used in the poem, in an autobiographical context:

> Kiwago is the big bull buffalo. The white buffalo is Kiwago. Wakonda is the great sky god, but also earth god. Wakonda takes in the whole shot, whereas Talako is the sky god. Talako would be like Horus in Ancient Egypt, Hermes in Greece. Wakonda is more the great spirit. I was a counselor at a boys' camp called Camp Kiwago. . . . I put on some little plays for them about a coyote man that brought fire, who made human beings, who was the Prometheus of the Indians. And through it I checked out the other gods. (155–56)

Little Richard (Richard Wayne Penniman, b. 1932), rock 'n' roll pioneer, is noted for his flashy, flamboyant style.

6. Jerry Falwell (b. 1933), a Baptist clergyman, founded the fundamentalist political group Moral Majority, Inc.; Billy Graham (b. 1918) is a Baptist evangelist and urban revivalist whose religious crusades have been worldwide; Oral Roberts (b. 1918), a clergyman and faith healer ordained in the Pentecostal and Methodist churches, founded Oral Roberts University in 1963 and the City of Faith Medical Research Center in 1981; Rex Humbard (b. 1919), a nondenominational fundamentalist, was one of the earliest of the televangelists, with an estimated 20 million viewers in 1972. In the *Mindfield* printing of this poem, the word *faggot* is eliminated (228). Elsewhere Corso has claimed, "Even the religious soul, Billy Graham, for example, makes a fortune" ("Some of My Beginning," *Poets* 40).

7. Walter Winchell (1897–1972) was the most famous syndicated gossip columnist from the early 1930s through the late 1950s, during which time he became a zealous anticommunist. In a 1977 interview with Tom Plante, Corso comments,

> Media like that is one of America's big black stains. They become the illustrious obscure, like Walter Winchell. . . . Winchell was a gossip columnist in the Forties and he could make or break people. The

powerheads caused no good at all. I'm 47. I read the papers in the
Forties. It was sensationalism for a gullible public. It was the poor
that suffered. The Hearst papers were judge and jury. Communists
became the scapegoat because Hearst and Scripps-Howard needed
headlines. (33)

In "The winds of Babylon," Corso offers ironic celebration that "[t]he last commie
/ lies in a state of grace," but he also prides himself on his decision not to endorse
Fidel Castro ("Upon My Refusal, *LL* 57). On the other hand, in 1965 Corso was
dismissed from a teaching position at the State University of New York at Buf-
falo for his refusal to sign the Feinberg certificate, which required either that he
deny that he was a Communist or that he had informed the authorities if he had
ever been a Communist (Cook 142). Corso commented to Cook, "Well, I was
teaching a course in Shelley. Imagine that. Of all the people who wouldn't sign a
loyalty oath it's Shelley" (144).

8. Thoth, the ibis-headed Egyptian god of wisdom, was associated with
Hermes as the messenger and scribe of the gods, and defended Horus, son of
Osiris, in the suit of bastardy brought against him by his uncle, Set, who murdered
his own brother, Osiris. Batman, a comic book hero created by Bob Kane (artist)
and Bill Finger (writer), first appeared in *Detective Comics* (DC) in 1939: as a boy
whose parents were killed, Bruce Wayne dedicated himself to "warring on crimi-
nals" and adopted a batlike disguise; his principal nemesis was the Joker, an inven-
tive, white-faced villain. Doris Day (Doris von Kappelhoff, b. 1924) was an
American singer with Les Brown's dance band and later an actress in a variety of
wholesome sex comedies, one of the best known being *Pillow Talk* (1959); Corso
uses the phrase "pillow talk" in "Love Poem for Three for Kaye & Me," in
"Gregorian RANT," and in a manuscript poem that Corso reads in the video *West
Coast: Beat and Beyond*.

9. W[illiam] C[laude] Fields (Claude William Dukenfield, 1880–1946) was
an American comic performer best known for his film work with director and
producer D. W. Griffith, for whose movies Fields played satiric rapscallions with
comedic melancholy. Charlie Chaplin (1889–1977) was a London-born performer
who moved to America and became a film maestro (as actor, writer, producer,
director, and composer) from 1914 to 1952; best known for his comic portrayal
of a sensitive, inventive, hard-luck tramp, Chaplin was eventually subjected to
severe criticism for his political leanings and left America for Switzerland in 1952.

10. In Greek mythology, Agamemnon, the leader of the Greek forces in the
Trojan War, sacrificed his daughter Iphigenia to the goddess Artemis and was
murdered by his wife, Clytemnestra. Johann Wolfgang von Goethe (1749–1832),
the German writer and scientist, is perhaps best known as the author of *The Sor-
rows of Young Werther* and *Faust*, and he wrote a poetic drama based on Iphigenia.

Rodion (Rodya) Romanovitch Raskalnikov is the protagonist of the novel *Crime and Punishment* by Fyodor Mikhailovitch Dostoyevsky (1821–81).

11. In a variant of this poem appearing in *Herald of the Autochthonic Spirit* as "Many Have Fallen," Corso specifically refers to his earlier poem "Bomb."

12. For reportorial analysis of American bombing of the United States itself, see Misrach and Misrach's *Bravo 20: The Bombing of the American West* and Goin's *Nuclear Landscapes*.

13. Ted Morgan has suggested that Corso is exceptional in avoiding this process:

> You could say this for Gregory—his street-urchin style was still intact. He had avoided ingestion by the Establishment, and remained an outsider, unfit for polite society. In that sense, he was closer to the original spirit of the Beats than the two others [Allen Ginsberg and William S. Burroughs], who now fitted better into the award-recipient, may-we-have-an-interview, poet-laureate mold. (604)

14. The Beats often did adopt measures designed to prevent their being co-opted by mainstream America. Abbie Hoffman recounts an incident in which he employed such a strategy: "I had painted the word *fuck* on my forehead as part of my costume. I didn't feel like having my picture in the mass media that day and that is the only way to do it and still be able to do your thing" (67). In addition, I can offer a personal incident testifying to the success of such calculated tactics by those associated with the Beat writers. Working on the Beat writers for my dissertation at the University of Illinois, I found that a number of these writers, including Corso, had appeared in an Ed Sanders–Tuli Kupferberg (of Fugs notoriety) periodical (thirteen issues from 1962 through 1965) that had a title unlikely to be cited in mainstream mass market publications and that the university library did not possess. Directed to the Acquisitions Department, I was met at the front desk by a middle-aged woman to whom I generally described my situation.

"Fine," she said to me, moving to her file cabinets. "What is the name of the periodical?"

Naive and disconcerted, I blurted out the title: "*Fuck You: A Magazine of the Arts.*"

She turned sharply to me: "I beg your pardon."

"*Fuck You: A Magazine of the Arts,*" I repeated, adopting what I hoped was an earnest expression.

She eyed me distrustfully: "How do you spell that?"

Now panicky, I stuttered, "*F-U-C-K Y-O-U! A Magazine of the Arts!*"

Continuing to glance at me suspiciously, she checked her files and told me what I already knew: "We don't have any periodical by that name." She added that I would have to see another person on the library staff, Mrs. B——, to find out whether copies of the periodical could be acquired.

"How old is Mrs. B——," I asked her, pointedly looking at the clock on the wall.

"Oh, she's about my age, maybe a year or two older."

I explained that I had to attend a meeting and that I would be sure to contact Mrs. B—— the following day.

The next day I went to Mrs. B——'s office. I scanned the workers there and saw a young secretary with long, loose hair. I went to her and again generally explained my situation.

"Well," she said, "you'll need to see Mrs. B—— ."

This time I had had the foresight to write out the name of the periodical on a slip of paper. "The problem is," I explained, "that this is the title," and handed her the slip.

She caught her breath reading the paper and scanned my face, perhaps suspecting me of a college prank.

"I'm serious," I told her, screwing as much seriousness into my expression as I could in a situation that was already possessing, even to me, a measure of surrealistic humor.

Suddenly her face brightened: "Oh, maybe you would like to see Mr. C—— ." She smiled in a way that seemed to enclose us both in a conspiracy and ushered me into another office. I sat there fearing that I might have misjudged her, that she might have called the campus police.

In a few minutes, Mr. C—— came excitedly into the office, apparently having been briefed by the secretary. "Dr. Skau?" he started. I explained that, no, I was only a graduate student, not a professor. "But you need *Fuck You* for your dissertation?" he asked.

I nodded.

"That's wonderful," he said. "I've been trying to get the library to pick up copies of it, but I couldn't get approval. If you need it for your dissertation, we're magic. Do you need anything else? Do you need *Screw?*"

15. Corso also blames this negative stereotype on Henry Luce (1898–1967), founder and publisher of Time, Inc., and his print media: "We're not against baths. Henry Luce thinks we're against baths. In order for him to distinguish, he has to say there are people who smell nice and there are people who don't" (Interview with A. Buchwald 154).

16. While denying the validity of the adjective "nationalistic," Corso expresses an attitude that seems to warrant it: "america is not a mean bad country, the people are kind of doltish and then again some are good spirited, smart, all kinds here, so it will be here the great event will occur, i feel this, i am not a nationalist, yet I believe it be this country will set things straight, allot heaven on earth" ("Dear Fathers" 13). Later, disappointed in the 1965 poetry reading at the Albert Hall in London, Corso introduces the nationalistic theme: "I thought I'd be reading

with poets. None of them were poets but the five Americans. Nationalistic, yes. There are some English poets, but they weren't there" (Interview with A. Ginsberg and D. Widgery).

In "The American Way," Corso says of America, "I am almost nationalistic about it!" (*EF* 69), but in a later interview with Michael Andre, he denies the accuracy of that assertion: "That's not my true feeling. I really didn't understand what that meant, and thought of the poet as the universal being. Being nationalistic about something is being geographical" (144–45). Here Corso is echoing a point he made in an earlier essay: "My concern is not just with American poets but with the poets of the world because a poet is first of all a universal being— that is why it is impossible for a true poet to be nationalistic" ("Some of My Beginning," *Poets* 179). Corso's poetic claim and later retraction seem to fit the phases of his ambivalence. He does, of course, sensibly object to "nationalistic madness" ("Variations," *Casebook* 96).

17. Abbie Hoffman notes some of the ironies involved in this situation:

> Thursday, I appeared in a commercially made shirt that has red and white stripes and stars on a blue background. Capitol police arrested me for mutilating the flag and proceeded to rip the shirt off my back . . . . The law I was arrested under would make everyone who dresses in an Uncle Sam costume and most drum majorettes criminals. The other night, I watched Phyllis Diller perform on national television in a miniskirt that looked more like an American flag than the shirt I wore. (94)

The complexity of the issue can be illustrated by an anecdote from Allen Ginsberg about an encounter between Jack Kerouac and Ken Kesey's Merry Pranksters (including Neal Cassady, the model for Kerouac's Dean Moriarty in *On the Road*):

> The Pranksters had a big throne of a sofa completely clear for Kerouac. . . . Kerouac came in. He was mute and quiet and they showed him to his couch seat but there was an American flag on it, so Kerouac, without making a big, noisy complaint but a little minor objection, turned around and took the flag and folded it up neatly and put it over the side of the couch so they wouldn't sit on it. He was very conscious of the flag as an image, and I think he misunderstood their use of it. They were appropriating the flag for their own Americana purposes and he thought they were insulting it. (qtd. in Perry 86)

On the other hand, in 1989 the Supreme Court ruled that mutilation of the American flag was protected freedom of speech as "the expression of an idea" (*Texas v. Johnson*). On 7 June 1995, however, the House Judiciary Committee voted to approve a constitutional amendment that would prohibit such expression.

18. On 14 August 1765, two effigies were found hanging from an elm tree in Boston as symbols of protest against the Stamp Act, after which the tree became known as the Liberty Tree. In August 1775, British soldiers cut the tree down before evacuating Boston.

4. Modes of Rebellion, Modes of Expression: The American Express

1. The novel suggests that the problem may stem at least in part from the universal human condition; thus, the description of the birth process at the beginning of the novel is unmistakably violent: "They wheeled her into the basement of the American Express, they held her down, they spread her legs, they plunged into her womb, they yanked the child from her, they punched it into life, they threw it out into the street, it lay there until dawn" (8). The situation of this rejected child symbolizes Corso's own beginnings, abandoned by his mother in his first year of life. Asked by an interviewer, "You were the central character; you were the young man who built the rooms under the American Express office?" Corso answered, "Yes. The birth was similar" (Interview with M. Andre 148).

2. Corso has indicated that Ginsberg is not specifically represented by any single character in *The American Express* (Interview with M. Andre 147).

3. See, for example, Grieg, "Beat Mystics," and O'Neil. *Newsweek* even felt compelled to devote a two-column article, "Bye, Bye Beatnik," to Corso's 1963 marriage (without a single reference to Corso's poem "Marriage"); the article pokes fun at Corso's marriage as a violation of the unidentified reporter's own ill-formed notions of Beat principles and behavior.

4. The *herald* of his surname, reflecting the poetic role that Corso has frequently claimed for himself, suggests that this character might be analogous to his author, as are several of the other characters.

5. In fact, the characters themselves sometimes even confuse each other. Describing Hinderov's reaction to Daphne's design for a new ship, Angus Plow claims, "He said Daphne was the true goddess of destruction, and that her main desire was to sink us all!" (221), combining Hinderov's comments about the more aptly named Shiva (89) and his complaints about Daphne (212).

6. Orlovsky (b. 1933) was Ginsberg's long-time lover and companion. "Simon would be more like Peter," Corso has said, corroborating the biblical Simon-Peter equation (Interview with M. Andre 147). In addition, Hinderov is "like a berserk secretary bird" (33), and in his remarks during a 1985 poetry reading, Corso said, "Peter looks like a secretary bird" (*Baraka/Corso Reading*). This suggests that a single, real-life model may have served as the basis for more than one

of his characters. Furthermore, Hinderov may be based in part on the Scottish writer and artist Alexander Trocchi (1925–84), who was also publishing novels (often under the pseudonym Frances Lengel) in Maurice Girodias's Traveller's Companion Series, the imprint of Olympia Press that published Corso's novel. In the early 1960s, Trocchi was a founding participant of Project Sigma, which he established to organize Underground forces globally. Corso says that Trocchi "was so chemically imbued that even with his great heavy coat you could see it all fuming in there" (qtd. in St Jorre 74); in *The American Express*, Hinderov is dressed in fur wraps and "in a huge brown coat" and a "huge coat." Thus, a single character in the novel may take on the characteristics of more than one real-life model.

7. Schumacher attributes the quotations as follows: an undated letter from Ginsberg to Kerouac and Neal Cassady, apparently written early in March 1952; a letter from Kerouac to Ginsberg dated 15 March 1952; and an undated letter from Kerouac to Ginsberg, apparently from late March or early April 1952. See *Selected Letters* 345. In 1952, John Clellon Holmes (1926–88) published his novel *Go*, the first work to appear in print focusing specifically on the group that came to be known as the Beat Generation. Robert Giroux (b. 1914) was Kerouac's editor at Harcourt Brace. Neal Cassady (1926–68) was the model for Kerouac's Dean Moriarty in *On the Road* and for Cody Pomeray in Kerouac's later novels. Among other references to the collaborative process in his early works, Ginsberg's afterword, "Hindsight," in *The Gates of Wrath* offers further testimony.

8. The *Pull My Daisy* text is a transcription of the ad-libbed voice-over narration that Kerouac provided for the film by Robert Frank and Alfred Leslie; the film is an adaptation of the last act of a three-act play written by Kerouac and entitled *The Beat Generation*. See Charters 301; Nicosia 582–83.

9. Kerouac's relationship to Catholicism was troubled and idiosyncratic. In the novel *The Dharma Bums*, Japhy Ryder confronts Ray Smith: "Oh, don't start preaching Christianity to me, I can just see you on your deathbed kissing the cross like some old Karamazov or like our old friend Dwight Goddard [editor of *The Buddhist Bible*] who spent his life as a Buddhist and suddenly returned to Christianity in his last days" (202). Gerald Nicosia indicates more specifically that Gary Snyder, the model for Japhy Ryder, "was convinced that Kerouac would be asking for Catholic last rites on his deathbed" (490). Corso reflects similar concerns when he has Carrol ask Wolfherald, "You think I'm still being Catholic, don't you?" (64). Corso seems to relent somewhat when Carrol, returning as a ghost, concedes, "Catholicism . . . a humane yet dark tribute to life. Its birth, this [Christmas] Eve we walk in, has meant a lot to man" (166).

10. Once again Corso indicates a parallel belief on his own part: "I do know that man changes, the consciousness changes, therefore his God must change, he cannot maintain the same old God" ("Dear Fathers" 8).

11. Cf. William S. Burroughs's comment, "Junkies always beef about *The Cold* as they call it" (*Naked* xlv).

12. In addition, as Richard S. Sorrell points out, "Frequently 'an angry, a HA-TING man,' Leo railed in much the same fashion, calling the world a 'pigsty'" (11).

13. See Charters 300; T. Morgan 116; Miles 249–50. Kerouac's father shared with his wife an antipathy toward his son's friends, a "bunch of dope fiends and crooks" (qtd. in Nicosia 160); Clark indicates that the dying "Leo enjoined his son against the art life, . . . telling him to beware of both Burroughs and Ginsberg" (72).

14. William Lee was the pseudonym that Burroughs used for his first published book, *Junkie*, and becomes the protagonist of *Naked Lunch*. Spectral characters recur throughout Burroughs's writings; in *Naked Lunch* alone, one encounters a "spectral" pusher (6), the Vigilante as "a ghost wanting what every ghost wants— a body" (8), the "spectral" Bradley the Buyer (15), and the narrator as "a ghost in the morning sunlight" (59) and as "a grey, junk-bound ghost" (66).

15. Corso has explained that Shiva, "the girl who is his [Hinderov's] antago-nist," was his girlfriend, "Sura, that's what she was like" (Interview with M. Andre 147). Corso has written a poem entitled "Sura" (*LL* 42–43), and his "Ode to Myself & Her" (*LL* 12–13) is a reprint of a poem earlier published as "Ode to Sura." In a 1956 letter to John Clellon Holmes, Kerouac wrote that "Surrah" [*sic*] was a "rich, young mistress" of Corso (*Selected Letters* 579).

16. L. Ron Hubbard (1911–86) was an author and founder of the Church of Scientology, a religio-scientific movement founded in 1954 and incorporating Hubbard's psychotherapeutic Dianetics. Burroughs was involved in Scientology during the late 1960s, but eventually left it, "impressed by the auditing techniques but disgusted by the authoritarian organization and the stupidly fascistic utter-ances of L. Ron Hubbard" (T. Morgan 443); Burroughs wrote a review of Robert Kaufman's *Inside Scientology* for *Rolling Stone*.

17. Corso's controlling image in this poem may derive originally from Burroughs. In his interview of Burroughs published in 1961, the same year that Corso's novel appeared, the elder writer comments, "I can make my feelings very clear, Gregory, I feel like I'm on a sinking ship and I want off. . . . You want to create a panic? That's top secret—want to swamp the lifeboats?" (81–82). In his untitled statement on Burroughs's death, Corso again introduces the maritime image: "Of the Beat Generation, Burroughs was kind of the captain of the ship."

18. For an elaborate treatment by Corso of his own idiosyncratic childhood experiences with time, see "The Times of the Watches." In addition, this essay relates Corso's story about being told by a convict in prison, "Son, don't you serve time, let time serve you" (94); he also relates this story in his interview with King, in "Written While Watching Lenny Bruce Obscenity Trial," and in "Some of My Beginning."

19. See Moore xxvii and xxix. The biographical model can help explain a detail about Dad Deform: early in the novel, he is questioned about his "going cheap class instead of first class like the rest" of the travelers (9). Moore addresses Ansen's frugality:

> Although he came from a well-to-do family, he was more than economical. As he himself put it, he did not want ever to work. He wished to spend his time as a gentleman and a scholar—and a poet— and that takes money. He had an inherited income, and he had to make it last. Therefore, he never spent a penny unwisely. (xv)

20. Subud is a religious movement founded in the 1930s by an Indonesian Sufi, Muhammed Subuh, who was called Bapak; followers of the Russian-born mystic Georges Ivanovitch Gurdjieff (1872–1949) introduced the movement in America and Europe during the 1950s. Adherents practice *latihan* (spontaneous singing, dancing, laughing, and shouting), activities that reportedly induce ecstatic release.

21. Albert Speer (1905–81), German architect and Nazi leader, recounted an episode at Obersalzberg, outside Berchtesgaden:

> Once, when we were seated at the round table in the teahouse, Hitler began staring at me. Instead of dropping my eyes, I took it as a challenge. Who knows what primitive instincts are involved in such staring duels. I had had others, and always used to win them, but this time I had to muster almost inhuman strength, seemingly forever, not to yield to the ever-mounting urge to look away—until Hitler suddenly closed his eyes and shortly afterward turned to the woman at his side. (119–20)

5. The Deathmonger and the Clown in the Tomb

1. Lipton cites a story illustrating the esteem in which Corso held Thomas: "And I remembered Allen Ginsberg telling me about the time Gregory Corso sneaked into the hospital at midnight and sat by Dylan Thomas' bed watching him die, till the nice, efficient, antiseptic nurses caught him at it and shooed him out" (20).

2. William and Anthony Esposito were executed in the electric chair at Sing Sing Prison in New York on 13 March 1942 for the murder on 14 January 1941 of a payroll messenger and a police officer in a hold-up on Fifth Avenue.

3. Theodoricus (Theodoric of Prague, fl. 1359–80) was a Bohemian painter with a severe, naturalistic style; many of his major religious paintings were executed for the Chapel of the Holy Cross of Karlstein Castle for Emperor Charles IV. The

work to which Corso refers appears to be the middle panel of a triptych, *The Man of Sorrows (Ecce Homo)*. *Ecce Homo* (literally, Latin for Behold the man) were the words of Pontius Pilate in presenting the scourged and tortured Christ to the Jews (John 19: 5); the words have become a label for a motif that was popular during the Renaissance as an artistic topic.

4. In an interview with Gavin Selerie, Corso, after reading this poem, pointed directly to the effect he had created: "See how cold that is?" (26).

5. Elsewhere, Corso cites a quotation from Theodore Roosevelt displayed at New York's American Museum of Natural History that seems to have inspired the concluding line of "For Those Who Commit Suicide": "*Only those are fit to live who do not fear to die and none are fit to die who have shrunk from the joy of life and the duty of life*" ("Moschops!" 53).

In a characteristically whimsical comment, Corso considers the methods of suicide, recalling "something I thought of when Marilyn Monroe died: They die, movie stars, by sleeping pills, it is a clean unugly nearly romantic way out; yet if all sleeping pills were suppositories . . . would they then so an absurd death commit?" ("Between" 38). Corso's comments also illuminate his treatment of Alexander Hamilton's death and illustrate his own susceptibility to (or affinity for) the romantic image. What is important is the stylish gesture. The possibility of regurgitative ugliness and vulgarity is ignored. The same spirit informs the stylized gestures and posturings of the eponymous male protagonist of the film *Harold and Maude* with his dramatic fake suicides.

6. Variations of this assertion include the following: "death is known in life not in death" ("Between" 39); "and ever ignorant of that death you'll never know" ("For Homer," *HA* 14); "If you wanna get somewhere you get there alive / dead you're up shit's creek!" ("Leaky Lifeboat," *HA* 15); "I will live / and never know my death" ("Getting," *HA* 35); and "yet you'll only know the death of another / never your own" ("Window," *M* 225).

7. Corso celebrates Poe for his artistic exploration of this realm: "O Poe, mad European! / death so wisely so beautifully / tackled" (♀ [*Ankh*]).

8. A 1959 letter from Corso to Ginsberg helps to illuminate (if not clarify) Corso's terms and images here: he recalls an incident in Greece when "I actually saw Death";

> I sat down and immediately said I KNOW I KNOW, people earth life this universe is going one way and I the other, yes, that's why I've been speaking death, well death is not bad, it's good, it's soul, there that what we think is soul in us is but death in us, lovely deaths, but man destroys that loveliness by morbidity and foundations and institutions and churches to aid life unto death, what they think is

death, they're all wrong, they have it all confused, they are going the wrong way, even the universe, it goes the wrong way; I saw there at that moment a skinless light, a naked brilliance and felt like I never felt before in my life; I had done a great thing, I stepped out of the circle and did not die, and outside the circle, dear friend, death holds its warrant; a summoning to something wonderful and beautiful I'm sure; I was scared and stepped back into the circle, but now I know I can go out of the circle anytime I want and always come back; no wonder I wrote all those poems about death, I knew I wasn't a morbid doomful person, I knew there had to be a reason behind it all.

9. Harpo (Adolph Arthur) Marx (1888–1964), one of the popular Marx Brothers of American radio, stage, and screen fame in the 1920s and 1930s, charmed audiences with his childlike (and childish) zaniness. *Vogue*, the popular American women's fashion magazine, published its first issue on 17 December 1892.

10. The Lone Ranger, eponymous hero of a radio program begun on WXYZ in Detroit in 1933, was the only survivor of an attack on six Texas Rangers; having recovered from his wounds, he dedicated himself to fighting for law and order in the West of "yesteryear." The program expanded to stations across the country and gained an audience of twenty million listeners. Earle W. Graser, who played the radio role of the Lone Ranger for nine years, was killed in an automobile accident on 8 April 1941. Corso would have barely turned eleven years of age at the time of Graser's death. Corso includes a concise poetic restatement of the Lone Ranger memory in "Field Report" (*M* 241).

11. This characterization appears in "Decal Poem" and "The Wise Fuckers" and perhaps explains the narrator's "Laughing" response in another poem after Death cries to him, "I'm not real," and "I'm just a rumor spread by life" ("The Whole Mess," *HA* 49).

12. A similar assertion appears in "The Doubt of Lie" (*M* 223).

13. These lines from a poem based on a 1975 poetry reading, as the title indicates, and published in *Herald* in 1981, include a passage that Wilson, in his 1966 bibliography of Corso's works, cited as a projected title for a new volume of Corso's poems: *There Is Still Time to Run Back Through Life and Expiate All That's Been Sadly Done* (6). Thus, the regrets and hope expressed in the passage were articulated by Corso fifteen years before they were finally incorporated into his published writings.

6. *"The Comedy Gone Mad": Corso's Surrealism and Humor*

1. Lamantia (b. 1927) is an American surrealist poet.

2. The first lines of this passage parallel an early line from Rimbaud's "A Sea-

son in Hell": "One evening I pulled Beauty down on my knees. I found her em-
bittered and I cursed her" (173). Corso used Rimbaud poems for several of his
cut-ups in the *Minutes to Go* collection and refers to him in "Marriage," among
other poems. Stephenson and Foster have both called attention to the influence
of Rimbaud on Corso.

3. Another version of this poem appears as "Hedgeville," *Elegiac* 81. Corso dis-
cusses the multiple appearance of the poem in his interview with Andre on p. 126.

4. The Mary Dare line also occurs in "Of One Month's Reading of English
Newspapers." The coincidence is likewise revealing of Corso's sensitivity. "Of One
Month's Reading" appeared in the American avant-garde periodical *Evergreen
Review* in the January/February 1962 issue; "Nature's Gentleman" first appeared
in the British collection of Corso's work *Selected Poems*, published in November
1962. The *Evergreen Review* publication includes a contributor's note in which
Corso asserts that he intended no offense to the English: "I love the English and
really mean no meanness." With a different title, the British publication, of course,
contains less possibility of offense and even turns the joke around on the narrator.

5. See also a Ferlinghetti postcard to Corso postmarked 27 September 1958
and a Ferlinghetti letter to Corso dated 5 March 1963, both held in a collection
housed in the Humanities Research Center at the University of Texas at Austin.
Corso responds to Ferlinghetti's objections in an undated (1957?) letter and in
letters from September 1958 and October 1958 held in the Bancroft Library at
the University of California at Berkeley.

6. Corso also refers to humor as a butcher earlier in the same interview on p.
124; in his interview with King on p. 6; in "Columbia U Poesy Reading—1975,"
HA 2; and in "Who I Am" 28.

7. In a letter to *Cambridge Opinion*, Corso explains, "politics and betterment
of earthly conditions is death to poetry, unless these newspaper subjects be treated
with light, love and laughter, like Allen's Howl and my Bomb."

8. Jeane (not Corso's Jeanne) Dixon (1918–97) was an American prophet,
psychic, and astrologer; among her many accurate predictions were the assassi-
nations of Mahatma Gandhi and John F. Kennedy, the suicide of Marilyn Mon-
roe, and the death in a plane crash of United Nations Secretary General Dag
Hammarskjöld.

9. In the original City Lights Pocket Poets Series publication of *Gasoline*, the
word *Dessert* was spelled as *Desert*.

10. On the other hand, the adolescently homophobic "White Swallow faggot
bar" of "Hi" (*WW* 8) is revised as the "White Swallow bar" in a later collection
(*M* 228).

11. Mercurio, Italian form of Mercury, the Roman renaming of Hermes dat-
ing from the fifth century, was the messenger of the gods. Hermes, son of Zeus,

was the Greek messenger of the gods and divine herald. Ganesha, the elephant-headed Hindu god, is "the lord of beginnings" and "is assigned the role of scribe for Vyasa's dictation of the *Mahabharata* in the eighth-century interpolation to this text" (Brown 1, 3). Thoth (Corso spells his name correctly in "Columbia U Poesy Reading—1975," among other references), the ibis-headed Egyptian moon god, was the messenger and scribe of the gods. Moses, the Hebrew prophet from the Old Testament of the Bible, is a messenger in transmitting God's laws, including the Ten Commandments, to the Israelites. In Norse mythology, Loki's role as messenger is less clear, but Thor sent him to negotiate with Thrym for the return of Thor's hammer; Loki also shares with Mercury and Hermes the role of mischief-maker or trickster. CBS is the acronym for the Columbia Broadcasting System, one of America's major television networks.

7. "The Poesy That Cannot Be Destroyed": Corso's Prosody

1. A manuscript of "In a Grecian Garden," a poem with lines later plundered for "Bomb," shows Corso's somewhat clumsy scansion of the first line as iambic pentameter. The manuscript is to be found in the Kenneth Spencer Research Library's Department of Special Collections at the University of Kansas.

2. FLN is an acronym for the National Liberation Front, a militaristic group active in the Algerian fight for independence from France.

3. The rhyme appears in an early version of the poem, "For Hope Savage," and is retained in the versions of "Sura" that appear in *The Beat Scene* and *Selected Poems*.

4. James Earl ("Jimmy") Carter Jr. (b. 1924) was the thirty-ninth U.S. president, from 1977 to 1981. Leonid Ilich Brezhnev (1906–82), Soviet statesman and Communist Party official, was virtually the leader of the Soviet Union from 1964 until the time of his death. MX (*M*issile, e*X*perimental) is an ICBM carrying multiple independently targeted nuclear warheads.

5. See p. 156. Corso reads still another slightly different form of this line in the video *Gang of Souls*.

6. The rhythms, the sound repetition, and even the dramatic positioning of the final word recall the opening couplet of Wallace Stevens's "Bantam in Pine-Woods" (1922): "Chieftain Iffucan of Azcan in caftan / Of tan with henna hackles, halt!" (Stevens, *Collected* 75).

7. In "Window," Corso uses the same image as in the last line of this poem, but without the internal or end rhyme: "with me the spirit has surfaced the human face" (*M* 226).

8. Sumer is a term used to indicate the southern part of ancient Mesopotamia.

9. Corso does not seem to have had a clear or thorough understanding of the purposes and tenets underlying Burroughs's methods. Among Corso's more ob-

vious cut-up attempts outside of *Minutes to Go*, see "Death of 1959" (*EF* 89–90) and the "It is past . . ." page of "Mutation of the Spirit" (*EF* 24).

10. I have been unable to locate a poem published by Corso entitled "Mind"; Ginsberg also comments on Corso's use of poetry as a "probe" in his interview with Barron on pp. 14–15.

11. This poem was first published as a looseleaf sheaf of pages, physically enabling readers to engage in such shuffling.

12. For an indication of the development of these poems, see Selerie 10–11. During his interview with Michael Andre, Corso is altering the version in "Eleven Times a Poem"; he explains, "It's not a revision, it's already been done, but I took it out, and now I want it back. . . . I had two different versions. I threw this in fast because I was getting the book together. I liked the 'Gay Fucketeer' better than, you know, the 'amputated rapist'" (148).

13. The latter poem is dated 1961, which would place its composition at roughly the same time as the first version.

14. In Corso's interview with Michael Andre, he relinquishes blame for this: "There is also a poem in the *Elegiac* that the publisher didn't know was already published in *Gasoline*, but it's a different version" (126).

15. The supporting example that Ginsberg provides does not involve verbal repetition.

16. Another shift in personal pronouns is evident in the work-papers that constitute "The Geometric Poem": in a section entitled "Heralding the Coming of Egypt," he asserts,

> Midst all that magenta delight
>   and sun-showery blue
> You bright mudangel
>   are the finer hue.

(EF 44)

Later, in the second of "3 Work Papers of Egypt Poem Book," he offers a pair of variants that move the pronoun from the second person to the first:

> When all great Circledom be splashed
> a sun-showery blue
> I'll return sweet point
> a finer hue
>
> . . . .
>
> when this mummificate cosmos unbandaged
> reskies sun-showery blue

I'll return, finky Harthor
a finer hue.

(*EF* 58; ellipsis added)

17. Howard's statement is suspiciously similar to a sentence by Geoffrey H. Hartman in a 1963 review of *Long Live Man*, "He [Corso] writes poetry but very few poems." (375), suggesting a more reprehensible form of plagiarism.

18. In Homer's *Odyssey*, the Cyclops Polyphemus, while drunk, is blinded by Odysseus and his men. Zeus, as the supreme god in Greek religion, would be the appropriate figure to petition for redress of Polyphemus's disability. Corso's poem "Mortal Infliction" (*HB* 69) is a powerful and moving treatment of Polyphemus's predicament.

19. St. Francis of Assisi (1182?–1226) is renowned for his gentleness and love for nature and humanity; Corso celebrates him in the poem "Saint Francis" (*LL* 36–40). In ancient Greece, the *agora* was a city's public square or market place used for public assembly; St. Paul (d. 64? A.D.) converted to Christianity and traveled as a missionary to, among many locations, Athens, where he preached "in the market daily" (Acts 17: 17). John Chapman (1774–1845) was known as Johnny Appleseed for distributing saplings and seeds to families heading westward and for sowing apple seeds himself on travels through Pennsylvania and Ohio. Kish was an ancient city of Mesopotamia; Virgil (Publius Vergilius Maro) (70–19 B.C.E.), the Roman poet who wrote the *Aeneid*, was Dante's guide through Hell and Purgatory in the *Divine Comedy*. Peter Pan is the eponymous flying hero of the play written in 1904 by the Scottish writer James M. Barrie; the play was a popular success in London and on Broadway and was made into a Walt Disney cartoon feature in 1953, and a musical version starring Mary Martin was broadcast live on NBC television in 1954. Albion is the ancient and literary name for Britain; Mercury was the Roman messenger of the gods; Jupiter was the supreme god in Roman religion; Minerva was the Roman goddess of the arts; Mars was the Roman god of war; and Dionysus, the Greek god of fertility and wine, is associated with drunken, orgiastic rituals and identified with divine, frenzied inspiration, and the festivals in his honor supposedly developed the form of the dithyramb.

20. In a variant publication of this passage, Corso cites the first four lines of Dickinson's poem; this time he correctly provides the first verb, but alters the original in other ways:

I taste a liquor never brewed—
From Tankards scooped in Pearl—
Not all the Vats upon the Rhine
Yield such an Alcohol!

(Dickinson 98–99)

I taste a liquor never brewed
From tankards scoped in pearl
Not all the vats along the Rhine
Can yield such an alcohol.

("Lines Between")

21. Cf. "The Hatter's remark seemed to her to have no sort of meaning in it, and yet it was certainly English" (Carroll 97).

22. Cf.

"'Then you should say what you mean,' the March Hare went on.
'I do,' Alice hastily replied; 'at least—at least I mean what I say— that's the same thing, you know.'
'Not the same thing a bit!' said the Hatter." (Carroll 95)

23. The strange fifth line of this section from "Army" is perhaps inspired by a passage from Thomas Hood's "The Bridge of Sighs": "Sisterly, brotherly, / Fatherly, motherly, / Feelings had changed" (52). Corso read from this Hood poem in a lecture with Ginsberg at the Naropa Institute in Boulder, Colorado, on 13 June 1975. Nebuchadnezzar (d. 562 B.C.E.) was a Babylonian king who defeated the Egyptian pharoah Necho in 605 B.C.E. to become the master of Western Asia.

24. A manuscript letter to Ferlinghetti indicates Corso's desire to change the archaic "thy" in "thy furcal mouth" and "thy baldy bean" in "Bomb" to "your," but the revisions were never incorporated. The letter, written in January of 1959, is held in Box 2 of the City Lights Books: Correspondence materials at the Bancroft Library of the University of California at Berkeley.

25. Antonio Vivaldi (1675?–1741) was a celebrated Italian baroque composer. Stanley ("Stan") Gayetzsky (Getz) (1927–91), American musician (saxophone) and orchestra leader, was known for his lyrical and technical proficiency in mainstream jazz. Johann Sebastian Bach (1685–1750) was an influential German composer and musician (organ). John Birks ("Dizzy") Gillespie (1917–93), American composer and musician (trumpet), was one of the principal figures of the jazz movement known as bebop.

26. In Thomas Parkinson's *Casebook*, the reprint of this poem substitutes the word "paradisiacal" (275), a form paralleling Joyce's usage in the Circe chapter of *Ulysses*, although nothing suggests that Corso approved this correction or that he is conversant with Joyce's novel. In an undated (1957?) letter to Lawrence Ferlinghetti, Corso attempts to defend his original spelling in terms of rhythm. The letter is collected in Box 2 of the City Lights Books: Correspondence section at the Bancroft Library of the University of California at Berkeley.

27. The latter misspelling was not used in the earlier version of "Sunrise" ("I am rich" 48), where the word was spelled as in the former case, suggesting the possibility of a typographical error that survived proofreading in the later version. On the other hand, in "Lines Between Past & Future," a poem that Corso apparently plundered for materials in "Columbia U Poesy Reading—1975," among other poems, he also uses the term "oralcry."

28. Although *Herald of the Autochthonic Spirit* was published in 1981 and *Wings, Wands, Windows* in 1982, Michael Frederick Annis, editor of the latter volume, assures me, in a personal letter dated 30 November 1983, that the original manuscript in his possession contains the negative and that the *Herald* version is the edited one. However, because *Mindfield* reprints the version without the negation, the *Wings* version seems more likely as the one that was later altered.

29. In his interview with Michael Andre, however, Corso states, "If they are already published, I don't correct anymore, although sometimes I am really tempted to. I know I could clean out a lot of them, and really set them aright, but then I let them go, and I don't bother" (126).

30. Charles ("Charlie") Christopher ("Bird") Parker (1920–55), American musician (alto saxophone) and composer celebrated for his improvisations, was one of the leaders of the jazz bebop movement. Miles Dewey Davis Jr. (1926–91), American musician (trumpet), was a major figure in the "cool" jazz movement.

Works Cited

Artaud, Antonin. *The Theater and Its Double.* Trans. Mary Caroline Richards. New York: Grove, 1958.

Auden, W. H. *Collected Poems.* Ed. Edward Mendelson. New York: Random, 1976.

Ball, Gordon. Rev. of *Herald of the Autochthonic Spirit,* by Gregory Corso. *American Book Review* 5.1 (Nov./Dec. 1982): 18.

"Bang Bong Bing." *Time* 7 Sept. 1959: 80.

Baraka, Imamu [LeRoi Jones]. Interview with Debra L. Edwards. *the unspeakable visions of the individual* 10 (1980): 129–44.

Barthes, Roland. *The Rustle of Language.* Trans. Richard Howard. New York: Hill, 1986.

"Beat Mystics." *Time* 3 Feb. 1958: 56.

Beiles, Sinclair, William Burroughs, Gregory Corso, and Brion Gysin. *Minutes to Go.* 1960. San Francisco: Beach, 1968.

Benedetto, Rosanne. "The Kerouac Symposium: An Afterword." *Soundings/East* [formerly *Gone Soft*] 2.2 (1979): 91–96.

Beyle, Bill. "Gregory Corso: Introductory Shot." *Unmuzzled Ox* 2.1–2 (1973): n. pag. Rpt. in *Unmuzzled Ox* 6.2 (#22) (Winter 1981): 73–78.

Blake, William. *The Complete Poetry and Prose of William Blake.* Ed. David Erdman and Harold Bloom. Rev. ed. Berkeley: U of California P, 1982.

Bogue, Merwyn, with Gladys Bogue Reilly. *Ish Kabibble: The Autobiography of Merwyn Bogue.* Baton Rouge: Louisiana State UP, 1989.

Bremser, Bonnie. *For Love of Ray.* London: London Magazine, 1971. Rpt. of *Troia: Mexican Memories.* New York: Croton, 1969.

Bremser, Ray. "A Listing of Ray Bremser's Poetry Readings & Treatments for Alcoholism since 1974." *Friction* 5–6 (Winter 1984): 5–7.

Breton, André. *Manifestoes of Surrealism.* Trans. Richard Seaver and Helen R. Lane. Ann Arbor: U of Michigan P, 1972.

Brossard, Chandler. *Who Walk in Darkness.* New York: Lancer, 1952.

Brown, Robert L. Introduction. *Ganesh: Studies of an Asian God.* Ed. Robert L. Brown. Albany: State U of New York P, 1991. 1–18.

Bryant, William Cullen. *The Poetical Works of William Cullen Bryant.* Ed. Henry C. Sturges. New York: Appleton, 1903.

Buck, William J. *History of the Indian Walk.* Philadelphia: Stuart, 1886.

Burns, Jim. "Gregory Corso: An Essay." *The Riverside Interviews 3: Gregory Corso.* Ed. Gavin Selerie. London: Binnacle, 1982. 48–61.

Burroughs, William S. *The Book of Breething.* Berkeley: Blue Wind, 1975. N. pag.

———. Interview with Conrad Knickerbocker [1965]. *Writers at Work: The* Paris Review *Interviews.* Ed. George Plimpton. Third Series. New York: Viking, 1967. 143–74.

———. "Introductory Notes." Corso, *Mindfield* xvii–xix.

———. *Naked Lunch.* 1959. New York: Grove, 1966.

———. Rev. of *Inside Scientology,* by Robert Kaufman. *Rolling Stone* 26 Oct. 1972: 66+.

Burroughs, William S., and Daniel Odier. *The Job: Interviews.* Rev. ed. New York: Grove, 1974.

"Bye, Bye, Beatnik." *Newsweek* 1 July 1963: 65.

Byron, Lord [George Gordon]. *Byron's Don Juan: A Variorum Edition.* Ed. Truman Guy Steffan and Willis W. Pratt. Vol. 2. Austin: U of Texas P, 1957. 4 vols.

Capote, Truman. *Other Voices, Other Rooms.* New York: Random, 1948.

Carroll, Lewis [Charles Lutwidge Dodgson]. *The Annotated Alice: Alice's Adventures in Wonderland & Through the Looking Glass.* Ed. Martin Gardner. New York: Potter, 1960.

Carruth, Hayden. "Poets without Prophecy." *Nation* 27 Apr. 1963: 354–57.

Cassady, Carolyn. *Off the Road: My Years with Cassady, Kerouac, and Ginsberg.* New York: Morrow, 1990.

Cassady, Neal. *The First Third & Other Writings.* Rev. ed. San Francisco: City Lights, 1981.

Chapman, Harold. *The Beat Hotel.* Montpellier, Fr.: Gil Blas, 1984.

Charters, Ann. *Kerouac: A Biography.* San Francisco: Straight Arrow, 1973.

Cherkovski, Neeli. "Revolutionary of the Spirit: Gregory Corso." *Whitman's Wild Children.* Venice, CA: Lapis, 1988. 175–95.

Clark, Tom. *Jack Kerouac.* San Diego: Harcourt, 1984.

Cook, Bruce. "An Urchin Shelley." *The Beat Generation.* New York: Scribner's, 1971. 133–49.

Cortázar, Julio. *Hopscotch.* Trans. Gregory Rabassa. New York: Signet, 1967.

Dickinson, Emily. *The Complete Poems of Emily Dickinson.* Ed. Thomas H. Johnson. Boston: Little, 1960.

diPrima, Diane. *Memoirs of a Beatnik.* Traveller's Companion Series. New York: Olympia, 1969.

Doris, John, ed. *The Suggestibility of Children's Recollections: Implication for Eyewitness Testimony.* Washington: American Psychological, 1991.

Dossey, Steve. "Gregory Corso: Another View." *Moody Street Irregulars: A Jack Kerouac Newsletter* 12 (Fall 1982): 6.

Dowden, George. *A Bibliography of Works by Allen Ginsberg: October, 1943 to July 1, 1967*. San Francisco: City Lights, 1971.

Emerson, Ralph Waldo. *The Complete Works of Ralph Waldo Emerson*. Vol. 2. Cambridge: Harvard UP, 1903–4. 12 vols.

"Every Man a Beatnik?" *Newsweek* 29 June 1959: 83.

Ferlinghetti, Lawrence. *Her*. New York: New Directions, 1960.

———. *Unfair Arguments with Existence*. New York: New Directions, 1963.

FitzGerald, Edward. *The Variorum and Definitive Edition of the Poetical and Prose Writings of Edward FitzGerald Including a Complete Bibliography and Interesting Personal and Literary Notes*. Ed. George Bentham. Vol. 3. 1902. New York: Phaeton, 1967. 7 vols.

Foster, Edward Halsey. *Understanding the Beats*. Columbia: U of South Carolina P, 1992.

France, Anatole. *The Crime of Sylvestre Bonnard*. Trans. Lafcadio Hearn. New York: Dodd, 1918.

Franklin, Benjamin. *A Narrative of the Late Massacres, in Lancaster County*. *Papers of Benjamin Franklin*. Ed. Leonard W. Labaree. Vol. 11. New Haven: Yale UP, 1967. 42–69. 31 vols.

Fraser, G. S. Rev. of *The Happy Birthday of Death*, by Gregory Corso. *Partisan Review* 27.4 (1960): 746–47.

Frost, Robert. *The Poetry of Robert Frost*. Ed. Edward Connery Lathem. New York: Holt, 1967.

Fuller, John. "The Poetry of Gregory Corso." *London Magazine* ns 1.1 (Apr. 1961): 74–77.

Gaiser, Carolyn. "Gregory Corso: A Poet the Beat Way." *A Casebook on the Beat*. Ed. Thomas Parkinson. New York: Crowell, 1961. 266–75.

Ginsberg, Allen. "Abstraction in Poetry." *It Is—A Magazine for Abstract Art* 3 (1959): 73–75.

———. *Airplane Dreams: Compositions from Journals*. San Francisco: City Lights, 1969.

———. "America." Ginsberg, *Howl and Other Poems* 31–34.

———. *The Fall of America: Poems of These States 1965–1971*. Pocket Poets Series 30. San Francisco: City Lights, 1972.

———. "Footnote to Howl." Ginsberg, *Howl and Other Poems* 21–22.

———. *The Gates of Wrath: Rhymed Poems: 1948–1952*. Bolinas: Grey Fox, 1972.

———. "Have You Seen This Movie?" Ginsberg, *Fall of America* 165–67.

———. "Howl." Ginsberg, *Howl and Other Poems* 9–20.

————. *Howl and Other Poems*. Pocket Poets Series 4. San Francisco: City Lights, 1956.

————. Interview with David Ossman. *The Sullen Art: Interviews with Modern American Poets*. Ed. David Ossman. New York: Corinth, 1963. 87–95.

————. Interview with Len Barron ["Introduction Overvue: An Interview with Allen Ginsberg"]. *Friction* 1.2–3 (Winter 1982): 7–19.

————. Interview with Thomas Clark [1965]. *Writers at Work: The* Paris Review *Interviews*. Ed. George Plimpton. Third Series. New York: Viking, 1968. 279–320.

————. Introduction. *Gasoline*. By Gregory Corso. Pocket Poets Series 8. San Francisco: City Lights, 1958. 7–10. Rpt. in *Gasoline/The Vestal Lady on Brattle and Other Poems*. San Francisco: City Lights, [1976]. 7–10.

————. "Journal Night Thoughts." *Planet News 1961–1967*. Pocket Poets Series 23. San Francisco: City Lights, 1968. 9–14.

————. *Journals Mid-Fifties: 1954–1958*. Ed. Gordon Ball. New York: Harper, 1995.

————. *Kaddish and Other Poems 1958–1960*. Pocket Poets Series 14. San Francisco: City Lights, 1961.

————. "Meditation and Poetics." *Spiritual Quests: The Art and Craft of Religious Writing*. Ed. William Zinsser. New York: Houghton, 1989. 145–65.

————. "Note." Ginsberg, *Kaddish* 100.

————. "On Corso's Virtues." Corso, *Mindfield* xiii–xv.

————. *Planet News 1961–1967*. Pocket Poets Series 23. San Francisco: City Lights, 1968.

————. "The Vomit of a Mad Tyger." *Shambhala Sun* 2.6 (July 1994): 14–23+.

Goin, Peter. *Nuclear Landscapes*. Baltimore: Johns Hopkins UP, 1991.

Grieg, Michael. "The Lively Arts in San Francisco." *Mademoiselle* Feb. 1957: 142–43+.

Haggard, H. Rider. *The Annotated* She: *A Critical Edition of H. Rider Haggard's Victorian Romance*. 1888. Ed. Norman Etherington. Bloomington: Indiana UP, 1991.

Hardy, Thomas. *The Complete Poetical Works of Thomas Hardy*. Ed. Samuel Hynes. Vol. 1. Oxford: Clarendon, 1982–95. 5 vols.

Hartman, Geoffrey H. Rev. of *Long Live Man*, by Gregory Corso. *Kenyon Review* 25.2 (Spring 1963): 374–79.

Hoffman, Abbie. *The Best of Abbie Hoffman*. New York: Four Walls Eight Windows, 1989.

Hölderlin, Friedrich. *Selected Verse*. Trans. Michael Hamburger. London: Anvil Press Poetry, 1986.

Hood, Thomas. *Selected Poems*. Ed. Clifford Dyment. London: Grey Walls, 1948.

Horovitz, Michael. "On the Beat with Gregory Corso." *The Riverside Interviews 3: Gregory Corso*. Ed. Gavin Selerie. London: Binnacle, 1982. 62–68.

Howard, Richard. "Gregory Corso." *Alone with America: Essays on the Art of Poetry in the United States since 1950*. Enlarged edition. New York: Atheneum, 1980. 76–83.

Hughes, Ted. *Crow*. New York: Harper, 1971.

Jennings, Francis. "The Scandalous Indian Policy of William Penn's Sons: Deeds and Documents of the Walking Purchase." *Pennsylvania History* 37.1 (Jan. 1970): 19–39.

Johnson, Joyce. *Minor Characters*. Boston: Houghton, 1983.

Jones, James T. Letter to Editor. *Blue Beat Jacket* 7 (1995): 6–12.

Joyce, James. *A Portrait of the Artist as a Young Man*. 1916. New York: Penguin, 1976.

———. *Ulysses*. Ed. Hans Walter Gabler. New York: Vintage, 1986.

Keats, John. *The Letters of John Keats (1814–1821)*. Ed. Hyder Edward Rollins. Vol. 2. Cambridge: Harvard UP, 1958. 2 vols.

———. *The Poems of John Keats*. Ed. Jack Stillinger. Cambridge: Harvard UP, 1978.

Kelly, Emmett, with F. Beverly Kelly. *Clown*. New York: Prentice, 1954.

Kerouac, Jack. "Belief and Technique for Modern Prose." *Good Blonde & Others*. Ed. Donald Allen. San Francisco: Grey Fox, 1993. 72–73.

———. *Book of Dreams*. San Francisco: City Lights, 1961.

———. *Desolation Angels*. 1965. New York: Bantam, 1966.

———. *The Dharma Bums*. 1959. New York: Penguin, 1976.

———. "Essentials of Spontaneous Prose." *Good Blonde & Others*. Ed. Donald Allen. San Francisco: Grey Fox, 1993. 69–71.

———. *Good Blonde & Others*. Ed. Donald Allen. San Francisco: Grey Fox, 1993.

———. *Lonesome Traveler*. 1960. New York: Grove, 1970.

———. *Maggie Cassady*. 1959. New York: Penguin, 1993.

———. *Mexico City Blues (242 Choruses)*. New York: Grove, 1959.

———. *On the Road*. 1957. New York: Penguin, 1976.

———. "The Origins of the Beat Generation." *Playboy* June 1959: 31–32+.

———. *Pull My Daisy*. New York: Grove, 1961.

———. *Scattered Poems*. San Francisco: City Lights, 1971.

———. *The Scripture of the Golden Eternity*. 1960. New York: Totem/Corinth, 1970.

———. *Selected Letters 1940–1956*. Ed. Ann Charters. New York: Penguin, 1995.

———. *The Subterraneans*. 1958. New York: Grove, 1981.

———. *The Town and the City*. New York: Harcourt, 1950.

———. *Vanity of Duluoz: An Adventurous Education, 1935–46*. New York: Coward-McCann, 1968.

Kerouac, Jack, Gregory Corso, and Allen Ginsberg. "Nixon." *Bombay Gin* 7 (Summer/Fall 1979): 1.

Knight, Brenda. *Women of the Beat Generation: The Writers, Artists and Muses at the Heart of a Revolution.* Berkeley: Conari, 1996.

Krim, Seymour. *Views of a Nearsighted Cannoneer.* New York: Dutton, 1968.

Lautréamont [Comte de] [Isidore Ducasse]. *Maldoror (Les Chants de Maldoror); Poesies.* Trans. Guy Wernham. New York: New Directions, 1966.

Leighton, Ralph. *Tuva or Bust! Richard Feynman's Last Journey.* New York: Penguin, 1992.

Lipton, Lawrence. *The Holy Barbarians.* New York: Grove, 1962.

Loftus, Elizabeth F. *Eyewitness Testimony.* Cambridge: Harvard UP, 1979.

Loftus, Elizabeth F., and James M. Doyle. *Eyewitness Testimony: Civil and Criminal.* New York: Kluever, 1987.

Marcuse, Herbert. Interview with Harvey Wheeler ["Varieties of Humanism"]. *Center Magazine* 1.5 (July 1968): 13–15.

Masheck, Joseph, ed. *Beat Art.* New York: Columbia U, 1977.

McClanahan, Thomas. "Gregory Corso." *American Poetry since World War II. Dictionary of National Biography.* Vol. 5. Part 1. Ed. Donald J. Greiner. Detroit: Gale, 1980.

McDarrah, Fred W., and Glenda S. McDarrah. *Beat Generation: Glory Days in Greenwich Village.* New York: Schirmer, 1996.

McNally, Dennis. *Desolate Angel: Jack Kerouac, the Beat Generation, and America.* New York: Random, 1979.

Miles, Barry. *Ginsberg: A Biography.* New York: Simon, 1989.

Misrach, Richard, and Myriam Weisang Misrach. *Bravo 20: The Bombing of the American West.* Baltimore: Johns Hopkins UP, 1990.

Moodnik, Arnold, and Mikhail Horowitz. "Ray Bremser." *The Beats: Literary Bohemians in Postwar America. Dictionary of Literary Biography.* Vol. 16. Part 1. Ed. Ann Charters. Detroit: Gale, 1983.

Moore, Steven. Introduction. *Contact Highs: Selected Poems 1957–1987.* By Alan Ansen. Elmwood Park: Dalkey Archive, 1989. xi–xxxiv.

Moraes, Dom. "Somewhere Else with Allen and Gregory." *Horizon* 11.1 (Winter 1969): 66–67.

Morgan, Bill. *The Works of Allen Ginsberg 1941–1994: A Descriptive Bibliography.* Bibliographies and Indexes in American Literature 19. Westport: Greenwood, 1995.

Morgan, Ted. *Literary Outlaw: The Life and Times of William S. Burroughs.* New York: Holt, 1988.

Nicosia, Gerald. *Memory Babe: A Critical Biography of Jack Kerouac.* New York: Grove, 1983.

Nuttall, Jeff. *Bomb Culture*. New York: Dell, 1968.

O'Neil, Paul. "The Only Rebellion Around." *A Casebook on the Beat*. Ed. Thomas Parkinson. New York: Crowell, 1961. 232–46.

Orwell, George. *The Collected Essays, Journalism, and Letters of George Orwell*. Ed. Sonia Orwell and Ian Angus. Vol. 3. New York: Harcourt, 1968. 4 vols.

Parkinson, Thomas, ed. *A Casebook on the Beat*. New York: Crowell, 1965.

Perloff, Marjorie. *Frank O'Hara: Poet among Painters*. New York: Braziller, 1977.

Perry, Paul. *On the Bus: The Complete Guide to the Legendary Trip of Ken Kesey and the Merry Pranksters and the Birth of the Counterculture*. New York: Thunder's Mouth, 1990.

Philip, Jim. "Journeys in the Mindfield: Gregory Corso Reconsidered." *The Beat Generation Writers*. Ed. A. Robert Lee. London: Pluto, 1996. 61–73.

Piaget, Jean. *Play, Dreams and Imitation in Childhood*. Trans. C. Gattegno and F. M. Hodgson. New York: Norton, 1962.

Rexroth, Kenneth. *American Poetry in the Twentieth Century*. New York: New Directions, 1971.

———. *Assays*. New York: New Directions, 1961.

Rimbaud, [Jean Nicholas Arthur]. *Complete Works, Selected Letters*. Trans. Wallace Fowlie. Chicago: U of Chicago P, 1966.

Sabatini, Rafael. *Scaramouche*. 1921. New York: Bantam, 1961.

Sargeant, Jack. *The Naked Lens: An Illustrated History of Beat Cinema*. London: Creation, 1997.

Schroeder, Terry. "Corso Advises Rome 'Tear Down Monuments.'" *San Francisco Chronicle* 24 Aug. 1966: 44.

Schumacher, Michael. *Dharma Lion: A Critical Biography of Allen Ginsberg*. New York: St. Martin's, 1992.

Schwartz, Marilyn. "Gregory Corso." *The Beats: Literary Bohemians in Postwar America. Dictionary of Literary Biography*. Vol. 16. Part 1. Ed. Ann Charters. Detroit: Gale, 1983.

Scully, James. "The Audience Swam for Their Lives." *Nation* 9 Mar. 1964: 244–47.

Selerie, Gavin. "Introduction." *The Riverside Interviews: 3—Gregory Corso*. Ed. Gavin Selerie. London: Binnacle, 1982. 5–20.

Shaw, George Bernard. *Major Barbara. Complete Plays with Prefaces*. Vol. 1. New York: Dodd, 1963. 297–446. 6 vols.

Shelley, Percy Bysshe. *The Complete Works of Percy Bysshe Shelley*. Ed. Roger Ingpen and Walter E. Peck. Vols. 2, 4, and 7. New York: Gordian, 1965. 10 vols.

———. "Death." Shelley, *Complete Works* 4: 59.

———. "A Defence of Poetry." Shelley, *Complete Works* 7: 109–40.

———. "Ode to the West Wind." Shelley, *Complete Works* 2: 294–97.

Smith, Henry Nash. *Virgin Land: The American West as Symbol and Myth.* Cambridge: Harvard UP, 1950.

Snyder, Gary. "'Notes on the Beat Generation' and 'The New Wind.'" *American Poetry* 2.1 (Fall 1984): 44–51.

Sorrell, Richard S. "Ti Jean and Papa Leo: Jack Kerouac's Relationship with His French-Canadian Father." *Moody Street Irregulars: A Jack Kerouac Newsletter* 11 (Spring/Summer 1982): 10–12.

Speer, Albert. *Inside the Third Reich.* Trans. Richard Winston and Clara Winston. New York: Macmillan, 1970.

Stephenson, Gregory. "'The Arcadian Map': Notes on the Poetry of Gregory Corso." *The Daybreak Boys: Essays on the Literature of the Beat Generation.* Carbondale: Southern Illinois UP, 1990. 74–89.

———. *Exiled Angel: A Study of the Works of Gregory Corso.* London: Hearing Eye, 1989.

Stevens, Wallace. *The Collected Poems.* New York: Vintage, 1990.

———. *Opus Posthumous.* Ed. Milton J. Bates. Rev. ed. New York: Knopf, 1989.

Stimpson, Catherine R. "The Beat Generation and the Trials of Homosexual Liberation." *Salmagundi* 58–59 (1982/1983): 373–92.

St Jorre, John de. *Venus Bound: The Erotic Voyage of the Olympia Press and Its Writers.* New York: Random, 1994.

Texas v. Johnson. 491 U.S. 397. U.S. Supreme Court, 1989.

Thurley, Geoffrey. "The Development of the New Language: Wieners, Jones, McClure, Whalen, Corso." *The American Moment: American Poetry in the Mid-Century.* London: Arnold, 1977. 187–209.

Tocqueville, Alexis de. *Democracy in America.* Trans. Henry Reeves. 1835. Vol. 2. New York: Vintage, 1945. 2 vols.

Trungpa, Chogyam. Lecture [1 July 1975]. *Compassion/3 Yanas.* Audiocassette 7. Boulder: Naropa, 1975.

Tytell, John. *Naked Angels: The Lives & Literature of the Beat Generation.* New York: McGraw, 1976.

Van Doren, Carl. *Benjamin Franklin.* New York: Viking, 1938.

Villar, Arturo del. "Gregory Corso, un Shelley *beat.*" *Arbor: Ciencia, Pensamiento y Cultura* 399 (1978): 99–103.

Wallace, Anthony F. C. *King of the Delawares: Teedyuscung 1700–1763.* Philadelphia: U of Pennsylvania P, 1949.

Watson, Steven. "Chronology." *Beat Culture and the New America 1950–1965.* Ed. Lisa Phillips. New York: Whitney, 1995. 249–61.

Weslager, C. A. *The Delaware Indians: A History.* New Brunswick: Rutgers UP, 1972.

Whitman, Walt. *Leaves of Grass.* Ed. Harold W. Blodgett and Sculley Bradley. Comprehensive Reader's Edition. New York: New York UP, 1965.

Williams, William Carlos. "The American Idiom." *New Directions in Prose and Poetry 17*. Ed. J. Laughlin. New York: New Directions, 1961. 250–51.

Wilson, Robert. *A Bibliography of Works by Gregory Corso*. New York: Phoenix, 1966.

Wordsworth, William. "The World Is Too Much with Us." *The Poetical Works of William Wordsworth*. Ed. E. de Selincourt and Helen Darbishire. Vol. 3. 2nd ed. Oxford: Clarendon, 1954. 5 vols. 18–19.

Yarney, A. David. *The Psychology of Eyewitness Testimony*. New York: Free, 1979.

Yeats, W. B. *The Collected Poems of W. B. Yeats*. New York: Macmillan, 1956.

Criticism, Reviews, and Commentary on Gregory Corso

Adler, Edward, and Bernard Mindich. *Beat Art: Visual Works by and about the Beat Generation*. New York: New York U School of Education, 1994. 12.

Akeroyd, Joanne Vinson. *Where Are Their Papers? A Union List Locating the Papers of Forty-Two Contemporary American Poets and Writers*. Bibliography Series 9. Storrs: U of Connecticut Library, 1976.

Algren, Nelson. "'Chicago Is a Wose.'" *Nation* 28 Feb. 1959: 191.

Anderson, Scott. "No Middle Ground in Poetry: Gregory Corso." *Rockstop Magazine* 10 (Spring 1985): 34–36.

Aronowitz, Alfred G. "The Beat Generation." Article 9. *New York Post* 18 March 1959: 64.

Ash, Mel. *Beat Spirit: The Way of the Beat Writers as a Living Experience*. New York: Tarcher/Putnam, 1997. 267–68.

B., P. L. Introduction. *The Vestal Lady on Brattle and Other Poems*. By Gregory Corso. Cambridge: Brukenfeld, 1955. N. pag. Facsimile edition by San Francisco: City Lights, 1969. Rpt. in *Gasoline/The Vestal Lady on Brattle and Other Poems*. San Francisco: City Lights, [1976]. 52.

Baker, A. T. "Poetry Today: Low Profile, Flatted Voice." *Time* 12 July 1971: 61+.

Balaban, Dan. "'Witless Madcaps' Come Home to Roost." *Village Voice* 13 Feb. 1957: 3. Rpt. in *The Village Voice Reader*. Ed. Daniel Wolf and Edwin Fancher. Garden City: Doubleday, 1962. 39–40.

Ball, Gordon. Rev. of *Herald of the Autochthonic Spirit*, by Gregory Corso. *American Book Review* 5.1 (Nov./Dec. 1982): 18.

"Bang Bong Bing." *Time* 7 Sept. 1959: 80.

Barone, Dennis. "Awakener to the Word." Rev. of *Mindfield: New and Selected Poems*, by Gregory Corso. *American Book Review* 12.4 (Sept./Oct. 1990): 17+.

Benedetto, Rosanne. "The Kerouac Symposium: An Afterword." *Soundings East* [formerly *Gone Soft*] 2.2 (1979): 91–96.

Berk, Larry. Rev. of *Mindfield*, by Gregory Corso. *Choice* 27.6 (1990): 948.

Bernard, Sidney. "A Reading and a Mourning." *New York Times Book Review* 24 Apr. 1977: 30+.

Beyle, Bill. "Gregory Corso: Introductory Shot." *Unmuzzled Ox* 2.1–2 (1973): n. pag. Rpt. in *Unmuzzled Ox* 6.2 (#22) (Winter 1981): 73–78.

Birnbaum, Henry. Rev. of *The Happy Birthday of Death*, by Gregory Corso. *Poetry* 97.2 (Nov. 1960): 119–20.

Bukowski, Charles. Letter to Editor. *Magazine* 3 (1966): 58–59.

Burnham, Geoffrey. "The Beats: Who Are These Guys?" *Brown Daily Herald Supplement* 12 Nov. 1962: 3–6.

Burns, Jim. "Gregory Corso: An Essay." *The Riverside Interviews 3: Gregory Corso*. Ed. Gavin Selerie. London: Binnacle, 1982. 48–61.

———. Rev. of *Exiled Angel*, by Gregory Stephenson. *Kerouac Connection* 19 (Spring 1990): 35–36.

Burroughs, William S. "Introductory Notes." *Mindfield*. By Gregory Corso. New York: Thunder's Mouth, 1989. xvii–xix.

———. *The Letters of William S. Burroughs 1945–1959*. Ed. Oliver Harris. New York: Viking, 1993.

"Bye, Bye, Beatnik." *Newsweek* 1 July 1963: 65.

Carroll, Paul. "Five Poets in Their Skins." *Big Table* 1.4 (Spring 1960): 133–38.

Carruth, Hayden. "Poets without Prophecy." *Nation* 27 Apr. 1963: 354–57.

Cassady, Carolyn. *Off the Road: My Years with Cassady, Kerouac, and Ginsberg*. New York: Morrow, 1990.

Challis, Chris. "The Fabulous Wordslinger: Gregory Corso & the Beat Coterie." *Palantir* 16 (1980): 30–34.

———. *Quest for Kerouac*. London: Faber, 1984.

Chapman, Harold. *The Beat Hotel*. Montpellier, Fr.: Gil Blas, 1984.

Charters, Ann. *Kerouac: A Biography*. San Francisco: Straight Arrow, 1973.

Cherkovski, Neeli. "Revolutionary of the Spirit: Gregory Corso." *Whitman's Wild Children*. Venice, CA: Lapis, 1988. 171–95.

Ciardi, John. "Epitaph for the Dead Beats." *Saturday Review* 6 Feb. 1960: 11–13+.

Clements, Robert J. "Botticelli's *Primavera* and *Venere*: Eighteen Literary Readings." *Forum Italicum* 13.4 (1979): 439–53.

Cocchi, Raffaele. "Gregory Corso: Poetic Vision and Memory as a Child of Italian Origin on the Streets and Roads of Omerica [sic]." *Rivista di Studi Anglo-Americani* 3.4–5 (1984/85): 343–52.

Congdon, Kirby. Rev. of *Exiled Angel*, by Gregory Stephenson. *Contact/II* 10.59–61 (Spring 1991): 76–77.

Contemporary Authors: A Bio-Bibliographical Guide to Current Authors and Their Works. Ed. Barbara Harte and Carolyn Riley. Vols. 5–8. 1st Rev. Detroit: Gale, 1969.

Contemporary Authors: A Bio-Bibliographical Guide to Current Writers in Fiction, General Nonfiction, Poetry, Journalism, Drama, Motion Pictures, Television, and Other Fields. Ed. Susan M. Trosky. New Revision Series. Vol. 41. Detroit: Gale, 1994.

Cook, Bruce. "An Urchin Shelley." *The Beat Generation*. New York: Scribner's, 1971. 133–49.

Cooper, Colin. "Where Are You Gregory Corso?" *Beat Scene* 26 (1996): 24.

Davidson, Michael. *The San Francisco Renaissance: Poetics and Community in Mid-Century*. Cambridge: Cambridge UP, 1989.

De Loach, Joan. "Gregory Comes to Visit." *Moody Street Irregulars: A Jack Kerouac Newsletter* 10 (Fall 1981): 14–15.

DeMott, Benjamin. Rev. of *The American Express*, by Gregory Corso. *Hudson Review* 14.4 (1961/62): 623–29.

Denney, Reuel. "Invitations to the Listener: Nine Young Poets and Their Audiences." Rev. of *The Vestal Lady on Brattle*, by Gregory Corso. *Poetry* 89.1 (Oct. 1956): 45–52.

Dickinson, Peter. Rev. of *Selected Poems*, by Gregory Corso. *Punch* 2 Jan. 1963: 31.

Dossey, Steve. "Gregory Corso: Another View." *Moody Street Irregulars: A Jack Kerouac Newsletter* 12 (Fall 1982): 6.

Dullea, Gerard J. "Ginsberg and Corso: Image and Imagination." *Thoth* 2.2 (Winter 1971): 17–27.

Efimov-Schneider, Lisa. "Poetry of the New York Group: Ukranian Poets in an American Setting." *Canadian Slavonic Papers* 23.3 (Sept. 1981): 291–301.

Ehrenpreis, Irvin. "Recent Poetry." Rev. of *The Happy Birthday of Death*, by Gregory Corso. *Minnesota Review* 1.3 (Spring 1961): 362–72.

"Every Man a Beatnik?" *Newsweek* 29 June 1959: 83.

Field, Arthur, and Paul Zindel. Rev. of *The Happy Birthday of Death*, by Gregory Corso. *Wagner Literary Magazine* 2 (1960/61): 97–98.

Fleischmann, Wolfgang B. "Those 'Beat' Writers." *America* 26 Sept. 1959: 766–68.

Fles, John. "The Great Chicago Poetry Reading." *Swank* 8.1 (Mar. 1961): 65–68+.

Fraser, G. S. Rev. of *The Happy Birthday of Death*, by Gregory Corso. *Partisan Review* 27.4 (Fall 1960): 746–47.

French, Warren. *The San Francisco Poetry Renaissance, 1955–1960*. Boston: Twayne, 1991.

Fuller, John. "The Poetry of Gregory Corso." *London Magazine* ns 1.1 (Apr. 1961): 74–77.

Furbank, P. N. Rev. of *Selected Poems*, by Gregory Corso. *Listener* 27 Dec. 1962: 1102.

Gaiser, Carolyn. "Gregory Corso: A Poet the Beat Way." *A Casebook on the Beat*. Ed. Thomas Parkinson. New York: Crowell, 1961. 266–75.

Gilbert, Jack. "Numbers." *Genesis West* 1.3 (Spring 1963): 251–52.

———. "Numbers." *Genesis West* 2.1 [#5] (Fall 1963): 39–40.

Ginsberg, Allen. "Abstraction in Poetry." *It Is—A Magazine for Abstract Art* 3 (1959): 73–75; revised in *Nomad/New York* 10–11 (Autumn 1962): 50–51.

———. "Act III." *Friction* 1.2–3 (Winter 1982): 97–98.

———. Interview with Len Barron ["Introduction Overvue: An Interview with Allen Ginsberg"]. *Friction* 1.2–3 (Winter 1982): 7–19.

———. Introduction. *Gasoline*. Pocket Poets Series 8. San Francisco: City Lights, 1958. 7–10.

———. "Meditation and Poetics." *Spiritual Quests: The Art and Craft of Religious Writing*. Ed. William Zinsser. New York: Houghton, 1988. 145–65.

———. "On Corso's Virtues." *Mindfield*. By Gregory Corso. New York: Thunder's Mouth, 1989. xiii–xv.

Gold, Herbert. *Bohemia: Digging the Roots of Cool*. New York: Touchstone, 1994.

Gooch, Brad. *City Poet: The Life and Times of Frank O'Hara*. New York: Knopf, 1993.

Goodman, Michael Barry. *Contemporary Literary Censorship: The Case History of Burroughs' Naked Lunch*. Metuchen: Scarecrow, 1981.

Gosciak, J. G. "Tales of Beatnik Lore: An Interview with Gregory Corso." *Contact II: A Poetry Review* 9.53–55 (Summer/Fall 1989): 33–35.

Grieg, Michael. "The Lively Arts in San Francisco." *Mademoiselle* Feb. 1957: 142–43+.

Grunes, Dennis. "The Mythifying Memory: Corso's 'Elegiac Feelings American.'" *Contemporary Poetry: A Journal of Criticism* 2.3 (1977): 51–61.

Gunn, Drewey Wayne. *American and British Writers in Mexico, 1556–1973*. Austin: U of Texas P, 1974.

Hamilton, Ian. *Robert Lowell: A Biography*. New York: Random, 1982. 459–60.

Harney, Steve. "Ethnos and the Beat Poets." *Journal of American Studies* 25.3 (1991): 363–80.

Hartman, Geoffrey H. Rev. of *Long Live Man*, by Gregory Corso. *Kenyon Review* 25.2 (Spring 1963): 374–79.

Hickey, Morgan. *The Bohemian Register: An Annotated Bibliography of the Beat Literary Movement*. Metuchen: Scarecrow, 1990. 66–71.

Holmes, John Clellon. "Gone in October." *Playboy* Feb. 1973: 96–98+. Rpt. in *Representative Men: The Biographical Essays*. Selected Essays. Vol. 2. Fayetteville: U of Arkansas P, 1988. 157–98.

Horowitz, Michael. "On the Beat with Gregory Corso." *The Riverside Interviews 3: Gregory Corso*. Ed. Gavin Selerie. London: Binnacle, 1982. 62–68.

Howard, Richard. "Gregory Corso." *Chelsea* 22–23 (June 1968): 148–57. Rpt. in *Alone with America: Essays on the Art of Poetry in the United States since 1950*. Enlarged edition. New York: Atheneum, 1980. 76–83.

Huncke, Herbert. *Guilty of Everything*. New York: Paragon, 1990.

Jarrell, Randall. *Randall Jarrell's Letters: An Autobiographical and Literary Selection.* Ed. Mary Jarrell and Stuart Wright. Boston: Houghton, 1985. 417–18.

Jerome, Judson. Rev. of *Long Live Man*, by Gregory Corso. *Antioch Review* 23.2 (Summer 1963): 243–44.

Jones, James T. Letter to Editor [14 June 1995]. *Blue Beat Jacket* 7 (1995): 6–12.

Kaganoff, Penny. Rev. of *Mindfield*, by Gregory Corso. *Publishers Weekly* 10 Nov. 1989: 57.

Kerouac, Jack. "The Last Word." *Escapade* June 1959: 72. Rpt. in *Good Blonde & Others*. Ed. Donald Allen. Rev. ed. San Francisco: Grey Fox, 1994. 145–48.

Knight, Arthur Winfield. "Gregory Corso and the Staff of Hermes." *Palantir* 23 (1983): 46–47. Rpt. in *Catching Up with Kerouac: Getting Boulder on the Road.* Ed. V. J. Eaton. The Literary Denim: A Journal of Beat Literature. Phoenix: Literary Denim, 1984. 99.

———. "Searching for Jack Kerouac." *Review of Contemporary Fiction* 3.2 (Summer 1983): 14–18.

Knight, Arthur, and Kit Knight, eds. *The Beat Vision: A Primary Sourcebook.* New York: Paragon, 1987.

———. *Kerouac and the Beats: A Primary Sourcebook.* New York: Paragon, 1988.

Knight, Brenda, ed. *Women of the Beat Generation: The Writers, Artists and Muses at the Heart of a Revolution.* Berkeley: Conari, 1996.

Kramer, Jane. *Allen Ginsberg in America.* New York: Vintage, 1970.

Krim, Seymour. "A Backward Glance O'er Beatnik Roads." *Triquarterly* 43 (1978): 324–37.

Kupcinet, Irv. "Kup's Column." *Chicago Sun-Times* 30 Jan. 1959: 52.

Leddy, Michael. Rev. of *Mindfield*, by Gregory Corso. *World Literature Today* 64.2 (Spring 1990): 312–13.

Leichtling, Jerry. "The Broadway Book of the Dead." *Village Voice* 28 Apr. 1975: 42.

Levine, Rosalind. Rev. of *Gasoline*, by Gregory Corso. *Poetry* 93.3 (Dec. 1958): 183–84.

Lipton, Lawrence. *The Holy Barbarians.* New York: Grove, 1962.

"Manners & Morals: Fried Shoes." *Time* 9 Feb. 1959: 16.

Masheck, Joseph, ed. *Beat Art.* New York: Columbia U, 1977; Masheck's introduction was published in adapted form in *Artforum* 15 (Apr. 1977): 58–59.

Maxwell, Glyn. Rev. of *Mindfield*, by Gregory Corso. *Times Literary Supplement* 31 May 1991: 12.

McClanahan, Thomas. "Gregory Corso." *American Poets since World War II. Dictionary of Literary Biography.* Vol. 5. Part 1. Ed. Donald J. Greiner. Detroit: Gale, 1980.

McCloskey, Mark. Rev. of *Long Live Man*, by Gregory Corso. *Wagner Literary Magazine* 4 (1963–64): 233.

McKenzie, James. "New Directions: On First Looking into Corso's *The Happy Birthday of Death*." *North Dakota Quarterly* 50.2 (Spring 1982): 85–93.

McNally, Dennis. *Desolate Angel: Jack Kerouac, the Beat Generation, and America*. New York: Random, 1979.

Messing, Gordon M. "Structuralist Analysis of Poetry: Some Speculations." *Lingua* 49 (1979): 1–10.

Miles, Barry. *Ginsberg: A Biography*. New York: Simon, 1989.

———. *William Burroughs, El Hombre Invisible: A Portrait*. New York: Hyperion, 1993.

Moraes, Dom. "Somewhere Else with Allen and Gregory." *Horizon* 11.1 (Winter 1969): 66–67.

Morgan, Bill. *The Beat Generation in New York: A Walking Tour of Jack Kerouac's City*. San Francisco: City Lights, 1997.

Morgan, Ted. *Literary Outlaw: The Life and Times of William S. Burroughs*. New York: Henry Holt, 1988.

Morris, Richard. "In Passing." *Hard Knoxville Review* 6 [1985?]: n. pag.

Napier, John. Rev. of *The Happy Birthday of Death*, by Gregory Corso. *Voices: An Open Forum for the Poets* 174 (Jan./Apr. 1961): 48–49.

Nicosia, Gerald. *Memory Babe: A Critical Biography of Jack Kerouac*. Berkeley: U of California P, 1994.

Norse, Harold. *Memoirs of a Bastard Angel*. New York: Morrow, 1989.

Nuttall, Jeff. *Bomb Culture*. New York: Delta, 1968.

Nygren, Dorothy. Rev. of *Elegiac Feelings American*, by Gregory Corso. *Library Journal* 1 Sept. 1970: 2811.

O'Hara, Frank. "Gregory Corso." *Standing Still and Walking in New York*. Ed. Donald Allen. Bolinas: Grey Fox, 1975. 82–85.

Olson, Kirby. "Gregory Corso." *Exquisite Corpse* 6.1–4 (Jan./Apr. 1988): 12.

O'Neil, Paul. "The Only Rebellion Around." *Life* 30 Nov. 1959: 114–16+. Rpt. in *A Casebook on the Beat*. Ed. Thomas Parkinson. New York: Crowell, 1961. 232–46.

Osborne, Charles. Rev. of *Selected Poems*, by Gregory Corso. *Spectator* 21 Dec. 1962: 969.

Parker, Derek. "Gregory Corso." *Contemporary Poets of the English Language*. Ed. Rosalie Murphy. Chicago: St. James, 1970. 236–37.

Pelias, Ronald J., and Jill Taft-Kaufman. "Performing Literary Works Judged Problematic." *Central States Speech Journal* 36.1–2 (Spring/Summer 1985): 82–91.

Perera, Victor. "At Sea with the Beats." *Partisan Review* 3 (Summer 1960): 569–76.

Philip, Jim. "Journeys in the Mindfield: Gregory Corso Reconsidered." *The Beat Generation Writers*. Ed. A. Robert Lee. London: Pluto, 1996. 61–73.

Plath, Sara. Rev. of *Herald of the Autochthonic Spirit*, by Gregory Corso. *Booklist* 15 Sept. 1981: 87–88.

Rashbaum, Burt. "Coursing through Corso's Course." *Water Row Review* 3 (1988): 11–12.

Ratner, Rochelle. Rev. of *Herald of the Autochthonic Spirit*, by Gregory Corso. *Library Journal* 1 Oct. 1981: 1930.

———. Rev. of *Mindfield*, by Gregory Corso. *Library Journal* 15 Oct. 1989: 85.

Reeves, Pauline. Rev. of *Mindfield*, by Gregory Corso. *Beat Scene* 9 (1990): 32.

Rety, John. "Gregory Corso's Bomb Poem." *Beat Scene* 30 (1998): 31.

Rev. of *Herald of the Autochthonic Spirit*, by Gregory Corso. *Publishers Weekly* 11 Sept. 1981: 71.

Rexroth, Kenneth. *American Poetry in the Twentieth Century*. New York: New Directions, 1971.

———. *Assays*. New York: New Directions, 1961. 194.

———. *With Eye and Ear*. New York: Herder, 1970.

Robinson, Murray. "Gregory Sends Us Poems That We Don't Get." *New York World Telegram & Sun* 16 June 1955, sec. 2: 1.

Ross, Alan. Rev. of *Selected Poems*, by Gregory Corso. *London Magazine* ns 2.10 (Jan. 1963): 88.

Sargeant, Jack. *The Naked Lens: An Illustrated History of Beat Cinema*. London: Creation, 1997.

Sawyer-Lauçanno, Christopher. *The Continual Pilgrimage: American Writers in Paris, 1944–1960*. Rev. ed. San Francisco: City Lights, 1998.

Sayre, Nora. "The Poets' Theatre: A Memoir of the Fifties." *Grand Street* 3.3 (Spring 1984): 92–105.

Schappell, Elissa. "The Craft of Poetry: A Semester with Allen Ginsberg." *Paris Review* 135 (Summer 1995): 212–57.

Schroeder, Terry. "Corso Advises Rome 'Tear Down Monuments.'" *San Francisco Chronicle* 24 Aug. 1966: 44.

Schumacher, Michael. *Dharma Lion: A Critical Biography of Allen Ginsberg*. New York: St. Martin's, 1992.

Schwartz, Marilyn. "Gregory Corso." *The Beats: Literary Bohemians in Postwar America. Dictionary of Literary Biography*. Vol. 16. Part 1. Ed. Ann Charters. Detroit: Gale, 1983. 117–40.

Scully, James. "The Audience Swam for Their Lives." *Nation* 9 Mar. 1964: 244–47.

Seigel, Catharine F. "Corso, Kinnell, and the Bomb." *University of Dayton Review* 18.3 (Summer 1987): 95–103.

Selerie, Gavin. Introduction. *The Riverside Interviews 3: Gregory Corso*. London: Binnacle, 1982. 5–20.

Seltzer, Joanne. "The King of the Cats: Eliot and Yeats." *Pre-Raphaelite Review* 1.1 (1977): 34–38.

Seymour-Smith, Martin. "Gregory Corso." *The Oxford Companion to Twentieth-Century Poetry in English*. Ed. Ian Hamilton. Oxford: Oxford UP, 1994. 101–2.

Simpson, Louis. Rev. of *Long Live Man*, by Gregory Corso. *Hudson Review* 16.1 (Spring 1963): 130–40.

Skau, Michael. "'Elegiac Feelings American': Gregory Corso and America." *McNeese Review* 32 (1989): 38–48.

———. "'To Dream, Perchance to Be': Gregory Corso and Imagination." *University of Dayton Review* 20.1 (Summer 1989): 69–78.

Skelton, Robin. Rev. of *Selected Poems*, by Gregory Corso. *Critical Quarterly* 5.2 (Summer 1963): 189–91.

Smalldon, Jeffrey. "Gregory Corso Closely Observed." *Beat Scene* 10 [1990]: 2–4.

Smilow, David. "Ginsberg Dialogue Compelling; Chapel Poetry Reading Mediocre." *Wellesley News* 12 Apr. 1973: 1+.

Sorrentino, Gilbert. "A Note on Gregory Corso's *To Black Mountain*." *Yūgen* (1959): 38.

Souster, Raymond. Rev. of *Bomb*, by Gregory Corso. *Combustion* 8 (Nov. 1958): 12.

Stauffer, Donald Barlow. "Gregory Corso." *Contemporary Poets*. Ed. James Vinson and D. L. Kirkpatrick. London: St. James, 1985. 160–61.

Stephenson, Gregory. "'The Arcadian Map': Notes on the Poetry of Gregory Corso." *Writers Outside the Margin: An Anthology*. Ed. Jeffrey H. Weinberg. Sudbury: Water Row, 1986. 21–36A. Rpt. in *The Daybreak Boys: Essays on the Literature of the Beat Generation*. By Gregory Stephenson. Carbondale: Southern Illinois UP, 1990. 74–89.

———. *Exiled Angel: A Study of the Work of Gregory Corso*. Toronto: Hearing Eye, 1989.

St Jorre, John de. *Venus Bound: The Erotic Voyage of the Olympia Press and Its Writers*. New York: Random, 1994.

Stock, Robert. "Letter from San Francisco." *Poetry Broadside* 1.2 (June 1957): 3–4+.

Sukenick, Ronald. *Down and In: Life in the Underground*. New York: Beech Tree/Morrow, 1987.

Thurley, Geoffrey. "The Development of the New Language: Wieners, Jones, McClure, Whalen, Corso." *The American Moment: American Poetry in the Mid-Century*. London: Arnold, 1977. 187–209.

Timm, Robert C. "Unleashing Language: The Post-Structuralist Poetics of Gregory Corso and the Beats." *Kerouac Connection* 27 (Winter 1995): 34–41.

Tytell, John. *Naked Angels: The Lives & Literature of the Beat Generation.* New York: McGraw, 1976.

Villar, Arturo del. "Gregory Corso: un Shelley *beat.*" *Arbor: Ciencia, Pensamiento y Cultura* 399 (1978): 99–103.

Vossen, Lesley Moore. Rev. of *Herald of the Autochthonic Spirit*, by Gregory Corso. *Best Sellers* Jan. 1982: 392.

Walden, John. Rev. of *Exiled Angel*, by Gregory Stephenson. *Beat Scene* 8 [1990]: 20.

Wallace, Ronald. *God Be with the Clown: Humor in American Poetry.* Columbia: U of Missouri P, 1984.

Warren, Kenneth. Rev. of *Mindfield*, by Gregory Corso. *Contact/II* 10.59–61 (Spring 1991): 74–78.

Watson, Steve. *The Birth of the Beat Generation: Visionaries, Rebels, and Hipsters, 1944–1960.* New York: Pantheon, 1995.

Whitmer, Peter O., with Bruce Van Wyngarden. *Aquarius Revisited: Seven Who Created the Sixties Counterculture that Changed America.* 1987. New York: Citadel, 1991.

Wilson, Robert. *A Bibliography of Works by Gregory Corso.* New York: Phoenix, 1966.

———. "Marching to a Different Drummer: Collecting 'Beat' Poets." *Biblio* 1.1 (July/Aug. 1996): 30–34.

Winters, Donald E., Jr. "Gregory Corso." *Critical Survey of Poetry.* Ed. Frank N. Magill. English Language Series. Englewood Cliffs: Salem, 1982. 574–79.

World Authors (1970–1975). Ed. John Wakeman. Wilson Authors Series. New York: Wilson, 1980.

Bibliography of Works by Gregory Corso

For variant printings of individual poems, I have employed a system intended to indicate progressively differing versions: unless otherwise indicated, printings are in the same form; variants are indicated as "printed in slightly different form," "printed in different form," or "printed in substantially different form." At times these distinctions may appear to be somewhat subjective, but my purpose is to give a general sense of differences rather than to establish indisputable categories. Where slight variations could be briefly explained, I have provided such explanation. All variants key off my first citation of a work in an entry.

I am indebted to the first published bibliography of Corso's works and make occasional references to it in my own bibliography:

Wilson, Robert. *A Bibliography of Works by Gregory Corso*. New York: Phoenix, 1965.

In 1977, the Butler Library of Columbia University exhibited drawings by Beat artists, including Corso. Critiques of these works, which I cite as "treated in Masheck," were published in the following monograph:

Masheck, Joseph, ed. *Beat Art*. New York: Columbia UP, 1977.

In addition, in a 1982 article, which I cite in a number of my entries, reference is made to some unpublished Corso poems; these allusions are from the following work:

Selerie, Gavin. Introduction. *The Riverside Interviews: 3—Gregory Corso*. Ed. Gavin Selerie. London: Binnacle, 1982. 5–20.

Also, several unpublished Corso volumes are cited in the following work:

Contemporary Authors: A Bio-Bibliographical Guide to Current Writers in Fiction, General Nonfiction, Poetry, Journalism, Drama, Motion Pictures, Television, and Other Fields. Ed. Susan M. Trotsky. New Revision Series. Vol. 41. Detroit: Gale, 1994.

Audio recordings of Corso's readings are indicated as [D] and are listed in the discography section of this bibliography. Filmed recordings are indicated as [F] and are listed in the filmography section.

"Abraham & Tribe Leaving Ur." Drawing. "Portfolio of Drawings"; "Portfolio of Drawings & Photographs" 93.

"Active Night." *Selected* 51; printed in slightly different form in *Long* 72 and *Mindfield* 114.

"After Another Reading of Dante." *Long* 73.

"After Reading 'In the Clearing.'" *Long* 89.

"Ah . . . Well." *Herald* 40; *Mindfield* 189.

"Air Is to Go." *Long* 67; printed in different form as "History Is Ended."

"Alchemical Poem." Broadside [holograph with drawings]. *Alchemical Spring; Stony Hills* [4.1] (#10) (1981): 16; printed with different lineation and without drawings as "Alchemy."

Alchemical Spring. Broadside poster of "Alchemical Poem" in holograph with Corso drawing illustrating poem. *the unspeakable visions of the individual* 9 (1979).

"Alchemy." *Herald* 50; *Mindfield* 202; printed with different lineation as "Alchemical Poem"; Corso reads this poem on *Johnson/Bremser* [D].

"ALGREINORSO." With Allen Ginsberg. *Journals Mid-Fifties: 1954–1958*. By Allen Ginsberg. Ed. Gordon Ball. New York: Harper, 1995. 313–14.

Allegorical drawing [Wilson's description (E3)]. *Brown Daily Herald Supplement* 12 Nov. 1962: 5.

Allen Ginsberg. Drawing. 1972. *The Beat Book*. Ed. Arthur Winfield Knight and Glee Knight. *the unspeakable visions of the individual* 4. California, PA: the unspeakable visions of the individual, 1974. 73.

"All Life Is a Rotary Club." *Happy Birthday* 72.

All Survived. Broadside, with Corso drawing. Englewood: Howling Dog, 1982 [similar in shape and design to "Child Saturn's Flower Is Up"]; printed without drawing in *Beatitude* 32 (1982): n. pag. and *Wings* 3; Corso reads a slightly different form of this poem in *West Coast* [F]; printed in different form as second stanza of "Many Have Fallen"; Corso reads a blend of the two versions as "All Survived" on *Johnson/Bremser* [D].

"All that is is finite" [among "Haiku"]. *Mind Field* 18.

The American Express [prose with Corso drawings]. The Traveller's Companion Series No. 85. Paris: Olympia, 1961; excerpt in *The Olympia Reader: Selections from The Traveller's Companion Series*. Ed. Maurice Girodias. New York: Ballantine, 1965. 677–83 [183–94, 197–98 from the novel]; chapters 20 and 2 in *Unmuzzled Ox* 12.3 (#25) (1988): 110+.

"The American Way." *The Outsider* 1.1 (Fall 1961): 9–14; printed in different form in *Elegiac* 69–75 and *Mindfield* 144–50.

"America Politica Historia, in Spontaneity." *Chelsea Review* 8 (Oct. 1960): 13–15; *Elegiac* 94–97; *Chelsea* 42/43 (1984): 62–64; and *Mindfield* 152–55.

"Amnesia in Memphis." *Evergreen Review* 1.3 (Winter 1957): 77; Corso reads this
poem on *Burroughs and Corso* [D]; printed in slightly different form variably in
Gasoline 22 and *Gasoline/Vestal* 22, *Selected* 19–20, and *Mindfield* 23 [with last
two lines eliminated in latter]; Corso reads the *Mindfield* form of this poem in
Beat Legends [F] and comments on the omitted lines, which he then also reads.

"Ancestry." *Herald* 20–21; last line printed in different form as conclusion of
"Earth Egg" and "Honor if you can."

"and life so." *Unmuzzled Ox* 6.2 (#22) (Winter 1981): 8; printed with corrected
possessives in *Unmuzzled Ox* 12.2 (1986): 21.

Angels. Watercolor painting. Exhibited at Research Conference on the Beat Gen-
eration, New York University School of Education, May 1994.

Angels Fighting Viral Flu Bugs. Watercolor painting. Exhibited at Research Con-
ference on the Beat Generation, New York University School of Education,
May 1994.

Angels Watching over Sick Gregory. Watercolor painting. Exhibited at Research Con-
ference on the Beat Generation, New York University School of Education,
May 1994.

⚥ [*Ankh*]. Oblong Octavo Series 13. New York: Phoenix, 1971. N. pag.; passages
printed in different form as "Poem Jottings in the Early Morn."

"Apples." *Rhinozeros* (1961): n. pag.; *Selected* 61; *Mindfield* 219; *Broadshirt Po-
etry Magazine* 1 (1994) [front of t-shirt]; printed in different form as "There
Can Be No Other Apple for Me."

"April Fool's Day." *Mind Field* 53.

"Ares Comes and Goes." *Long* 70–71; *Penguin* 32–33.

"Army." *Big Table* 1.1 (1959): 144–48; printed with corrected spelling of "appre-
ciatively" in *Happy Birthday* 81–85 and *Mindfield* 93–96; printed in different
form in *Junge* 26+.

"Arrogance." *Mind Field* 10.

"Artemis." *Gregorian*; *Poems*.

Artwork [includes drawings identified as Cnidius Wand, Salamis, Porus, Hydra,
Ibis Stick, and Aegina]. *Contact II: A Poetry Review* 9.53–55 (Summer/Fall
1989): 34–35.

"The Ass" [Ginsberg refers to a Robert Frank short video of Corso reading this
poem]; see Sargeant, Jack. *The Naked Lens: An Illustrated History of Beat Cin-
ema*. London: Creation, 1997.

Atlas and Herakles. Ink drawing; treated in Masheck 14.

"Attention!" [holograph]. *Rhinozeros* (1961): n. pag.

"At the Big A." *Fuck You: A Magazine of the Arts* 8.5 (Spring 1965): n. pag. [Wil-
son (C91) cites this as "At Big A"].

"authothonic like earth my hand" [holograph]. *Poets at Le Metro* 3 [1963]: n. pag. [Wilson (C82) identifies the title of one of Corso's drawings for the title of this poem].

"Autobiography of Gregory Nunzio Corso, 1930–1975." *Purple Moonlight Pages.* [Ed. Stephen Ronan.] N.p.: Subterraneous Archives, [1997]. N. pag.

"Away One Year." *Yūgen* 4 (1959): 22; *Happy Birthday* 62; *Selected* 41–42.

"Azegbequx." *Long* 91.

Balthus. Watercolor painting. Exhibited at Research Conference on the Beat Generation, New York University School of Education, May 1994.

"Bath." *Mind Field* 27; printed in different form as section of "From Rome to Boulder—landing thoughts" 45; printed in different form as section of "Field Report" 264.

Baths of Caracalla. Watercolor painting. Exhibited at Research Conference on the Beat Generation, New York University School of Education, May 1994.

"A Beatnik's Britain." *Sunday Times Colour Magazine* [London] 24 Feb. 1963: 13.

"Beauty swells within me." *Bombay Gin* 4 (Summer/Fall 1977): n. pag.

"A Bed's Lament." *Selected* 49; *Mindfield* 213.

"Berlin Impressions" [prose]. *Evergreen Review* 5.16 (Jan./Feb. 1961): 69–83.

"Berlin Zoo." *Mindfield* 215; printed in same form as "Berlin Zoo—2."

"Berlin Zoo—2." *Selected* 54; printed in same form as "Berlin Zoo."

"Between Childhood and Manhood" [prose]. *Cavalier* Jan. 1965: 36–37+ [Wilson (C90) cites only pages 36–37].

"Beyond Delinquency." *Between Worlds* 1.1 (Summer 1960): 87–88; *Selected* 47–48; printed in slightly different form in *Long* 16–17.

Biographical Note [prose]. *The New American Poetry.* Ed. Donald M. Allen. New York: Grove, 1960. 429–30; revised and updated in *The Postmoderns: The New American Poetry Revised.* Ed. Donald Allen and George F. Butterick. New York: Grove, 1982. 384–85.

"Birthplace Revisited." *Gasoline* 31; *Selected* 24–25; *Gasoline/Vestal* 31; printed in slightly different form in *Mindfield* 31; Corso reads the early version of this poem on *William Burroughs* [D] and comments on an objection that apparently led to the changed *Mindfield* form; Corso reads the latter version of this poem on *Burroughs and Corso* [D] and in *NY Beat* [F], Vols. 1 and 3.

"Blake." *Mind Field* 56.

"The blood the semen spat by madness." *Bombay Gin* [2] (Winter/Spring 1977): 55.

Blurb [prose]. *Clear Wind.* By Neeli Cherkovski. San Diego: Avant, 1984.

Blurb [prose]. *Sacred Fix.* By Sinclair Beiles. Rotterdam: Cold Turkey, 1975.

"Body Fished from the Seine." *Olympia* 4 (1963): 25; *Elegiac* 109.

"Bomb." Broadside. San Francisco: City Lights, 1958; *Happy Birthday* as foldout between pp. 32 and 33; *Junge* [n. pag.], accompanied by a record on which Corso reads the poem; *Mindfield* 65–69; excerpt recorded on *ESP* [D]; according to Wilson [F4], Corso reads this poem on *Allen Ginsberg* [D]; also recorded on *Corso, Ferlinghetti* [D] and *Pictures* [D]; Corso reads a slightly different form of an excerpt from "Bomb" [approximately the last third of the poem] in the video *Fried Shoes, Cooked Diamonds* [F]; Corso reads an excerpt from the poem in the video *Beat Legends* [F], identified on tape and box as "O Bomb"; Corso reads three lines from the poem in the video *Gang of Souls* [F].

"Bombed Train Station, 80 Killed." *Herald* 27–28.

"Botticelli's Spring." *Tempo Presente* 6.8 (Aug. 1961): n. pag.; printed in same form as "Botticelli's 'Spring'" in *Gasoline* 27, *Selected* 22–23 with omission of *a* in line 4, *Gasoline/Vestal* 27, and *Mindfield* 28; Corso reads this poem on *Howls* [D] and in the video *Beat Legends* [F].

"Brecht & Benn." *Long* 63.

"But I Do Not Need Kindness." *Gasoline* 33–34; *Gasoline/ Vestal* 33–34; *Mindfield* 32–33.

"But Surely Yahweh's Not Dead?" *Vice* 1.1 [1966–67]: n. pag.

"By Oscar Wilde's Grave." *Long* 31.

"The Calabrese Are Noted for Having Hard Heads (Testa Dura)." *Mind Field* 12–14; printed omitting lines 22–23 as "Noted for Having Hard Heads (Testa Dura)."

"Cambridge, First Impressions." *Vestal* 33–35; *Gasoline/Vestal* 97–99; *Mindfield* 15–17.

"Cambridge Sky." *Two Cities* 4 (Summer 1960): 41; *Elegiac* 85.

"Canto Corso with Rings." *Unmuzzled Ox* 6.2 (#22) (Winter 1981): 5; printed in different form as untitled poem in *Unmuzzled Ox* 12.2 (1986): 20.

"Canto with Typo." *Unmuzzled Ox* 6.2 (#22) (Winter 1981): 5–7; printed with corrected spellings as "There is no god"; printed in different form as "Hi."

"Capt. Poetry & His Magical Lyre & Pegasus." Drawing. *Mindfield* 198.

Caricatures. Drawings. From 1982 Naropa Institute Kerouac Festival. *New Blood* 8 (Nov. 1982): 37.

"Carrol's Ghost Walking in Snow." Drawing. *Wormwood Review* 4.3 (#15) (1964): 18–19 [Wilson (E6) misspells the title character's name and misidentifies the issue as "IV, 13"]; *American Express* 165; *Unmuzzled Ox* 2.1–2 (1973): n. pag. and 6.2 (#22) (Winter 1981): 146.

Cast of characters from *In This Hung-up Age*. Drawing. *Encounter* Jan. 1962: 90.

"Child Saturn's Flower Is Up." Drawing. *Saturn*.

Church. Unpublished "conceptual book" cited in Chapman, Harold, *The Beat Hotel*. Montpellier, France: Gil Blas, 1984, 38.

"A City Child's Day." *Long* 81–83.

"Cityscape." Ink drawing. "Portfolio of Drawings"; "Portfolio of Drawings & Photographs" 92; treated in Masheck 16–17.

"Clone 3[61]." Holograph broadside, with Corso drawings in right-hand margin in portfolio: despite printed date, portfolios were not issued until July 1978. *Five/ 1/'77*. Oakland: Archer, 1977. N. pag.; printed in different form as "I Gave the Sky Away."

"Close Call." Unpublished poem cited by Selerie 7–8.

"Clown." *Happy Birthday* 52–61; *Mindfield* 76–84; Corso reads the first two pages of the *Happy Birthday* printing on *William Burroughs* [D].

"Clumping in Soho" [prose]. *Nugget* June 1962: 16–23.

Collected Plays; cited in *Contemporary Authors*, New Revision Series, 83, as a 1980 Corso text.

"Columbia U Poesy Reading—1975." *Herald* 1–5; printed in slightly different form in *Mindfield* 161–65; passages from this poem printed in substantially different form in sections 3 and 4 of "Lines Between Past & Future."

"Commission Unfulfilled." *Selected* 61; *Mindfield* 219.

"Concourse Didils." *3 Arts Quarterly* 4 (Winter 1960): 27–28 [Wilson (C56) indicates this as only page 27]; printed in slightly different form in *Elegiac* 100–101.

"Coney Island." *Vestal* 4–5; *Gasoline/Vestal* 59–61.

Contributor's note [prose]. *Evergreen Review* 6.22 (Jan./Feb. 1962): 6.

Corso of LaVigne in Herb's. Ink drawing; treated in Masheck 13.

Corso's grave. Drawing. *Intrepid Anthology: A Decade & Then Some; Contemporary Literature—1976*. Ed. Allen DeLoach. *Intrepid* 25–35. Buffalo: Intrepid, 1976. 48.

"cosmos entire" [among "Haiku"]. *Mind Field* 17.

Cover drawing. Multi-colored illustration. *Mindfield* front and back cover.

Cowboy and Horse. Ink drawing. "Portfolio of Drawings"; "Portfolio of Drawings & Photographs" 79; treated in Masheck 15–16.

"Crete." *10 Times a Poem* [holograph]; printed in different form as #7 in "Eleven Times a Poem."

"The Crime." *Vestal* 18; *Gasoline/Vestal* 76.

"Cut Up." With Dwight Eisenhower. *Locus Solus* 2 (Summer 1961): 152; printed in same form as "Cut Up of Eisenhower Speech & Mine Own Poem."

"Cut Up of Eisenhower Speech & Mine Own Poem." *Minutes* 33; printed in same form as "Cut Up."

"Cut Up of Ginsberg Letter & Herald Trib Paris Editorial." *Minutes* 34.

"Cut Up of One of My Poems." *Minutes* 35.

"Danger." *Long* 88; *Mindfield* 118.

"The Day after Human Kind." Letter to Vojo Sindolic; printed in slightly differ-

ent form as "The Day after Humankind—a Fragment"; Corso reads the first
two stanzas of this poem as the beginning of part 2 of "The Day after Human-
kind—a Fragment" on *Johnson/Bremser* [D].

"The Day after Humankind." Manuscript poem Corso reads on *Johnson/Bremser*
[D]; the poem consists of prefatory lines, part 1 ("The Day Before"), and part
2 ("The Day After")]; part 2 begins with the first two stanzas of "The Day after
Human Kind" and "The Day after Humankind—a Fragment."

"The Day after Humankind—a Fragment." *Alpha Beat Soup* 6 (Winter 1989/90):
40; printed in slightly different form as "The Day after Human Kind"; Corso
reads the first two stanzas of this poem as the beginning of part 2 of "The Day
After Humankind."

"The Day Before the Phenomenon." *Herald* 35.

"Daydream." *Herald* 49; broadside, Minneapolis: Bookslinger, 1982; Corso reads
this poem in the video *Beat Legends* [F]; printed in substantially different form
as fifth entry in "A Small Notebook," as #9 of "Eleven Times a Poem," and as
"Reading about Nicaraguan & Mid East Wars."

"Dear Fathers." Letter. *Magazine* 5 (1972), part 2: 7–15; printed with original
misspellings as "Poetry and Religion."

"Dear Girl." *Selected* 52; *Long* 11; *Mindfield* 104 [listed as p. 102 in Table of
Contents].

"Dear Villon." *Wings* 19; printed in substantially different form as "Dear Villon,
Dear Milarepa"; printed in slightly different form in *Herald* 24 and *Mind-
field* 181.

"Dear Villon, Dear Milarepa" [identified as "unfinished poem"]. *Unmuzzled Ox*
2.1–2 (1973): n. pag.; *Unmuzzled Ox* 6.2 (#22) (Winter 1981): 103–4; printed
in substantially different form as "Dear Villon"; passage printed in slightly
different form as "Proximity."

"Death." *Happy Birthday* 38–42; first five sections of this poem reproduced as
inscribed typescript with Roman numerals rather than Arabic in Schwartz,
Marilyn, "Gregory Corso," *The Beats: Literary Bohemians in Postwar America.
Dictionary of Literary Biography*, vol. 16, part 1, ed. by Ann Chanters (Detroit:
Gale, 1983), 132.

"Death Comes at Puberty." *Long* 53; Corso reads this poem in the video *Beat
Legends* [F].

"Death of a Revolutionary." Drawing [of dead Abbie Hoffman]. *Mindfield* 248.

"Death of 1959." *Between Worlds* 1.1 (Summer 1960): 88–89; *Elegiac* 89–90.

"Death of the American Indian's God." *Selected* 59; printed in slightly different
form in *Long* 18; last stanza printed in different form as prose passage in "De-
tective Frump's Spontaneous & Reflective Testament" 72.

"Decal Poem." *Unmuzzled Ox* 3.2 (#10) (1975): 11–12; printed in slightly different form in *Unmuzzled Ox* 6.2 (#22) (Winter 1981): 106–7.

"Delacroix Mural at St. Sulpice." *New York Quarterly* 28 (Fall 1985): 41.

"Dementia in an African Apartment House." *Vestal* 3; printed with omission of fifth line in *Gasoline/Vestal* 58; Corso reads the latter form in the video *Beat Legends* [F].

"Destiny." *Herald* 46; *Mindfield* 197.

"Detective Frump's Spontaneous & Reflective Testament" [prose]. *Transatlantic Review* 5 (Dec. 1960): 69–76; sections printed in different form as "Air Is to Go," "Horses," "Death of the American Indian's God," and "Man"; Corso reads a slightly different form of an excerpt from the passage on the American Indian in the video *Gang of Souls* [F].

"Dialogue." *3 Arts Quarterly* 4 (Winter 1960): 26; *Elegiac* 99.

"Dialogues from Children's Observation Ward." *Vestal* 16; *Gasoline/Vestal* 74.

"Dialogue—2 Dollmakers." *The New American Poetry*. Ed. Donald M. Allen. New York: Grove, 1960. 206–7.

"Dichter und Gesellschaft in Amerika." *Akzente* 5 (1958): 101–12 [German translation of "The Literary Revolution in America," with no translator cited].

"A Difference of Zoos." *Selected* 57; printed in substantially different form in *Long* 62, *Penguin* 31, and *Mindfield* 111, with misspelling of *Frankenstein* in latter; Corso reads a slightly different form on *Burroughs and Corso* [D].

"Direction Sign in London Zoo." *Selected* 51; *Mindfield* 213.

"Discord." *Happy Birthday* 21.

"Discussion following poetry reading April 1973, Salem State College." With Allen Ginsberg and Peter Orlovsky. Panel discussion. *Gone Soft* 1.3 (Spring 1974): 19–32.

"Dogod Meopoem." *Beatitude* 31 (1981): 3; printed in same form as "The Meop Poem and Doggod" and "Fire Report—No Alarm."

"Doll Poem." *Gasoline* 45; *Selected* 27–28; *Gasoline/Vestal* 45; *Mindfield* 41.

"Don't Shoot the Warthog." *Gasoline* 35; *Gasoline/Vestal* 35; *Mindfield* 34.

"The Double Axe." *Long* 71.

"The Doubt of Lie." *the unspeakable visions of the individual* 10 (1980): 127–28; *Mindfield* 223–24; printed in substantially different form as part of section 2 of "Lines Between Past & Future"; Corso reads a substantially different form as part of an unidentified poem on *Burroughs and Corso* [D]; first two stanzas printed in different form in "Poem" ["I say"], "Window," and "Gregorian RANT."

"The Doubt of Truth" [postcard poem]. California, PA: the unspeakable visions of the individual, 1979; several lines printed in different form in "Who I Am"; printed without final two lines in *the unspeakable visions of the individual* 10 (1980): 127 and *Mindfield* 222.

"Do we preside over the death of poesy? . . ." Unpublished poem cited by Selerie 19.

"Down Old Greece Way." *Contact II: A Poetry Review* 9.53–55 (Summer/Fall 1989): 35.

Drawings: Pen & Ink. Cited in *Intrepid* 23/24 (Summer/Fall 1972), p. 96, as volume 8 in a new book series (Beau Fleuve) by Intrepid Press; by the next issue, *Intrepid Anthology: A Decade & Then Some; Contemporary Literature—1976* (*Intrepid* 25–35), the Corso volume disappears from the list of works in the Beau Fleuve Series.

"A Dreamed Poem, Thanksgiving Morn—1973—." *Bombay Gin* 4 (Summer/Fall 1977): n. pag.

"A Dreamed Realization." *Happy Birthday* 49; *Mindfield* 74.

"Dream of a Baseball Star." Drawing. *Mindfield* 72.

"Dream of a Baseball Star." *Happy Birthday* 45; *Mindfield* 71–72.

"D. Scarlatti." *Gasoline* 30; *Gasoline/Vestal* 30.

"Earliest Memory." *Herald* 11; *Mindfield* 170; printed in substantially different form as "The occurence is in the remembrance"; printed in substantially different form as passage in section 2 of "Lines Between Past & Future"; the poem recreates an incident Corso relates in "Between Childhood and Manhood" 91 and "When I Was Five I Saw a Dying Indian" 29–30.

"Earliest Record of Hell." *10 Times a Poem* [holograph]; printed in different form as conclusion of #2 in "Eleven Times a Poem."

"An Early Dutch Scene." *Long* 72; Corso reads this poem on *William Burroughs* [D].

"Early Morning Writings." *Happy Birthday* 43–44.

"Earth Egg." *The Japanese Notebook Ox. Unmuzzled Ox* 2.4–3.1 (#8/9) (1974): n. pag. [boxed edition of a chapbook in both holograph and print, and five folded, unpaged sheets of drawings]; first poem printed in slightly different form as "Holiday Greetings from Gregory Corso"; sections printed in different form in "Return," "Ancestry," "Honor if you can," and "Inter & Outer Rhyme."

"Eastside Incidents." *The Needle* 1.3 (Nov. 1956): 4; *Elegiac* 80.

"Ecce Homo." *Gasoline* 28; *Gasoline/Vestal* 28; printed without last two lines in *Selected* 23.

"Eden Were Elysium." *Long* 49.

Edgar Allan Poe. Watercolor painting. Exhibited at Research Conference on the Beat Generation, New York University School of Education, May 1994.

"An Egyptian Mistress' Loveglyphs." *Bombay Gin* 4 (Summer/Fall 1977): n. pag.

Elegiac Feelings American. New York: New Directions, 1970.

"Elegiac Feelings American (for the dear memory of John Kerouac)." *Elegiac* 3–12; *Mindfield* 125–34; printed in substantially different form as "Spontaneous Requiem."

"Eleven Times a Poem." *Elegiac* 31–36; printed in substantially different form as *10 Times a Poem*; #6 printed in substantially different form as sixth entry in

"A Small Notebook" and as "A 2-Pathed Omen"; #9 printed in substantially different form as fifth entry in "A Small Notebook," printed in substantially different form as "Reading about Nicaraguan & Mid East Wars," and printed in substantially different form as "Daydream"; in his interview with Corso, Michael Andre cites still another variant of this section on p. 148.

"Emily Dickenson the Trouble with You Is—." *Big Table* 4 (Spring 1960): 87 [Wilson (C53) corrects the misspelling in the title]; printed with corrected spelling in title in *Mindfield* 210 [misspelling retained in Table of Contents].

"Ergastolini." *New Departures* 3.3 (1960): 114–15 [Wilson (C37) cites pagination only as far as page 114].

"Errol Flynn—On His Death." *Two Cities* 4 (Summer 1960): 41–42; *Elegiac* 86.

"European Thoughts—1959." *Long* 34–35; *Mindfield* 106; last stanza printed in different form as #10–11 of "Random Writings, Fiesole and Geneva 1960."

"Everywhere March Your Head." With William Burroughs. *Locus Solus* 2 (Summer 1961): 148–49, cut-up of Rimbaud's "To a Reason (A Une Raison)"; *Minutes* 23.

"Eyes." *New Directions in Prose and Poetry 31*. Ed. J. Laughlin, Peter Glassgold, and Frederick R. Martin. New York: New Directions, 1975. 23–25; printed in slightly different form in *Bombay Gin* [#2?] (Winter/Spring 1977): 51–52; printed in different form in *Herald* 37–39.

"The Fairy Tale Hero." *Long* 60.

"Falls the Sun like a Shot Circle." Drawing. *Mindfield* 167.

"Family." Corso reads this poem on *Baraka/Corso* [D].

"Feelings on Getting Older." *Herald* 51–53; *Mindfield* 203–5; printed in different form as "Feelings on Growing Old."

"Feelings on Growing Old." *New Directions in Prose and Poetry 31*. Ed. J. Laughlin, Peter Glassgold, and Frederick R. Martin. New York: New Directions, 1979. 143–46; printed in different form as "Feelings on Getting Older."

"Field Report." *Mindfield* 238+; sections printed in different form as "On Gregory Being Double the Age of Shelley" and "Bath."

"The 5th Estate." *Mind Field* 54–55.

Find It So Hard to Write the How Why & What. Cited in *Contemporary Authors*, New Revision Series, p. 83, as a Corso text published by the Paterson Society in 1961.

"Fire Report—No Alarm." *Mind Field* 31–33; printed with misspelling of "brethren" in *Mindfield* 234–35; printed in slightly different form as "Dogod Meopoem" and "The Meop Poem and Doggod."

"First Night in the White House." *Selected* 51; printed in different form in *Long* 58.

"First Night on the Acropolis." *Long* 19; printed in different form as concluding stanza of "On the Acropolis."

"First Reading at the Six Gallery, October 7, 1955" [prose]. With Allen Ginsberg. *Howl*. By Allen Ginsberg. Ed. Barry Miles. New York: Harper, 1986. 165–66; abridged printing of "The Literary Revolution in America."

"5oems & drawings of birds & cats." *Unmuzzled Ox* 3.2 (#10) (1975): 94–103; printed with misspelling of "suits" in first poem in *Unmuzzled Ox* 6.2 (#22) (Winter 1981): 108–17; fourth poem printed in different form as "Spirit."

"Flight." *Long* 90.

"Fluctuation." *10 Times a Poem* [holograph].

"Flu Ramblings Sequence '91." Corso reads this manuscript poem in the video *Beat Legends* [F].

"Food." *Yūgen* 5 (1959): 31–32; *Happy Birthday* 33–35.

"For ——." *Long* 88; *Mindfield* 117.

"For Allen" [prose]. *Best Minds: A Tribute to Allen Ginsberg*. Ed. Bill Morgan and Bob Rosenthal. New York: Lospecchio, 1986. 72.

"For Black Mountain." *Yūgen* 4 (1959): 28.

"For Black Mountain—2." *Yūgen* 7 (1961): 30.

"For Bunny Lang." *i.e.* [*Cambridge Review*] 1.6 (Dec. 1956): 24; *Happy Birthday* 67.

"For Homer." *Herald* 13–14; *Mindfield* 172–73.

"For Hope Savage." *Between Worlds* 1.1 (Summer 1960): 90; printed in same form as "Sura."

"For Ignorance." *Bombay Gin* 4 (Summer/Fall 1977): n. pag.

"For John Lennon." *Unmuzzled Ox* 6.2 (#22) (Winter 1981): 121; printed with misspelling of *hosannahs* in *Herald* 28; printed in different form as "Piffle" and "Metaphor."

"For K. R. Who Killed Himself in Charles Street Jail." *Happy Birthday* 50.

"For Lisa." *Beatitude* 29 (1979): 3; printed in same form as "For Lisa, 1."

"For Lisa, 1." *Herald* 54; printed in same form as "For Lisa."

"For Lisa, 2." *Herald* 54; *Mindfield* 206; printed in same form as "I saw an angel today."

"For Lorenzo." Drawing. *Poets at Le Metro* 5 (June 1963): n. pag.

"For Mary Rogers." *Mind Field* 42–44; Corso reads a different form of the first half of this poem on *Baraka/Corso* [D].

"For Miles." *Gasoline* 44; *Gasoline/Vestal* 44; *Mindfield* 40; printed without final stanza in *Selected* 27.

"For Miranda." *Wings* 34; printed in different form in *Herald* 14 and *Mindfield* 174.

"For My Pregnant Wife, Be It Girl or Boy." *New Directions Books Fall-Winter 1964–5* [catalog]. New York: New Directions, 1964. 14.

"For Those Who Commit Suicide." *Long* 87.

"Fortune came to Society's rat." Corso reads this poem on *Baraka/Corso* [D].

Four Poems. New York: Paradox, 1981.

"Four Reasons Why You Should Not Renew Your Subscription to Evergreen Review." N. p.: n. p., 1962.

"Fragment from Mutation of the Spirit." *City Lights Journal* 3 (1966): 201; printed in same form as "the decencies of life . . ." poem in "Mutation of the Spirit."

"Fragment from the Decadence." *Vestal Lady* 20; *Renaissance* 1.3 (1962): inside back cover; *Gasoline/Vestal* 80.

"A French Boy's Sunday." *Olympia* 4 (1963): 25; *Elegiac* 110.

"Friend." *Long* 54; *Penguin* 30; *Mindfield* 108; Corso reads the last seven lines of this poem in the video *Beat Legends* [F] [identified on tape and box as "Friends"]; printed in different form as first poem in "Triptych: Friend, Work, World"; Corso reads a slightly different form of this poem on *Burroughs and Corso* [D].

"The Frightening Difference." *Poetry London—New York* 1.4 (Summer 1960): 32–33; *Happy Birthday* 37; *Selected* 40.

"From an Interview: On the 'Beat Movement'" [prose]. *Nomad New York* 10–11 (Autumn 1962): 49 [Wilson (C76) identifies the date as Aug.].

"From Another Room." *Happy Birthday* 69; *Mindfield* 86.

"From Rome to Boulder—landing thoughts." *Bombay Gin* ns 1.4 (Summer 1989): 106–8; printed in slightly different form in *Mind Field* 45–52; early section printed in different form as "Bath."

"from *The Mutation of the Spirit.*" *C: A Journal of Poetry* 1.10 (1965): n. pag.; printed in same form as five of the poems from the larger work.

"Galactic Birth." *Herald* 42; *Mindfield* 192.

"The Game." *Vestal* 21; *Gasoline/Vestal* 81.

"Gargoyles." *Happy Birthday* 67.

Gasoline. Pocket Poets Series 8. San Francisco: City Lights, 1958; printed in different form by City Lights bound with *Vestal* in 1976.

Gasoline/The Vestal Lady on Brattle. San Francisco: City Lights, [1976], printing in different form of the two books bound in a single volume.

"The Geometrician of Milano." *Herald* 29; Selerie cites an earlier draft (19–20).

The Geometric Poem [holograph poem sequence with drawings]. Milan: Pivana, 1966; printed without the multiple colors of the original in *Elegiac* 37–68.

"German Visitations of Music Men." *Herald* 30–31; last stanza printed in different form as "Writ When I Found Out His Was an Unmarked Grave" and as stanza in *Way Out.*

"Getting to the Poem." *Wings* 10; printed in different form in *Herald* 34–35 and *Mindfield* 187–88; Corso reads a slightly different form of the latter version in the video *Beat Legends* [F]; last three lines removed to conclusion of "Return."

"Giant Turtle." *Happy Birthday* 49; *Mindfield* 73.

"God." *Nomad* 5/6 (Winter/Spring 1960): 25.

"God Is a Masturbator." *Fuck You: A Magazine of the Arts* 7.5 (Sept. 1964): n. pag.; *Elegiac* 112; *Mindfield* 156.

"God? She's Black." *Selected* 52; *Penguin* 25; printed in different form in *Long* 44; Corso reads a slightly different form of the first four stanzas of the latter version in the video *Beat Legends* [F] [identified on tape and box as "O God, She's Black!"].

The Golden Dot. Cited as "forthcoming book" in Phoenix Bookshop Catalog 200 (Sept. 1986); Corso discusses "the golden dot" in his interview with Gavin Selerie 34; Corso reads poems from this projected volume on *Baraka/Corso* [D].

"Gone the Last Danger on Earth." *Long* 45.

"Good News for Sad Saturn in San Francisco." Drawing. *Beatitude* 32 (1982): n. pag.

"The grass was written." *Beatitude* 29 (1979): 2.

"Greece." *New Departures* 3.3 (1960): 108–14; printed with corrected spellings in *New Directions in Prose and Poetry 17*. Ed. J. Laughlin. New York: New Directions, 1961. 330–37; printed in different form in *Long* 20–27; printed in substantially different form as "On the Acropolis."

"Greenwich Village Suicide." *Vestal* 5; *Gasoline/Vestal* 61; printed without final line in *Selected* 9–10; printed in slightly different form in *Mindfield* 3; Corso reads the latter form of this poem in the video *Beat Legends* [F].

"Gregorian RANT." *Gregorian*; printed with several typographical errors and altered stanza break in *Poems*; printed as a poster with several typographical errors as Published in Heaven Poster Series 27 (Louisville: White Fields, 1995); section in stanza 2 printed in different form as passages in "The Doubt of Lie," "Poem" ["I say unto you"], and "Window"; pair of lines in penultimate stanza printed in slightly different form as conclusion of "Leda."

Gregorian RANT. Published in Heaven Chapbook Series 18. Louisville: White Fields, 1993. N. pag.

"Gregory Corso being interviewed by Roger Richards, NY Cable TV host, of Greenwich Books Ltd." Drawing. *The Beat Journey.* Ed. Arthur and Kit Knight. *the unspeakable visions of the individual* 8. California, PA: the unspeakable visions of the individual, 1978. 140.

"Gregory reading mss." Drawing. *Wings* 18.

"Growing Pains." *Long* 80.

"A Guide for My Infant Son." *Herald* 56; *Mindfield* 206.

"A Guy." Drawing. *Wings* 29.

"Haiku" ["All that is is finite"]. *Mind Field* 18.

"Haiku" ["cosmos entire"]. *Mind Field* 17.

"Haiku" ["I get uncomfortable"]. *Mind Field* 23.

"Haiku" ["In quickest moment"]. "Things to Cut Up." *Minutes* 57.

"Haiku" ["Life begins in micro"]. *Mind Field* 22.

"Haiku" ["the nearer you arrive"]. *Mind Field* 19.

"Haiku" ["Police act like"]. *Mind Field* 7.

"Haiku" ["There are enough stars"]. *Mind Field* 21.

"Haiku" ["were we to reach a galaxy"]. *Mind Field* 20.

"Hair." *Happy Birthday* 14–16; *Selected* 32–34; printed with misspelling of "merchant" in *Mindfield* 51–53.

"Halloween." *Selected* 50; *Long* 55; *Mindfield* 109.

"Happening on German Train." *Selected* 53; printed in substantially different form as "Happening on a German Train" in *Long* 33 and *Mindfield* 105.

The Happy Birthday of Death. New York: New Directions, 1960.

Happy Death [filmscript]. With Jay Socin. Produced in New York in 1965.

"Having Fun with Myself at the Expense of Others Poem: Things in Life I Know Most Others Don't Know" [manuscript poem]. Corso reads this poem on *Johnson/Bremser* [D]; includes "Women."

"Head of Christ." Crayon drawing. "Portfolio of Drawings"; reproduced with border in "Portfolio of Drawings & Photographs" 90; treated in Masheck 11–12.

"Heave the Hive with New Bees." *Happy Birthday* 71.

"Hedgeville." *Combustion* 2 (Apr. 1957): 3; *Elegiac* 81; printed in different form as "Last Night I Drove a Car."

Heirlooms from the Future. Cited in Summer 1976 Naropa Institute Catalog, p. 19, as title of Corso's next book to be published by New Directions; Corso discusses this projected volume in his interviews with Gavin Selerie 32, 34, and with Misurella (passim) and uses the title as a phrase in "Decal Poem" and "Lines Between Past & Future."

"Hello . . ." *Gasoline* 40; printed lacking one period in ellipsis in title in *Gasoline/Vestal* 40; printed without ellipsis in title in *Mindfield* 37; Corso reads this poem in the video *Beat Legends* [F].

Herald of the Autochthonic Spirit. New York: New Directions, 1981 [Selerie says this volume was once called *Heirlooms* and *Revolutionary of the Autochthonic Spirit*, see p. 18].

"Herman Saturn." Drawing. *Saturn.*

"H. G. Wells." Unpublished poem cited by Ginsberg, "Introduction," *Gasoline* 7; the Butler Library at Columbia University holds a manuscript poem by Corso entitled "After Reading H. G. Wells".

"Hi." *Wings* 8–9; printed with several changes from lower case to upper case in *The Spirit That Moves Us* 11 (1991): 204–5; Corso reads a slightly different form of this poem on *Johnson/Bremser* [D]; printed in slightly different form in *Mindfield* 228–29; printed in different form as "Canto with Typo" and "There is no god."

"History Is Ended." *Nomad* 5/6 (Winter/Spring 1960): 24; *Elegiac* 82; first stanza printed in different form as prose passage in "Detective Frump's Spontaneous & Reflective Testament" 71; printed in different form as "Air Is to Go."

Hitting the Big 5-0. New York: Catchword, 1983. N. pag.

Holiday Greetings from Gregory Corso. New York: Phoenix, 1972. N. pag.; printed in slightly different form as "Holiday Greetings from Gregory Corso"; printed in slightly different form as first poem in "Earth Egg" and as "Inter & Outer Rhyme."

"Holiday Greetings from Gregory Corso." *World* 26 (Winter 1973): n. pag.; printed in slightly different form as *Holiday Greetings from Gregory Corso*; printed in slightly different form as first poem in "Earth Egg" and as "Inter & Outer Rhyme."

"Honor if you can." *Sitting Frog: Poetry from the Naropa Institute.* Ed. Rachel Peters and Eero Ruuttila. Brunswick: Blackberry, 1976. N. pag.; concluding line printed in slightly different form in "Earth Egg" and "Ancestry."

"Horses." *Long* 29; printed in slightly different form as passage in "Detective Frump's Spontaneous & Reflective Testament" 71.

"The Horse Was Milked." *Vestal* 17; *Gasoline/Vestal* 75; *Mindfield* 7.

"How Happy I Used to Be." *Happy Birthday* 12–13; *Selected* 30–31; *Mindfield* 48–49.

"How Not to Die." *Four Poems*; *Wings* 1; *Herald* 17; *Mindfield* 177.

"How One Looks at It." *Selected* 58.

"Hunch." *Herald* 57.

"I Am Colors: Fragment from Epic in Progress." *Aylesford Review* 5.3 (Summer 1963): 128.

"I am rich." *Bombay Gin* 8 (Summer/Fall 1980): 48; printed in substantially different form as "Sunrise."

"I Am 25." *Gasoline* 36; *Selected* 25–26; *Gasoline/Vestal* 36; *Mindfield* 35; printed in slightly different form on *Broadshirt Poetry Magazine* 1 (1994) [front of t-shirt]; Corso reads this poem on *Howls* [D].

"Ich bin Dichter . . ." *Loose Blätter Sammlung* 6 (Spring 1979): 11, German translation of first ten lines of "Dichter und Gesellschacht in Amerika" broken into poetic lines.

"I Dream in Daytime." *Floating Bear* 28 (Dec. 1963): 3; printed in same form as "I Dream in the Daytime."

"I Dream in the Daytime." *Elegiac* 111; printed in same form as "I Dream in Daytime."

"I feel there is an inherent ignorance in me." *Beatitude* 29 (1979): 1; printed in different form as "Wisdom."

"I Gave Away . . ." *Herald* 41; *Mindfield* 191; Corso reads a slightly different form of this poem in the video *Beat Legends* [F] [identified on tape and box as "Arrogant Poem"]; printed in different form as "I Gave the Sky Away."

"I Gave the Sky Away." *Renegade: The West Coast Review of Unlimited American Literature and Art* (1978): 30; *Bombay Gin* 6 (Summer 1978/Spring 1979): 39; printed in different form as "Clone 3⁶¹"; printed in slightly different form without title in *Birthstone* 4 (1978): 5; printed in different form as "I Gave Away . . ."

"I get uncomfortable" [among "Haiku"]. *Mind Field* 23.

"I Held a Shelley Manuscript." *Happy Birthday* 22; *Selected* 34–35; *Mindfield* 58.

Imaginary Classical Landscape. Oil painting; treated in Masheck 17–19.

"Imagination." With Allen Ginsberg. *Beatitude* 29 (1979): 50.

"I Met This Guy Who Died." *Herald* 10; *Mindfield* 169; printed in same form as "JLK" with this title as first line; conclusion printed in slightly different form in section 3 of "Lines Between Past & Future"; Corso reads this poem on *Johnson/Bremser* [D] and in the video *Beat Legends* [F].

I Might Be Count Balsomo, or Might Be Mozart, or Yet Might Be the Macky de Sade. Watercolor painting. Exhibited at Research Conference on the Beat Generation, New York University School of Education, May 1994.

"I Miss My Dear Cats." *Gasoline* 32; printed in slightly different form in *Gasoline/Vestal* 32.

"Immutable Moods." *Elegiac* 116–20.

"In a Way" [first poem in "Some Greek Writings"]. *Long* 68.

"I never knew we existed in a hazardous time." Corso reads this poem on *Baraka/Corso* [D].

"In Honor of Those the Negroes Are Revolting Against." *Vice* 1.1 [1966–67]: n. pag.

"In My Beautiful . . . And Things." *Vestal* 15; *Gasoline/Vestal* 73.

"In Praise of Neadnderthal Man." *New Blood* 4 (1981): 72–73; printed in slightly different form with corrected spelling of title in *Wings* 4–5; printed in slightly different form with corrected spelling of title in *Herald* 43–45 and *Mindfield* 194–96.

In Ran the Moonlight and Grabbed the Prunes. Projected title for Corso's second book of poems cited in *i.e.* [*Cambridge Review*] 6 (Dec. 1956): 7; used in concluding line of "This Was My Meal."

"Inter & Outer Rhyme." *Herald* 21; *Mindfield* 178; printed in slightly different form as "Holiday Greetings from Gregory Corso" and first poem of "Earth Egg."

Interview ["Radio Interview"]. KBCO-FM 97, Boulder, CO. 16 Aug. 1981. *Wings* 20–29.

Interview of William Burroughs. With Allen Ginsberg. *Journal for the Protection of All Beings* 1 (1961): 79–83.

Interview with Allen Ginsberg. *Journal for the Protection of All Beings* 1 (1961): 21–29.

Interview with Allen Ginsberg ["Beat Rap"]. *Interview* Dec. 1989: 64–67+.

Interview with Allen Ginsberg and David Widgery. *U—University & College Magazine* 3.7 (Oct. 1965): 13.

Interview with Art Buchwald ["Art Buchwald in Paris: The Upbeat Beatnik"]. *New York Herald Tribune* 14 Jan. 1960: 19; *Evergreen Review* 14 (Sept./Oct. 1960): 153–54; *Kerouac and Friends: A Beat Generation Album*. By Fred W. McDarrah. New York: Morrow, 1985. 100–102 [McDarrah mistakenly cites the original publication date as 4 Jan. 1960].

Interview with Barry Gifford and Lawrence Lee. *Jack's Book: An Oral Biography of Jack Kerouac*. Ed. Barry Gifford and Lawrence Lee. New York: St. Martin's, 1978. passim; excerpt in *Wings* 30.

Interview with Danny O'Bryan [19 Nov. 1993]. *Poems*.

Interview with Edmundo Bracho ["¿Qué Sabes Tú de la Vida, Muchacho?"]. *Quimera* 121 (1993): 34–39.

Interview with Fred Misurella ["Entretien avec Gregory Corso"]. Translated from English into French by Nancy Blake. *Tel Quel* (1977): 59–71.

Interview with Gavin Selerie. *The Riverside Interviews: 3—Gregory Corso*. London: Binnacle, 1982. 21–47.

Interview with J. G. Gosciak ["Tales of Beatnik Lore: An Interview with Gregory Corso"]. *Contact II: A Poetry Review* 9.53–55 (Summer/Fall 1989): 33–35.

Interview with Michael Andre. *Unmuzzled Ox* 2.1–2 (1973): n. pag.; *Unmuzzled Ox* 6.2 (#22) (Winter 1981): 123–58.

Interview with Murray Robinson ["Gregory Sends Us Poems That We Don't Get"]. *New York World Telegram & Sun* 16 June 1955, sec. 2: 1.

Interview with Robert King [1974] ["'I'm Poor Simple Human Bones': An Interview with Gregory Corso"]. In *The Beat Diary*. Ed. Arthur and Kit Knight. *the unspeakable visions of the individual* 5. California, PA: the unspeakable visions of the individual, 1977. 4–24; *The Beat Vision: A Primary Sourcebook*. Ed. Arthur and Kit Knight. New York: Paragon, 1987. 152–84.

Interview with Tom Plante [1977] ["Gregory Corso in California"]. *Renegade: The West Coast Review of Unlimited American Literature and Art* (1978): 32–35.

Interview with [Victor] Bockris and [William T.] Wylie. *Unmuzzled Ox* 4.1 (#13) (1976): 139.

"In the Early Morning." *Vestal* 13; *Selected* 12–13; *Gasoline/Vestal* 71; printed in same form as "Poem" ["In the early morning"].

"In the Fleeting Hand of Time." *Partisan Review* 25.2 (Spring 1958): 226–27; printed in slightly different form in *Selected* 15–16 and *Penguin* 12–13; printed with misspellings in *Gasoline* 15–16; *Gasoline/Vestal* 14–15; *Mindfield* 21–22; Corso reads this poem on *Howls* [D] [*Partisan Review*, *Selected*, and *Penguin* use the spelling "fiery," and the others employ "firey"; *Gasoline*, *Selected*, and *Penguin* use "paradiscal," and the others "paradisical"; the recorded version favors the latter spelling and changes "Milanese" to "Calabrian"].

"In the Morgue." *Vestal* 6; *Selected* 10; *Gasoline/Vestal* 62; printed with added subtitle "a dream" in *Mindfield* 4.

"In the Tunnel-Bone of Cambridge." *i.e.* [*Cambridge Review*] 1.1 (1954): 28–29 [Wilson (C3) cites only page 28]; printed with altered position of dash in lines 22–23 in *Vestal* 9–10, *Gasoline/Vestal* 66–67, and *Selected* 11–12.

"In This Hung-up Age" [play, with Corso drawings of characters; identified in subtitle as "A One-Act Farce Written 1954"]. *Encounter* 18.1 (Jan. 1962): 83–90; printed in different form and without drawings as "In This Hung-Up Age" in *New Directions in Prose and Poetry 18*. Ed. J. Laughlin. New York: New Directions, 1964. 149–61; in his interview with Michael Andre, Corso states that this play was produced at Harvard in 1954, see p. 128.

"Into the Aperture of an Unlikely Archimage." *Vestal* 30; printed with misspelling of "again" in line 16 in *Gasoline/Vestal* 92–93.

Introduction [prose]. *Junge* 246+.

"Introduction to Peter Orlovsky's Poems" [prose]. *Clean Asshole Poems & Smiling Vegetable Songs: Poems 1957–1977*. By Peter Orlovsky. San Francisco: City Lights, 1978. 7–8.

"I saw an angel today." *Beatitude* 29 (1979): 2; printed in same form as "For Lisa, 2."

"Italian Extravaganza." *Gasoline* 31; *Selected* 24; *Gasoline/Vestal* 31; *Mindfield* 30; Corso reads this poem on *Burroughs and Corso* [D] and *William Burroughs* [D].

"Italian Park." *Oxford Magazine* 15 May 1958: 434; printed in substantially different form as "Park."

"It was the happy birthday of Death." *Wednesday Paper and 2 Days Later* [1960?]: 7.

"I Where I Stand." *Long* 41.

"Japanese Notebook." Drawings on five folded sheets. *Japanese Notebook Ox.*

Japanese Notebook Ox. Unmuzzled Ox 2.4–3.1 (#8/9) (1974): n. pag. [boxed edition includes "Earth Egg" poems and Japanese Notebook drawings].

"JLK." *Unmuzzled Ox* 6.2 (#22) (Winter 1981): 120; *Four Poems*; printed with first line removed to title and with dedication "For J. L. K." as "I Met This Guy Who Died."

Junge Amerikanische Lyrik. Edited with Walter Höllerer. Munich: Hanser, 1961.

"Kerouac." Reproduction of painting. *Mindfield* 124.

"King Crow." *Audience* 13 May 1955: 10; printed with inserted stanza break in *Vestal* 14, *Gasoline/Vestal* 72, and *Selected* 13 [with italicized *is* in line 6 in latter].

"Kingfish in Waterfield." Drawing. *Mindfield* 46.

"The Last Gangster." *Gasoline* 32; *Selected* 25; *Gasoline/Vestal* 32; *Mindfield* 31; Corso reads this poem on *Burroughs and Corso* [D].

"Last Night I Drove a Car." *Gasoline* 46; *Selected* 28; *Gasoline/Vestal* 46; printed with subtitle "*a dream*" in *Mindfield* 42; Corso reads this poem in the video *Beat Legends* [F]; printed in different form as "Hedgeville."

"Last Night in Milano." *Alpha Beat Soup* 6 (Winter 1989/90): 40.

"The Last Warmth of Arnold." *Gasoline* 20–21; *Selected* 18–19; *Gasoline/Vestal* 19–21; Corso reads the first part of this poem on *Burroughs and Corso* [D] and the whole poem on *Howls* [D].

"Latest Indian Poem." *Unmuzzled Ox* 6.2 (#22) (Winter 1981): 105.

"The Leaky Lifeboat Boys." *Four Poems*; printed in slightly different form in *Herald* 15–16 and *Mindfield* 175–76; first five stanzas printed in different form as "The Wise Fuckers."

"Leda." *Gregorian*; printed correcting several typographical errors while creating others, altering some lineation, and omitting a line in stanza 4 in *Poems*; concluding lines printed in slightly different form in penultimate stanza of "Gregorian RANT."

Letter to Allen Ginsberg [8 Oct. 1959]. *Trembling Lamb* 1.1 (1960): 1.

Letter to Allen Ginsberg [13 Oct. 1961]. *Beat Angels*. Ed. Arthur and Kit Knight. *the unspeakable visions of the individual* 12. California, PA: the unspeakable visions of the individual, 1982. 105–6.

Letter to Carolyn Cassady [excerpt]. "Poor God." By Carolyn Cassady. *Kerouac and the Beats: A Primary Sourcebook*. Ed. Arthur and Kit Knight. New York: Paragon, 1988. 1–2; *Off the Road: My Years with Cassady, Kerouac, and Ginsberg*. By Carolyn Cassady. New York: Morrow, 1990. 314.

Letter to Editor. *Cambridge Opinion* 14 (1959): 12.

Letter to Editor. *Genesis West* 1.4 (Summer 1963): 370, a response to Jack Gilbert's disparaging comments about Corso in the previous issue, p. 252.

Letter to Editor. *Outsider* 1.3 (Spring 1963): 35.

Letter to Editor. *Village Voice* 26 Nov. 1958: 4+ [Wilson (C21) cites only page 4]; *The Village Voice Reader*. Ed. Daniel Wolf and Edwin Fancher. Garden City, NY: Doubleday, 1962. 46.

Letter to Editor. *Village Voice* 26 Nov. 1958: 13.

Letter to Editor. With Allen Ginsberg and Peter Orlovsky. *Nation* 4 Apr. 1959: 2.

Letter to Editor. With Allen Ginsberg and Peter Orlovsky. *Time* 9 Mar. 1959: 5.

Letter to Gary Snyder [c. 30 June 1958]. *The Beat Road*. Ed. Arthur and Kit Knight. *the unspeakable visions of the individual* 14. California, PA: the unspeakable visions of the individual, 1982. 35.

Letter to Gerard Malanga [22 Apr. 1979]. *Little Caesar* 9 (1979): 239+.

Letter to Irving Rosenthal. *Big Table* 1.1 (Spring 1959): 3.

Letter to Jack Kerouac. *Brown Daily Herald Supplement* 12 Nov. 1962: 4.

"Letter to Kerouac." Corso reads this poem on *Baraka/Corso* [D].

Letter to Neal Cassady [3 Dec. 1957]. *As Ever: The Collected Correspondence of Allen Ginsberg and Neal Cassady.* Ed. Barry Gifford. Berkeley: Creative Arts, 1977. 191–92.

Letter to Philip Rahv. *Partisan Review* 3 (Summer 1960): 576.

Letter to Vojo Sindolic [1982]. "Beat Letters to Yugoslavia." *Writers Outside the Margin: An Anthology.* Ed. Jeffrey H. Weinberg. Sudbury, MA: Water Row, 1986. 104–5.

Letter to Warren Hinkle. *Argonaut* ns 3 (Spring 1994): 82.

Letter to William S. Burroughs [1962]. *The Beat Diary.* Ed. Arthur and Kit Knight. *the unspeakable visions of the individual* 5. California, PA: the unspeakable visions of the individual, 1977. 158–61.

"Let Us Inspect the Lyre." *Happy Birthday* 17–18.

"Liability." *Herald* 47.

"Life a Battlefield." Drawing. *Mindfield* 265.

"Life begins in micro" [among "Haiku"]. *Mind Field* 22.

"Life, Death and Dancing: A Buffalo Shindig" [prose]. *Esquire* July 1965: 34–35.

"Lines Between Past & Future" [1975?]. *Purple Moonlight Pages.* [Ed. Stephen Ronan.] N.p.: Subterraneous Archives, [1997]. N. pag.; part of section 2 printed in substantially different form as "The Doubt of Lie"; passages from sections 3 and 4 printed in substantially different form in "Columbia U Poesy Reading—1975"; lines from section 3 printed in slightly different form as conclusion of "I Met This Guy Who Died"; lines from section 4 printed in same form as "Truth is eternity"; Corso reads parts of sections 4 and 2 in substantially different form as an unidentified poem on *Burroughs and Corso* [D] [if one judges by the recorded version, the manuscript pages of the published poem may have been misarranged].

"Lines Written Nov. 22, 23—1963—in Discord—." *Of Poetry and Power: Poems Occasioned by the Presidency and the Death of John F. Kennedy.* Ed. Erwin A. Glikes and Paul Schwaber. New York: Basic, 1964. 115–18; printed in slightly different form in *Elegiac* 27–30 and *Mindfield* 140–43.

"The Literary Revolution in America" [prose]. With Allen Ginsberg. *Litterair Paspoort* [Amsterdam] 110 (Nov. 1957): 193–96 [Corso's byline, but Ginsberg "wrote much of this article," according to B. Morgan, *The Works of Allen Ginsberg 1941–1994: A Descriptive Bibliography*, Bibliographies and Indexes in American Literature 19 (Westport: Greenwood, 1995), 231]; opening passage was translated into German and broken into poetic lines as "Ich bin dichter . . ." and attributed to Corso; printed in abridged form as "First Reading at the Six Gallery, October 7, 1955."

"A Little Lost." *Folio* 25.1 (Winter 1960): 37; *Happy Birthday* 48.

"Little Mozart has nowhere to go." Reproduction of drawing with some paint shadings. *Mindfield* 103.

"Logos Logos Logos." *Long* 78–79.

Long Live Man. New York: New Directions, 1962.

"Looking at the Map of the World." *Happy Birthday* 70.

"Love." *Selected* 57; printed in different form as "Love Dirge."

"Love Dirge." *Long* 32; printed in different form as "Love."

"Loveglyph." *Herald* 45.

"The Love of Two Seasons." *Long* 51; *Mindfield* 107.

"Love Poem for Three for Kaye & Me." *Beatitude* 33 (1985): 5; *Mindfield* 230–31.

"Lyres Tell the Truth!" Drawing. *Poets at Le Metro* 3 (1963): n. pag.

"MacLaine." Portrait drawing. "Portfolio of Drawings"; "Portfolio of Drawings & Photographs" 87.

"Made by Hand." *Playboy* July 1959: 45; *The Bedside Playboy.* Ed. Hugh M. Hefner. Chicago: Playboy, 1968. 393.

"The Mad Yak." *Gasoline* 42; *Penguin* 11; *Gasoline/Vestal* 42; *Mindfield* 38; Corso reads this poem on *Burroughs and Corso* [D] and in the video *Beat Legends* [F].

"The Makers of God." *City Lights Journal #4.* Ed. Mendes Monsanto [Lawrence Ferlinghetti]. San Francisco: City Lights, 1978. 79–80.

"Making a Move." *10 Times a Poem*; printed in different form as #5 in "Eleven Times a Poem."

"Man." *Gemini* 3.3 (Summer 1960): 47; printed in substantially different form in *Penguin* 26–27, *Long* 9–10, and *Mindfield* 101–2; sections printed in different form as passages in "Detective Frump's Spontaneous & Reflective Testament" 75–76; Corso reads a different form of this poem with "Mortal Infliction" appended as part of the poem on *World's Great Poets* [D].

"Man about to Enter Sea." *Selected* 50; *Penguin* 24; printed in substantially different form as "Man Entering the Sea, Tangier."

"Man Entering the Sea, Tangier." *Long* 66–67; printed in substantially different form as "Man About to Enter Sea"; Corso reads this poem on *Burroughs and Corso* [D].

Manifesto [prose]. With Allen Ginsberg and Peter Orlovsky. "Art Buchwald: P.S. From Paris." *Chicago Sun-Times* 17 May 1961, sec. 2: 10 [Wilson (C64) cites this item as appearing on page 9].

"Man Seated Outside My Window." *Vestal* 26; *Gasoline/Vestal* 88.

"Many Have Fallen." *Herald* 26; *Mindfield* 182; printed in different form as "All Survived"; Corso reads a blend of the two different forms as "All Survived" on *Johnson/Bremser* [D]; Corso reads a slightly different form of the *Mindfield* version in the video *Beat Legends* [F] twice, in different readings [identified on tape and on box as "Prophesy 1958" and then as "The Slow Bullets of Radiation"].

"Marriage." *Evergreen Review* 3.9 (Summer 1959): 160–63; printed in different
   form (and without original dedication "for Mr. and Mrs. Mike Goldberg") in
   Happy Birthday 29–32, *Wings* 31–33, and *Mindfield* 61–64 [Table of Contents
   in latter cites the poem as beginning on p. 62]; printed in slightly different form
   (again without dedication) in *Selected* 36–39; printed in slightly different form
   (again without dedication) in *Penguin* 15–19; Corso reads a slightly different
   form of this poem on *Disconnected* [D].

"Masterpiece." *Long* 60.

"Medieval Anatomy." *Happy Birthday* 42.

"The Meop Poem and Doggod." *Pearl* 8 (Summer 1981): 21; printed in same form
   as "Dogod Meopoem" and "Fire Report—No Alarm."

"Messenger Boy." Drawing. *Wings* 9.

"Metaphor." Cited in Selerie 9; printed in different form as "Piffle"; printed in
   different form as "For John Lennon."

"Mexican Impressions." *Gasoline* 23–24; *Selected* 20–21; *Gasoline/Vestal* 23–24;
   Mindfield 24–25 [Table of Contents cites the title as "Mexican Impression"];
   Corso reads this poem on *Howls* [D]; Corso reads parts 5 and 2 on *William
   Burroughs* [D]; Corso reads part 5 on *Johnson/Bremser* [D].

"Miasma." *10 Times a Poem*; printed in different form as #2 in "Eleven Times
   a Poem."

"Middleton Gardens." *Combustion* 2 (Apr. 1957): 3; *Elegiac* 81.

Mind Field. Madras, India: Hanuman, 1989.

Mindfield. Marker painting. Exhibited at Research Conference on the Beat Gen-
   eration, New York University School of Education, May 1994.

Mindfield. New York: Thunder's Mouth, 1989.

The Minicab War [under pseud. de la Rue]. With Sykes [Anselm Hollo] and
   O'Moore [Ron Haworth]. London: Matrix, 1961.

Minutes to Go. With Sinclair Beiles, William Burroughs, and Brion Gysin. San
   Francisco: Beach, 1968. Rpt. of Paris: Two Cities, 1960.

"The Mirror Within." *Herald* 39.

"A Moment's Wish." *Happy Birthday* 63.

"Money/Love." *Herald* 36.

"Moon Prevention" [excerpt]. With Allen Ginsberg and Peter Orlovsky. *Journals
   Mid-Fifties: 1954–1958*. By Allen Ginsberg. Ed. Gordon Ball. New York:
   Collins, 1995. 379–85.

"Moroccan Writings." *Outburst* 2 (1963): n. pag.; printed in different form as
   "Some Moroccan Writings."

"Mortal Infliction." *Open Space* 1 (1964): n. pag.; printed in slightly different form
   in *Happy Birthday* 69, *Selected* 46, and *Mindfield* 86; Corso reads the latter form

of this poem in the video *Beat Legends* [F] and as the conclusion of "Man" on *World's Great Poets* [D].

"Moschops! You Are a Loser!" [prose]. *Nugget* Oct. 1962: 52–53+.

"Mr. Moneybag's Lament." *Long* 50; printed in different form in second poem of "Triptych: Friends, Work, World."

"Ms Saturn Offers Hankie to Mr Saturn Who's Sad." Drawing. *Beatitude* 32 (1982): n. pag.

"The muse is my doppelganger." Corso reads this poem on *Baraka/Corso* [D].

"Muse on Firing Range." Drawing. *Mindfield* 239.

"Musician." Ink drawing on yellow paper. "Portfolio of Drawings"; reproduced with border in "Portfolio of Drawings & Photographs" 91; treated in Masheck 14–15.

The Mutation of the Spirit: A Shuffle Poem. New York: Death, 1964. N. pag.; the Dusty Bright poem printed in different form in *dimas* 3 (196?): n. pag.; five of the poems printed in same form as "from *The Mutation of the Spirit.*" *C: A Journal of Poetry* 1.10 (1965): n. pag.; the "decencies of life" poem printed in same form as "Fragment from Mutation of the Spirit." *City Lights Journal* 3 (1966): 201; the "O walking crucifix" poem printed in same form in *Poetry USA* 4.16 (Fall 1989): 5; printed in slightly different form as "Mutation of the Spirit" in *Wholly Communion: International Poetry Reading at the Royal Albert Hall London June 11, 1965* (New York: Grove, 1965), 32–42 and *Elegiac* 18–26; Corso reads a different form of the "Last night" poem and of the last section of the "O there is burning snow" poem in the video *Wholly Communion* [F].

"My Grandmother Was a Cavewoman." Corso reads this poem on *Baraka/Corso* [D].

"My Hands Are a City." *Vestal* 7; *Renaissance* 1.4 (1962): 4; *Gasoline/Vestal* 63.

"My Visit to Concord." *Combustion* 2 (Apr. 1957): 3; *Elegiac* 81.

The Names I Drop Bounce. Cited in Gosciak interview as a collection of Corso's essays projected to be published by Paragon Press (34).

"Nature's Gentleman." *Selected* 49–50; printed in slightly different form in *Long* 49; Corso reads the latter version in the video *Beat Legends* [F]; the Mary Dare line printed in same form in "Of One Month's Reading of English Newspapers."

"the nearer you arrive" [among "Haiku"]. *Mind Field* 19.

"Nevermore Baltimore." *Herald* 32–33; *Mindfield* 183–84.

"New York Man." *Vestal* 13; *Gasoline/Vestal* 70.

"1959." *Jabberwock: Edinburgh University Review* (1959): 28–29 [Wilson (C32) identifies the title of this journal as *Jabberwock 1959*]; printed with altered stanza break and change of "debauchee" to "debauché" in *Happy Birthday* 90–91 and *Mindfield* 97–98.

"1953." *Happy Birthday* 23–24; printed without last six lines in *Selected* 35–36.

"Nixon" [1958]. With Jack Kerouac and Allen Ginsberg. *Bombay Gin* 7 (Summer/Fall 1979): 1.

"No Doubt What He Saw." *Happy Birthday* 46; *Selected* 40–41.

"Noted for Having Hard Heads (Testa Dura)." *Mindfield* 232–33; printed in different form as "The Calabrese Are Noted for Having Hard Heads (Testa Dura)."

"Notes after Blacking Out." *Happy Birthday* 11; printed omitting lines 10–11 in *Selected* 30; *Mindfield* 47.

"Notes from the Other Side of April: With Negro Eyes, with White—Four Moments from a Poet's Life" [prose]. *Esquire* July 1964: 86+.

"Not This." *Vice* 1.1 [1966–67]: n. pag.

"No Word." *Gasoline* 41; *Selected* 26; *Gasoline/Vestal* 41.

"The occurence is in the remembrance." *New Departures* 12 (1980): 20; printed in substantially different form as "Earliest Memory"; printed in substantially different form as passage in section 2 of "Lines Between Past & Future"; the poem recreates an incident Corso relates in "Between Childhood and Manhood" 91 and "When I Was Five I Saw a Dying Indian" 29–30.

"Ode to Coit Tower." *Gasoline* 11–14; *Gasoline/Vestal* 11–13; Corso reads this poem on *Howls* [D].

"Ode to Myself." *Between Worlds* 1.1 (Summer 1960): 86–87; printed in different form as "Ode to Sura" and "Ode to Myself & Her."

"Ode to Myself & Her." *Long* 12–13; printed in different form as "Ode to Myself"; printed in same form as "Ode to Sura."

"Ode to Old England & Its Language." *New Directions in Prose and Poetry 19.* Ed. J. Laughlin. New York: New Directions, 1966. 260–62; *Elegiac* 113–15; first page of latter text printed under this title in *Mindfield* 157–58; sections of the poem printed in different form as passages in *American Express* 40–42.

"Ode to Sura." *Two Cities* 4 (Summer 1960): 40–41; *Elegiac* 83–84; printed as "Ode to Myself & Her"; printed in different form as "Ode to Myself."

"Of One Month's Reading of English Newspapers." *Evergreen Review* Jan./Feb. 1962: 48; *Elegiac* 77; *Mindfield* 151; the Mary Dare line printed in same form in "Nature's Gentleman."

"An Old Man Said He Once Saw Emily Dickinson." *Vestal* 28; *Gasoline/Vestal* 90.

"O Mighty Tug." *Vice* 1.1 [1966–67]: n. pag.

"On Cave Wall at Trois Freres, Shaman with Antler Headgear." Ink drawing. "Portfolio of Drawings"; "Portfolio of Drawings & Photographs" 136; treated in Mascheck 13–14.

"On Chessman's Crime." *Yūgen* 7 (1961): 29–30; printed with corrected possessive in *Mindfield* 212.

"One Day . . ." *Beatitude* 15 (17 June 1960): 23; *Beatitude Anthology*, ed. by Lawrence Ferlinghetti (San Francisco: City Lights, 1960), 31; printed with corrected spelling of "Gulf" as "One Day" in *Two Cities* 4 (Summer 1960): 43; printed with corrected spellings in *Elegiac* 88; printed with "friend" for "fiend" as "One Day" in *Penguin* 23; printed in slightly different form in *Mindfield* 211.

"On Gregory Being Double the Age of Shelley." *Mind Field* 11; printed in different form as section of "Field Report" 259.

"On My Way Here." *Gregorian*; *Poems*.

"On Palatine." *Happy Birthday* 63; *Selected* 42–43.

"On Pont Neuf." *Happy Birthday* 24; *Mindfield* 59.

"On the Acropolis." *Beatitude* 17 (Oct./Nov. 1960): n. pag.; printed in different form in *Penguin* 21–22; early stanzas printed in substantially different form as early section of "Greece"; last stanza printed in different form as "First Night on the Acropolis."

"On the Death of a Lucky Gent." *Front Unique* 2 (Inverno 1960): 25; printed in slightly different form in *New Departures* 4 (1962): 59, and with corrected spelling of "Nicholas" as "On the Death of the Lucky Gent" in *Elegiac* 98.

"On the Walls of a Dull Furnished Room . . ." *Gasoline* 30; printed in slightly different form in *Tempo Presente* 6.8 (Aug. 1961): n. pag.; printed in slightly different form without ellipsis in title in *Gasoline/Vestal* 30; printed in slightly different form without ellipsis in title and with inversion of last two lines in *Mindfield* 30; Corso reads this poem on *Burroughs and Corso* [D] and *William Burroughs* [D] [on the latter, Corso comments on the possibility of reversing the last two lines].

"O orb of time." *Beatitude* 32 (May 1982): n. pag.

"Open Letter to Life Magazine" [prose]. With Brion Gysin, Bill Burroughs, and Sinclair Beiles. *Nomad* 5/6 (Winter/Spring 1960): 22.

"Open the Gate." *Harvard 1956* 2.2 (1956): 57–60 [Wilson (C9) cites only the first two pages of this poem, mistaking the last two pages for a separate poem].

Orpheus. Drawing. *The Stiffest of the Corpse: An Exquisite Corpse Reader*. Ed. Andrei Codrescu. San Francisco: City Lights, 1989. 64–65.

"Outside Prison." Pen and ink drawing. *Intrepid* 18–19 (Winter 1971): 35.

"Overlooking Bay Bridge, 6 am, 14 Hours After Birth of Nile." Corso reads this poem on *Baraka/Corso* [D].

"Owl." *Folio* 25.1 (Winter 1960): 37; printed in slightly different form in *Happy Birthday* 71.

"Paranoia in Crete." *Evergreen Review* 2.8 (Spring 1959): 58; *Happy Birthday* 51; *Mindfield* 75.

"Paris." *Gasoline* 48; *Selected* 28–29; *Gasoline/Vestal* 48.

"Paris—1960." *Two Cities* 4 (Summer 1960): 42–43; printed in slightly different form in *Elegiac* 87.

"Park." *Happy Birthday* 64–65; printed in substantially different form as "Italian Park"; printed with altered line break in *Selected* 43–44.

"A Pastoral Fetish." *Vestal* 31; *Gasoline/Vestal* 94; *Mindfield* 13.

Penguin Modern Poets 5. London: Penguin, 1963 [includes poems by Corso, Lawrence Ferlinghetti, and Allen Ginsberg].

"the people i used to like." *Unmuzzled Ox* 12.2 (1986): 20; printed in different form as "Canto Corso with Rings."

"Peter Orlovsky Allen Ginsberg Gregory Corso." Drawing. *Wings* 6.

"Phaestos Is a Village with 25 Families" [third poem of "Some Greek Writings"]. *Long* 69; Corso reads a slightly different form of this poem on *Burroughs and Corso* [D], *William Burroughs* [D], and *World's Great Poets* [D] [identified on latter as "Phaestos"].

"Piffle." *Ins and Outs* 4–5 (1980): 37; printed in different form as "Metaphor"; printed in different form as "For John Lennon."

"The Plight of Iacchus." *Long* 90.

"Poem" ["Down a lane in Heaven"]. *Fervent Valley* 4 (Summer 1974): n. pag.

"Poem" ["In the early morning"]. *Harvard Advocate* 138.1 (Autumn 1954): 22; printed as "In the Early Morning."

"Poem" ["I say unto you"]. Broadside. Englewood: Howling Dog, 1982; *Wings* 13–14; Corso reads a slightly different form of this poem on *Johnson/Bremser* [D]; printed in slightly different form as "Window"; early passage printed in slightly different form as beginning of "The Doubt of Lie"; early passage printed in slightly different form in "Gregorian RANT."

"A Poem Begun to See How Good My Head Still Is." *Mind Field* 34–41.

"Poem Jottings in the Early Morn." *Herald* 55–56; printed in substantially different form as ♀ [*Ankh*].

"Poems from Berlin." *Outsider* 1.2 (Summer 1962): 21–23 [Wilson (C73) cites the entry as extending through page 24]; printed with corrected possessive and misspelling of "like" in fourth poem in *Elegiac* 102–5.

Poems, Interview, Photographs. Published in Heaven Chapbook Series 30. Louisville: White Fields, 1994. N. pag.

"Poetry and Religion: An Open Letter" [prose]. *Aylesford Review* 5.3 (Summer 1963): 119–26; printed with original manuscript misspellings as "Dear Fathers."

"Poet Saturn." Drawing. *Saturn*; *Beatitude* 33 (1985): 4.

"Poet Saturn Writing Poem with Favorite Cat Looking On." Drawing. *Beatitude* 32 (1982): n. pag.

"Poets Hitchhiking on the Highway." *Coastlines* 2.3 (#7) (Spring/Summer 1957): 27; *Evergreen Review* 1.3 (Winter 1957): 79; *Happy Birthday* 28; *Mindfield* 60; Corso reads a slightly different form of this poem in the video *Beat Legends* [F].

Poets (Old and Beat). Watercolor painting. Exhibited at Research Conference on the Beat Generation, New York University School of Education, May 1994.

"Poet Talking to Himself in the Mirror." *Mind Field* 24–26; printed in slightly different form and expanded in *Mindfield* 236–37.

"Police." *Big Table* 1.1 (Spring 1959): 148–52; printed in different form in *Happy Birthday* 86–89.

"The Poor Bustard." *i.e.* [*Cambridge Review*] 1.5 (Mar. 1956): 63–64; *Elegiac* 78–79 [listed in Table of Contents as "The Pure Bastard"].

"A Portfolio of Drawings." Drawings. *Unmuzzled Ox* 2.1–2 (1973): n. pag.; reproduced in slightly different form in "A Portfolio of Drawings & Photographs." *Unmuzzled Ox* 6.2 (#22) (Winter 1981): 79–94.

Portrait of Allen Ginsberg and Gregory Corso. Drawing. *Brown Daily Herald Supplement* 12 Nov. 1962: front cover.

"Portrait of Kerouac." Reproduction of acrylic painting. *Lips* 6 (1983): 15.

"Portrait of Laura [Boss]." Reproduction of acrylic painting. *Lips* 6 (1983): 17.

"Portrait of Robert LaVigne." Ink drawing [13 Sept. 1956]. "Portfolio of Drawings"; "Portfolio of Drawings & Photographs" 86; *Beat Culture and the New America: 1950–1965.* By Lisa Phillips. New York: Whitney Museum, 1995. 48; treated in Masheck 12–13.

"Post-script from Gregory Corso:—Note for my contribution to the Cut-Up System" [prose]. *Minutes* 63.

"Pot." *Schrif-Taal* [Amsterdam] 50 (1961): n. pag.; *Elegiac* 76; printed in substantially different form as reproduction of manuscript in Fred W. McDarrah and Gloria S. McDarrah, *Beat Generation: Glory Days in Greenwich Village* (New York: Schirmer, 1996), 210, with dedication "for Bill Barker who suggested the poem."

"Power." *Big Table* 1.1 (Spring 1959): 138–44; excerpted in different form by Ginsberg in "Introduction," *Gasoline* 8–9; printed in slightly different form in *Happy Birthday* 75–80; printed in slightly different form in *Mindfield* 87–92.

"PPS Haiku." *Mind Field* 9.

"The Prognosticator of 64999." *Herald* 19.

"Proximity." *Herald* 26; *Wings* back cover; *Mindfield* 182; Corso reads this poem in the video *Beat Legends* [F] twice in separate readings; printed in slightly different form as section of "Dear Villon, Dear Milarepa."

"P.S. 42." *Long* 85–87.

"PS Haiku." *Mind Field* 8.

A Pulp Magazine for the Dead Generation. With Henk Marsman. Paris: Dead Language, 1959, prints in slightly different form four poems (mistakenly identified as "five poems") from *Vestal*: "In My Beautiful . . . and Things," "In the

Tunnel-Bone of Cambridge," "Cambridge, First Impressions," and "Dementia in an African Apartment House."

"Puma in Chapultepec Zoo." *Gasoline* 26; *Selected* 21; *Gasoline/Vestal* 26; *Mindfield* 27; Corso reads this poem on *Burroughs and Corso* [D], *William Burroughs* [D], and in the video *Beat Legends* [F].

"Purple Subway Ride (based on the works of Takis)." *Magnetic Sculpture*. By Takis. New York: Howard Wise Gallery, 1967. N. pag.

"Quick Egyptics." Drawing. "Portfolio of Drawings"; "Portfolio of Drawings & Photographs" 138.

"A Race of Sound." *Long* 73; *Mindfield* 114.

"Random Writings, Fiesole and Geneva 1960." *3 Arts Quarterly* 3 (Autumn 1960): 16–18; sections printed in different form as "3," "Thought," and "European Thoughts—1959."

Rarely, Rarely, Comest Thou Spirit of Delight, Keats and Shelley 1980. Oil painting on canvas. Exhibited at Research Conference on the Beat Generation, New York University School of Education, May 1994; reproduced in black and white in *Beat Art: Visual Works by and about the Beat Generation*. By Edward Adler and Bernard Mindich. New York: New York U School of Education, 1994. 12.

"Reading about Nicaraguan & Mid East Wars." *New Departures* 12 (1980): 20; printed in substantially different form as fifth entry in "A Small Notebook" 18 and as #9 in "Eleven Times a Poem"; printed in substantially different form in Michael Andre's interview with Corso 148; printed in substantially different form as "Daydream."

"The Rebel." Drawing. *Poets at Le Metro* 3 (1963): n. pag.; untitled in *New Departures* 4 (1962): 59; variation of this drawing appears as panel in *Unmuzzled Ox* 6.2 (#22) (Winter 1981): front cover and in "5oems & drawings of birds & cats" 114–15.

"Red fire rose blood scream crash sun bloom splash" [among "Things to Cut-Up"]. *Minutes* 56.

"Reflection." *Selected* 55–56; printed without last four lines in *Mindfield* 218 [the last four lines appear alone on p. 56 of the original source].

"Reflection in a Green Arena." *Long* 28–29; *Penguin* 28–29; first three lines of third stanza printed in same form as section 3 of "Three Loves"; Corso reads a different form of first half of this poem [identified as "Reflections in a Green Arena"] on *World's Great Poets* [D].

"Regarding America Going or Being Nuts." *Argonaut* 138.4214 ns #3 (Spring 1994): 82.

"Rembrandt—Self-Portrait." *Big Table* 4 (Spring 1960): 86; *Selected* 60; *Mindfield* 209.

"Reply From" [prose]. With Allen Ginsberg and Peter Orlovsky. *Wagner Literary Magazine* [formerly *Nimbus*] (Spring 1959): 30–31 [according to Wilson

(C23), written *in toto* by Corso]; *Beat Literature*. By Gregor Roy. Monarch
Notes and Study Guide 809–4. New York: Monarch, 1966. 117–18 [without
salutation].

"Requiem for 'Bird' Parker." *i.e.* [*Cambridge Review*] 1.3 (Spring 1955): 104–6;
printed in slightly different form as "Requiem for 'Bird' Parker: Second Ver-
sion" in *Vestal* 22–24 [listed in Contents as "Requiem for 'Bird' Parker, Musi-
cian," under which title printed in *Gasoline/Vestal* 82–86]; printed in slightly
different form in *Intrepid* 4 (Dec. 1964): n. pag.; printed in slightly different
form in Mindfield 8–11.

"Return." *Herald* 8–10; ninth stanza printed in different form as second poem in
"Earth Egg"; concluding lines printed in same form as conclusion of "Getting
to the Poem."

Review of *Doctor Sax* [prose]. By Jack Kerouac. *Kulchur* 3 (1961): 96–98.

"The Runaway Girl." *Vestal* 29; *Gasoline/Vestal* 91.

"The Sacré-Coeur Café." *Happy Birthday* 66; *Mindfield* 85; printed in different
form in *Selected* 44–45.

"Saint Francis." *Long* 36–40.

"Saturnal Ball." Drawing. *Beatitude* 32 (1982): n. pag.

"Saturn and Family." Drawing. *Saturn*.

"Saturn at the Guitar." Drawing. *Saturn*.

The Saturn Family. Charleston: Parchment Gallery, 1981, folio of six reproduced
line drawings ("Herman Saturn," "Poet Saturn," "Child Saturn's Flower Is Up,"
"Saturn at the Guitar," "The Sorrow of Mr. & Mrs. Saturn," and "Saturn and
Family") by Corso, in celebration of Corso's art and the achievements of Voy-
ager I's exploration among the stars. N. pag.

"Satyr's Chant." *Grecourt Review* 11.3 (Apr. 1959): 178; printed with an altered
spelling in *Happy Birthday* 73.

"The Sausages." *Vestal* 31; *Gasoline/Vestal* 95.

"The Saving Quality." *Selected* 56; printed in different form in *Long* 59 and *Mind-
field* 110; Corso reads the latter form of this poem in the video *Beat Legends* [F].

"Sea Chanty." *Vestal* 7; *Gasoline/Vestal* 64; first six lines printed under this title in
Selected 11; printed in different form in *Mindfield* 5; Corso reads a slightly dif-
ferent form of the first stanza on *Burroughs and Corso* [D]; Corso reads a slightly
different form of the entire poem in the video *Gang of Souls* [F] and the
Mindfield form of the poem in the video *Beat Legends* [F].

"Seaspin." *Happy Birthday* 13; *Selected* 32; *Penguin* 14; *Mindfield* 50.

"Second Night in N. Y. C. after 3 Years." *Long* 91; *Mindfield* 119 [Table of Con-
tents identifies title as "The Second Night in NYC After 3 Years"]; printed in
slightly different form in *Penguin* 38; Corso reads the *Penguin* form on *Will-
iam Burroughs* [D], in the video *Beat Legends* [F], and as "Second Night in
N.Y.C. after 2 Years" on *Burroughs and Corso* [D].

"Seed Journey." *Selected* 53; printed in different form in *Long* 59; printed in different form in *The Beat Journey*. Ed. Arthur and Kit Knight. *the unspeakable visions of the individual* 8. California, PA: the unspeakable visions of the individual, 1978. 175; printed in slightly different form in *Mindfield* 110; Corso reads a slightly different form of the *Long* version on *William Burroughs* [D]; Corso reads the *Beat Journey* form on *Burroughs and Corso* [D]; Corso reads the *Mindfield* form in the video *Beat Legends* [F] [identified on tape and box as "Sea Journey"].

Selected Poems. London: Eyre, 1962 [Wilson (A9) points out that the last section cites 29 poems from *Long*, but that *Long* was published after *Selected* (5); thus, despite the Contents of *Selected*, these poems are not in *Long*: "A Bed's Lament," "Direction Sign in London Zoo," "St Tropez Early Morning," "Berlin Zoo—2," "Vermeer," "Reflection," "Upon Leaving France," "Something There Is," "How One Looks At It," "Rembrandt—Self-Portrait," "Commission Unfulfilled," and "Apples"].

Self-portrait. Drawing. *Broadshirt Poetry Magazine* 1 (1994): front of t-shirt.

Self-portrait. Drawing. *Brown Daily Herald Supplement* 12 Nov. 1962: 5.

Self-portrait. Drawing. *Mindfield* vi.

"Self-portrait." Ink drawing. "Portfolio of Drawings"; "Portfolio of Drawings & Photographs" 85; *Beat Culture and the New America 1950–1965*. By Lisa Phillips. New York: Whitney Museum, 1995. 48.

Self-Portrait. Signed drawing dated 1 May 1974 [with inscription: "The Spirit is a charitable thief—"]. *Self-Portrait: Book People Picture Themselves*. Ed. Burt Britton. New York: Random, 1976. 93.

Self Portrait 1961. Drawing. Catalog 17. New York: Carr, 1963. Front cover.

"A Self-portrait Originally in Color." Painting. "Portfolio of Drawings"; without title in "Portfolio of Drawings & Photographs" 84.

"The Senile Genius." *Long* 52–53.

"The Shakedown." *Vestal* 11; *Gasoline/Vestal* 68; printed with last line split into two in *Mademoiselle* Feb. 1957: 191.

"She Doesn't Know He Thinks He's God." *Happy Birthday* 36; printed in slightly different form in *Mindfield* 70.

Shelley. Drawing. *Buffalo Stamps* 3/4 (1972): front cover.

Shelley. Drawing [1971]. "Portfolio of Drawings"; "Portfolio of Drawings & Photographs" 94.

"Shelley." Drawing. *Wings* 11.

Shelley into Ventures. Unpublished manuscript cited by Raffaele Cocchi, "Gregory Corso: Poetic Vision and Memory as a Child of Italian Origin on the Streets and Roads of Omerica [sic]," *Rivisti di studi anglo-americani* 3.4–5 (1984–1985): 344, note 4.

"Shots of Verse." *Long Shot* 16 (1994): 6–9.

"6 Poems Untitled." *Intrepid Anthology: A Decade & Then Some, Contemporary Literature—1976.* Ed. Allen DeLoach. *Intrepid* 25–35. Buffalo: Intrepid, 1976. 47.

"A Small Notebook." *Fubbalo* 1.2 (Summer 1965): 17–18; fifth entry printed variably in substantially different form as #9 in "Eleven Times a Poem," in interview with Michael Andre 148, as "Reading about Nicaraguan & Mid East Wars," and as "Daydream"; sixth entry printed in substantially different form as "A 2-Pathed Omen" and #6 of "Eleven Times a Poem."

"The Sniper's Lament." *Vestal* 18; *Gasoline/Vestal* 77.

"Socratic Poetry Rap, August 3, 1977 Naropa Institute." Discussion with students. *Rocky Ledge* 4 (Feb./Mar. 1980): 4–11.

"Some Greek Writings" [three poems: "In a Way," "When President Eisenhower," and "Phaestos Is a Village with 25 Families"]. *Long* 68–69; *Mindfield* 112–13; Corso reads a slightly different form of the third poem on *Burroughs and Corso* [D] and *World's Great Poets* [D].

"Some Moroccan Writings." *Long* 64–65; printed in different form as "Moroccan Writings."

"Some of My Beginning—and What I Feel Right Now" [prose]. *Magazine* 2 (1965): 36–41; Portree, Isle of Skye, Scotland: Aquila, 1982; printed in substantially different form in *Poets on Poetry*. Ed. Howard Nemerov. New York: Basic, 1966. 172–81.

"Something There Is." *Selected* 56–57.

"Song." *Vestal* 8; *Gasoline/Vestal* 65; *Mindfield* 6.

"Song of the Feast." *A New Folder: American Poems and Drawings*. Ed. Daisy Aldan. New York: Folder, 1959. 27.

"Sons of Your In" [cut-up of Rimbaud's "To A Reason"]. With William Burroughs. *Locus Solus* 2 (Summer 1961): 150–51; *Minutes* 24–25.

"The Sorrow of Mr. & Mrs. Saturn." Drawing. *Saturn.*

"The Sorrow of Saturn." Drawing. "Portfolio of Drawings"; "Portfolio of Drawings & Photographs" 88.

"Sorrow of Saturn." Drawing. *Wings* 12.

"Soul." *Long 80.*

"Sources." Ed. Douglas Calhoun. Post-reading comments to audience at State University College at Cortland, New Jersey, Spring 1971. *Athanor* 5 (Winter 1973): 1–6.

"Spirit." *Herald* 41; *Mindfield* 190; printed in different form as fourth poem in "5oems & drawings of birds & cats" 101; Corso reads this poem in the video *Beat Legends* [F]; Corso reads a slightly different form in the video *Gang of Souls* [F].

"Spontaneous Piece on the '50's in America." *Minutes* 32.

"Spontaneous Poem after Having Seen the Metropolitan Museum." *Happy Birthday* 25–27.

"Spontaneous Requiem." *Ramparts* 8 (Mar. 1970): 23–25; expanded as "Elegiac Feelings American."

"A Spontaneous Requiem for the American Indian." *Yūgen* 2 (1958): 2+; printed in slightly different form as "Spontaneous Requiem for the American Indian" in *Elegiac* 13–17 and *Mindfield* 135–39.

"Spooksville." *Mind Field* 28–30.

"Spring's Melodious Herald." *Grecourt Review* 11.3 (Apr. 1959): 179; *Happy Birthday* 74; *A New Directions Reader*. Ed. Hayden Carruth and J. Laughlin. New York: New Directions, 1964. 207–8.

"Standing on a Streetcorner: A Little Play" [with Corso drawings]. *Evergreen Review* 6.23 (Mar./Apr. 1962): 63–78; *The Evergreen Review Reader: A Ten-Year Anthology*. Ed. Barney Rosset. N.p.: Castle, 1968. 456–63; a 1953 manuscript of this work in the Department of Special Collections of the Kenneth Spencer Research Library, University of Kansas at Lawrence, indicates that it was once titled "Power".

"Stars." *Long* 55; *Mindfield* 109.

Statement [prose]. *Input* 1.3 (Sept. 1964): front cover.

"St. Lukes, Service for Thomas." *Vestal* 32; *Selected* 13–14; *Gasoline/Vestal* 96; printed as "St. Luke's, Service for Thomas" in *Mindfield* 14.

"St Tropez Early Morning." *Selected* 54; *Mindfield* 214.

Stylized Figure (Skull or Mask). Ink drawing in five colors. "Portfolio of Drawings"; "Portfolio of Drawings & Photographs" 81; treated in Masheck 15.

"Suburbia Mad Song." *Long* 11.

"Sun" [with subtitle "(*Automatic Poem*)"]. *Gasoline* 25–26; printed in different form in *Selected* 21–22; printed in slightly different form in *Gasoline/Vestal* 25–26 and *Mindfield* 26; Corso reads this poem on *Howls* [D].

"Sunrise." *Unmuzzled Ox* 6.2 (#22) (Winter 1981): 118; printed in substantially different form as "I am rich"; printed in slightly different form in *Herald* 6 and *Mindfield* 166 [with misspelling of "thereon" in latter volume]; Corso reads a slightly different form of the latter version in *Beat Legends* [F].

"Sunset." *Unmuzzled Ox* 6.2 (#22) (Winter 1981): 119; *Mindfield* 168; printed with a change of "sura" to "sutra" in *Herald* 7; Corso reads this poem in the video *Beat Legends* [F].

"Sura." *The Beat Scene*. Ed. Elias Wilentz. New York: Corinth, 1960. 175; printed in slightly different form in *Selected* 48–49, which is printed in the same form as "For Hope Savage"; printed in slightly different form in *Long* 42–43.

Symposium on Kerouac [1973]. With others. *Soundings—East* [formerly *Gone Soft*] 2.2 (Fall/Winter 1979): 1–89.

"Take Sophia's mom." Corso reads this poem on *Baraka/Corso* [D].

"Ten Angry Men" [prose]. With Allen Ginsberg. *Esquire* June 1986: 260–62.

10 Times a Poem [holograph poem sequence with drawings, identified by Corso on title page as "Collected at random from 2 suitcases filled with poems—the gathering of 5 years"]. New York: Poets, 1967. N. pag.; printed in substantially different form as "Eleven Times a Poem."

"That Little Black Door on the Left" [play]. *Pardon Me, Sir, But Is My Eye Hurting Your Elbow?* Produced by Bob Booker and George Foster. New York: Gies, 1968. 159–63.

"There are enough stars" [among "Haiku"]. *Mind Field* 21.

"There Can Be No Other Apple for Me." *Long* 74; printed in different form as "Apples."

"There is no god." *Unmuzzled Ox* 12.2 (1986): 22; printed in slightly different form as "Canto with Typo"; printed in different form as "Hi."

There Is Still Time to Run Back through Life and Expiate All That's Been Sadly Done. Book title projected for Feb. 1965 in New Directions Books (Fall/Winter 1964–65); variant of this title appears as lines in "Columbia U Poesy Reading—1975" 5.

"There's a chinaman in my dreams." Drawing. *Mindfield* 221.

"They." *Long* 83; *Mindfield* 117; Corso reads a slightly different form of this poem on *William Burroughs* [D].

"Things to Cut-Up, Collected by Gregory Corso." *Minutes* 55–58.

"Thinking China." *Herald* 18.

"The Thin Thin Line." *Long* 56–57.

"30th Year Dream." *Residu* 2 (Spring 1966): 20; printed with typographical errors in *American Poetry Review* 18.6 (Nov./Dec. 1989): 56 and *Mindfield* 220 [the poem treats an incident Corso recounts in "Poetry and Religion: An Open Letter" 121, "Dear Fathers" 9, and Letter to William S. Burroughs 160]; Corso reads an abridged form in the video *Beat Legends* [F].

"This Is America." *Vestal* 19; *Gasoline/Vestal* 78–79.

"This Was My Meal." *Evergreen Review* 1.3 (Winter 1957): 78; printed in different form in *Gasoline* 43, *Selected* 26–27, *Gasoline/Vestal* 43, and *Mindfield* 39 [corrected spelling of "Dessert" in last three volumes; "upsidedown" split into two words in last volume].

"Thought." *Long* 46; printed in slightly different form as middle stanza of "3"; printed in different form as first poem in "Random Writings, Fiesole and Geneva 1960."

"Thoughts on a Japanese Movie." *Vestal* 2; *Gasoline/Vestal* 56.

"A Thousand Words" [prose]. *Photographs.* By Allen Ginsberg. Altadeena, CA: Twelvetrees, 1990. N. pag.

"Three." *Gasoline* 39; *Tempo Presente* 6.8 (Aug. 1961): n. pag.; *Gasoline/Vestal* 39; *Mindfield* 36.

"3." *Selected* 55; second and third stanzas printed in different form as first and sixth poems in "Random Writings, Fiesole and Geneva 1960"; second stanza printed in slightly different form as "Thought"; printed in different form in *Mindfield* 217.

"Three Loves." *Long* 14; section 3 printed as first three lines of third stanza of "Reflection in a Green Arena."

"3 Saturnal Graces." Drawing. *Beatitude* 32 (1982): n. pag.

"The Times of the Watches" [prose]. *Cavalier* Dec. 1964: 36–37+.

"To a Downfallen Rose." *Gasoline* 37–38; *Gasoline/Vestal* 37–38.

"To Die Laughing(?)." *Long* 58.

"To H. S." *Long* 30.

"Train Wreck." *Olympia* 4 (1963): 24–25; printed in slightly different form in *Elegiac* 106–8.

"Transformation & Escape." *Happy Birthday* 19–21; printed with change of "on" to "in" in third line from end in *Mindfield* 55–57.

"Triptych: Friend, Work, World." *The Hasty Papers: A One-Shot Review* (1960): 7; printed with corrected spelling of "vengeance" in *Elegiac* 91–93; first poem printed in slightly different form as "Friend"; passages from second poem printed in different form in "Mr. Moneybag's Lament."

"Truth is eternity." *New Departures* 7–8 10–11 (1975): 145; printed in section 4 of "Lines Between Past & Future."

"The Turning Tide." *10 Times a Poem* [holograph]; printed in different form as #4 in "Eleven Times a Poem."

"12 Ash St. Place." *Vestal* 25; *Gasoline/Vestal* 87; printed in slightly different form in *Mindfield* 12.

Two drawings. *Unmuzzled Ox* 2.3 (1974): 74–75.

"Two Drawings for Barney [Rosset]." *Review of Contemporary Fiction* 10.3 (Fall 1990): 93–94.

"A 2-Pathed Omen." *10 Times a Poem* [holograph]; printed in substantially different form as sixth entry in "A Small Notebook"; printed in substantially different form as #6 in "Eleven Times a Poem."

"Two Weather Vanes." *Folio* 25.1 (Winter 1960): 37; printed in slightly different form in *Kulchur* 2 (1960): 34 [Wilson (C36) mistakenly cites this issue as #3; in line 5 "fags" is apparently a misprint for "flags"] and *Elegiac* 82 ["fags" is here emended to "fogs"].

"2 Weird Happenings in Haarlem." *Gasoline* 19; printed in slightly different form in *Selected* 17; printed in slightly different form in *Gasoline/Vestal* 18.

"Uccello." *Gasoline* 29; *Gasoline/Vestal* 29; *Mindfield* 29; printed with altered line endings in *Selected* 23–24; printed as broadside with altered spacing, reproduction of *La Batalla de Sant Roma*, and Spanish and Catalan translations by Agusti Barta (Poetry Pamphlet 14). Terrassa, Sp.: Mirall de Glaç, 1987; Corso reads this poem on *William Burroughs* [D].

"UFO on Rooftops." Drawing. *Intrepid Anthology: A Decade & Then Some; Contemporary Literature—1976*. Ed. Allen DeLoach. *Intrepid* 25–35. Buffalo: Intrepid, 1976. 49.

"Under Peyote." *Happy Birthday* 18; *Mindfield* 54.

Untitled. Ink painting on paper. Poem entitled "A Complaint By a City Dweller" exhibited at Research Conference on the Beat Generation, New York University School of Education, May 1994.

Untitled [c. 1962]. Collage of color reproductions of steepled architecture against starred sky, exhibited at Beat Culture and the New America: 1950–1965, Walker Art Center, Minneapolis, Summer 1996.

Untitled drawing. *New Departures* 4 (1962): 59; printed as "The Rebel," *Poets at Le Metro* 3 (1963): n. pag.; printed in slightly different form as panel in *Unmuzzled Ox* 6.2 (#22) (Winter 1981): front cover and in "5oems & drawings of birds & cats" 114–15.

Untitled drawing [appears to be illustration of "Alchemy," but not opposite this poem]. *Mindfield* 185.

Untitled drawing [Egyptian motif; identified as "A sketch drawn by Gregory Corso from one of his working notebooks, 1980" and as "a pilfered sketch" in Contents]. *Catching Up with Kerouac: Getting Boulder on the Road*. Ed. V. J. Eaton. *The Literary Denim: A Journal of Beat Literature*. Phoenix: Literary Denim, 1984. 100.

Untitled drawing [embracing couple]. "Portfolio of Drawings"; "Portfolio of Drawings & Photographs" 89.

Untitled drawing [5 strip panels]. *Unmuzzled Ox* 6.2 (#22) (Winter 1981): front cover; "5oems & drawings of birds & cats"; one panel printed in different form as untitled drawing that later appeared as "The Rebel."

Untitled drawing [human figure]. *The Beat Book*. Ed. Arthur Winfield Knight and Glee Knight. *the unspeakable visions of the individual* 4. California, PA: the unspeakable visions of the individual, 1974. 33.

Untitled drawing [pen and ink]. Musicians: guitarist, bassist, and drummer identified on drum as the ♀ (*Ankh*) Bros. *Intrepid* 18–19 (Winter 1971): 34.

Untitled drawing [processional featuring Messenger Spirit and Orpheus]. *The Stiffest of the Corpse: An Exquisite Corpse Reader*. Ed. Andrei Codrescu. San Francisco: City Lights, 1989. 64–65.

Untitled drawing [Saturn family with flowers, with child Saturn's flower the only one not drooping]. "Portfolio of Drawings"; "Portfolio of Drawings & Photographs" 83.

Untitled drawing [surreal family living-room scene]. "Portfolio of Drawings"; "Portfolio of Drawings & Photographs" 82.

Untitled drawing [variety of animals with trumpeting angel]. "Portfolio of Drawings"; "Portfolio of Drawings & Photographs" 80.

Untitled drawing [Villon and Milarepa]. "Portfolio of Drawings"; "Portfolio of Drawings & Photographs" 102 [appears opposite the first page of "Dear Villon, Dear Milarepa"].

Untitled poem ["At Allen Ginsberg's sukhavati ceremony, New York Shambhala Center, April 7, 1997"]. *Shambhala Sun* July 1997: 40.

Untitled poem ["Snapped in the past"]. *Angels, Anarchists & Gods.* By Christopher Felver. Baton Rouge: Louisiana State UP, 1996. 205.

Untitled statement [prose in holograph]. *The Poet Exposed.* Ed. Chris Felver. New York: Van Der Marck, 1986. 108.

Untitled statement [prose reminiscence on Burroughs]. *Rolling Stone* 18 Sept. 1997: 55.

Untitled statement [prose reminiscence on Ginsberg]. *Rolling Stone* 29 May 1997: 40+.

"Upon Leaving France." *Selected* 56.

"Upon My Refusal to Herald Cuba." *Long* 57.

"The Vanity of the Bright Young Men." *Residu* 2 (Spring 1966): 19–20.

"Variations on a Generation" [prose]. *Gemini* 2.6 (Spring 1959): 47–51 [Wilson (C33) omits date and page numbers]; *A Casebook on the Beat.* Ed. Thomas Parkinson. New York: Crowell, 1961. 88–97.

"Venice 1958—." *Beat Coast East: An Anthology of Rebellion.* Ed. Stanley Fisher. New York: Excelsior, 1960. 27; printed in slightly different form as section of "Food" 35.

"Vermeer." *Selected* 55; *Mindfield* 216.

"Verse." *Adventures in Poetry* 12 (Summer 1975): n. pag.; printed in slightly different form as last two stanzas of "Who I Am"; printed in slightly different form in *Herald* 25.

"The Vestal Lady on Brattle." *Vestal* 1; *Selected* 9; *Gasoline/Vestal* 55.

The Vestal Lady on Brattle and Other Poems. Cambridge: Brukenfeld, 1955; facsimile edition San Francisco: City Lights, 1969; printed in slightly different form and with altered pagination bound with *Gasoline* San Francisco: City Lights, [1976].

"Vision Epizootic." *Vestal* 12 [listed in contents as "Vision Epizootics"]; as "Vision Epizootics" in *Gasoline/Vestal* 69–70.

"Vision of Rotterdam." *Gasoline* 17–18; printed in slightly different form in *Selected* 16–17; printed with corrected spellings in *Gasoline/Vestal* 16–17; Corso reads this poem on *Howls* [D].

"Walk." *Big Table* 4 (Spring 1960): 88; *Selected* 59–60; printed in different form in *Long* 15.

"Walrus-Bird." Drawing. *Intrepid Anthology: A Decade & Then Some; Contemporary Literature—1976*. Ed. Allen DeLoach. *Intrepid* 25–35. Buffalo: Intrepid, 1976. 50.

"War-Babies War." *Zeitgeist* 1.3 (Apr. 1966): 15–16.

"War of birds & cats." Drawing. *Wings* 34.

"Was Papa Haydn Born April 1st?" *New Directions in Prose and Poetry 50*. Ed. J. Laughlin, Peter Glassgold, and Griselda Ohannessian. New York: New Directions, 1986. 236.

"Waterchew!" *Happy Birthday* 27.

Way Out: A Poem in Discord. Starstreams Poetry Series Number 1. Kathmandu, Nepal: Bardo Matrix, 1974. N. pag.; stanza on sixth page printed in different form as "Writ When I Found Out His Was an Unmarked Grave" and printed in different form as passage in "German Visitations of Music Men" 31; line 3 printed in same form as last line of penultimate stanza of "Yaaaah:" [characters from *Way Out* also appear in "Yaaaah:"].

"were we to reach a galaxy" [among "Haiku"]. *Mind Field* 20.

"What Chance Command?" *Long* 61.

"What the Child Sees." *Herald* 12; *Mindfield* 171.

"When a Boy . . ." *Herald* 33; *Mindfield* 186 [last two lines repeat an incident from "The Geometric Poem" 61]; Corso reads this poem in the video *Beat Legends* [F] [identified on tape and box as "When a Boy I Monitored the Stairs"].

"When Better Women Are Made Harvard Men Will Make Them Banner" [Wilson (C10) identifies a portion of "Open the Gate" beginning with this line as a separate poem].

"When I Think To Refrain." *Long* 13.

"When I Was Five I Saw a Dying Indian" [prose]. *Evergreen Review* 11.48 (Aug. 1967): 29–30+; Corso treats incidents from this autobiographical essay in his poems "The occurence is in the remembrance," "Earliest Memory," and "Youthful Religious Experiences."

"When President Eisenhower"; second poem in "Some Greek Writings" 68.

"When We All . . ." *Herald* 50; *Mindfield* 201.

Who am I—Who I am [see his interview with Gavin Selerie 32, where Corso cites this as a lost manuscript volume].

"Who I Am." *Renegade: The West Coast Review of Unlimited American Literature and Art* (1978): 28–29; *Bombay Gin* 6 (Summer 1978/Spring 1979): 37–38;

several lines printed in different form in "The Doubt of Truth"; last two stanzas printed in slightly different form in "Verse."

"The Whole Mess . . . Almost." *New Departures* 12 [1980?]: 19; printed in substantially different form in *Herald* 48–49 and *Mindfield* 199–200; Corso reads the latter form of this poem in the video *Beat Legends* [F] [identified on tape and box as "The Whole Mess, Almost"] and a slightly different form of that version of the poem again in the same video, but at a different reading; Corso reads a slightly different form of lines 11–14 of the latter version in the video *Gang of Souls* [F].

William Burroughs with Cat. Watercolor painting. Exhibited at Research Conference on the Beat Generation, New York University School of Education, May 1994; on the painting Corso titles this piece *Juna negat sibi nata, nihil How.*

William Burroughs with Cat. Watercolor painting. Exhibited at Research Conference on the Beat Generation, New York University School of Education, May 1994; on the painting Corso titles this piece *Portrait of William S. Burroughs: Nude of a Good-Hearted Sage.*

"Window." *Mindfield* 225–27; printed in slightly different form as "Poem" ["I say unto you"]; early passage printed in different form in "The Doubt of Lie" and "Gregorian RANT."

"The winds of Babylon" [holograph, with untitled drawings by the author, one of which he identifies elsewhere as an Ibis Stick]. *War Poems.* Ed. Diane di Prima. New York: Poets, 1968. 1.

Wings, Wands, Windows. Ashes Chapbook 2. Englewood: Howling Dog, 1982.

"Wisdom." *Unmuzzled Ox* 6.2 (#22) (Winter 1981): 122; printed in different form as "I feel there is an inherent ignorance in me"; *Herald* 12; *Mindfield* 171.

"The Wise Fuckers." *Bombay Gin* 7 (Summer/Fall 1979): 43; printed in substantially different form as "The Leaky Lifeboat Boys."

"With Proxima Centuri harbor." *Bombay Gin* [#2?] (Winter/Spring 1977): 53–54.

"Women." Manuscript poem read by Corso as part of "Having Fun . . ." on *Johnson/Bremser* [D] and in the video *West Coast* [F].

"The Wreck of the Nordling." *Vestal* 26; *Selected* 13; *Gasoline/Vestal* 88; printed without punctuation in *Mindfield* 13; Corso reads this poem in the video *Beat Legends* [F].

Writings from Unmuzzled Ox Magazine; this volume reproduces all the materials that appeared in *Unmuzzled Ox* 22 (Winter 1981), including the Corso poems and drawings and the interview of Corso by Michael Andre.

"Writings in the Early Morn and Early Night in Calabria." *Mind Field* 15–16.

"Writ in Horace Greeley Square." *Long* 84–85; printed with misprint of "drove" for "dove" in *Penguin* 36–37.

"Writ on the Eve of My 32nd Birthday." *Long* 92–93; *Penguin* 39–40 [identified in Contents as beginning on page 32]; *Mindfield* 120–21; Corso reads a slightly different form of this poem in the video *Beat Legends* [F].

"Writ on the Steps of Puerto Rican Harlem." *Long* 77–78; *Penguin* 34–35; *Mindfield* 115–16.

"Written at a Rock Star's Gravesite, in Spontaneity." Corso reads this poem on *Baraka/Corso* [D].

"Written in Nostalgia for Paris." *Happy Birthday* 68; *Selected* 45–46; printed with omission of article "a" in penultimate line in *Penguin* 20.

"Written While Watching Lenny Bruce Obscenity Trial." *East Side Review* 1.1 (Jan./Feb. 1966): 56–57 [identified in Contents as "Notes on Lenny Bruce Obscenity Trial"].

"Written While Watching the Yankees Play Detroit." *Happy Birthday* 47–48.

"Writ When I Found Out His Was an Unmarked Grave." *Long* 32; printed in slightly different form in *Way Out*; printed in slightly different form as last stanza of "German Visitations of Music Men" 31; *Mindfield* 104; Corso reads this poem as "Written When I Found Out His Was an Unmarked Grave" [cited on record label as "Written on Finding an Unmarked Grave"] on *World's Great Poets* [D].

"Yaaaah:." *Measure* 2 (Winter 1958): 42–43; last line of penultimate stanza printed as third line of *Way Out* [Yaaaah and the Ratface and Sweetface of this poem are characters in *Way Out*].

"You Came Last Season." *Vestal* 2; *Gasoline/Vestal* 57.

"Youthful Religious Experiences." *Four Poems*. New York: Paradox, 1981. N. pag.; printed in slightly different form in *Herald* 22–23 and *Mindfield* 179–80 [the poem treats a series of incidents Corso recounts in "When I Was Five I Saw a Dying Indian].

"You, Whose Mother's Lover Was Grass." *Vestal* 27; printed without period in line 14 in *Gasoline/Vestal* 89.

"Zizi's Lament." *Gasoline* 47; *Gasoline/Vestal* 47; *Mindfield* 47; Corso reads this poem in the video *Beat Legends* [F].

Notes

In *Desolate Angel: Jack Kerouac, the Beat Generation, and America*. New York: Random, 1979, Dennis McNally asserts that two articles that appeared with Kerouac's byline were actually written in collaboration with Corso, Ginsberg, and Orlovsky (268):

"The Roaming Beatniks." *Holiday* Mar. 1960: 60–61+; "The Vanishing American Hobo." *Holiday* Oct. 1959: 82+.

Whatever contributions the other writers may have made, Kerouac's prose style dominates. In "The Vanishing American Hero," reference is made twice to "gasoline, power, Army, or police" (112, 113), each noun a title of a Corso work.

The credit page of *Long Live Man* indicates that poetry from that volume earlier appeared in *Evergreen Review*, but I have not discovered there a source for any of those poems.

The credit page of *Elegiac Feelings American* indicates that poetry from that volume appeared in the Amsterdam publication *Quadrat-Prints*.

Steven Watson lists Corso among the contributors to the final issue (#7) of *The Black Mountain Review* ("Chronology" 254), but that issue contains no work by Corso.

Discography

Allen Ginsberg Lawrence Ferlinghetti Gregory Corso Andrei Voznesensky. LP. London: Lovebooks, 1965 [according to Wilson (F4), Corso reads "Marriage" and "Bomb" (6/15/65)].

Baraka/Corso Reading [4 August 1985]. Audiocassette. Naropa Summer Series. Boulder: Naropa, 1985 [Corso comments and reads "new poems" from the projected volume *The Golden Dot*: "Written at a Rock Star's Gravesite, in Spontaneity," "Overlooking Bay Bridge, 6 am, 14 Hours After Birth of Nile," "My Grandmother Was a Cavewoman," "For Mary Rogers," "Letter to Kerouac," "Family," "I never knew we existed in a hazardous time," "Take Sophia's mom," "The muse is my doppelganger," and "Fortune came to Society's rat"].

Blake's Greatest Hits. EP. By Allen Ginsberg. Kansas City: Blue Moon, 1982 [Corso accompanies Ginsberg on Blake's "Nurses Song," recorded 28 November 1979].

Burroughs and Corso Reading [11 June 1975]. Audiocassette. Naropa Institute Archives Project 003. Boulder: Naropa, 1975 [Corso reads "Sea Chanty," excerpt from "The Last Warmth of Arnold," "Amnesia in Memphis," "Puma in Chapultepec Zoo," "On the Walls of a Dull Furnished Room," "Italian Extravaganza," "Birthplace Revisited," "The Last Gangster," "The Mad Yak," "Friend," "Seed Journey," "A Difference of Zoos," "Man Entering the Sea, Tangier," excerpt from "Some Greek Writings," "Second Night in N. Y. C. after 3 Years," and unidentified poem "put together today from my notebook"— see "The Doubt of Lie" and "Lines Between Past & Future"].

Corso, Ferlinghetti, Voznesensky, & Others: The Lovebook Record. LP. New York: ESP, 1967 [cited on *The ESP Sampler*; this appears to be the same item as the above 1965 Lovebooks record].

Disconnected. LP. New York: Giorno Poetry Systems, 1974 [Corso reads "Marriage" (recorded 7 March 1973)].

The ESP Sampler. LP. New York: ESP, 1969 [Corso reads excerpt from "Bomb"].

Gatē: Two Evenings with Allen Ginsberg, Peter Orlovsky, Gregory Corso and Stephen Taylor. LP. Vol. 1. Munich: Loft, 1980 [Corso accompanies Ginsberg in performance].

Holy Soul Jelly Roll: Poems and Songs 1949–1993. CD. By Allen Ginsberg. 4 vols. Los Angeles: Rhino, 1994 [at the beginning and end of "Death to Van Gogh's Ear" on Vol. 1, Corso talks with Ginsberg].

Howls, Raps & Roars: Recordings from the San Francisco Poetry Renaissance. CD. Berkeley: Fantasy, 1993 [Disc 3 contains recordings of Corso's readings of "In the Fleeting Hand of Time," "Vision of Rotterdam," "The Last Warmth of Arnold," "Mexican Impressions," "Botticelli Spring," "Sun—A Spontaneous Poem," "Ode to Coit Tower," and "I Am 25"].

Johnson [Joyce]/Bremser [Ray]/Kerouac [Jan]/Corso/Orlovsky. Naropa Institute Archives 57 A and B. Audiocassette (2 tapes). Boulder: Naropa, 1982 [A: Corso comments and reads a manuscript poem "recently written" entitled "Having Fun with Myself at the Expense of Others Poem: Things in Life I Know Most Others Don't Know," "Poem" ["I say unto you"]; B: "All Survived," "Hi," "The Day after Humankind," excerpt from "Mexican Impressions," "Alchemy," and "I Met This Guy Who Died"].

Junge Amerikanische Lyrik. Munich: Carl Hanser, 1961 [this book anthology co-edited by Corso includes a 7" record, on one side of which Corso reads "Bomb"].

Pictures from the Gone World. LP. N.p.: Pesky Serpent, [1996] [Corso reads a passage from "Bomb" (from line 8 into line 13) on side 1].

Tenderness Junction. LP. By The Fugs. Burbank: Reprise, 1968 [Corso plays harmonium on the song "Hare Krishna"].

William Burroughs, William Burroughs, Jr., and Gregory Corso [July 1977]. Audiocassette. Naropa Institute Archives Project. Boulder: Naropa, 1991 [Corso comments and reads excerpts from "Mexican Impressions," "Puma in Chapultepec Zoo," "Uccello," "On the Walls of a Dull Furnished Room," "Italian Extravaganza," "Birthplace Revisited," excerpt from "Clown," "They," "An Early Dutch Scene," "Seed Journey," "Phaestos Is a Village with 25 Families," and "Second Night in N. Y. C. after 3 Years"].

The World's Great Poets, Vol. 1: America Today! Gregory Corso, Allen Ginsberg, Lawrence Ferlinghetti. LP. New York: CMS, 1971 [Corso reads "Man," "Reflection in a Green Arena," "Writ When I Found Out His Was an Unmarked Grave," and "Phaestos Is a Village with 25 Families"].

The World's Great Poets Reading at the Festival of Two Worlds, Spoleto, Italy—American Poets: Ginsberg, Berryman, Corso. LP. New York: Applause, 1968 [Corso's readings are the same as those on *World's Great Poets, Vol. 1*].

Filmography

Beat Legends: Gregory Corso [a medley of readings: April 1991 NYU; April 1989 NYU; 1978 Naropa Institute; April 1989 NYU; and April 1991 NYU]. Prod. Mitch Corber. New York: Thin Air, n.d. [Corso comments and reads "Flu Ramblings Sequence '91," "Greenwich Village Suicide," "Sea Chanty," "The Wreck of the Nordling," "Amnesia in Memphis," "Puma in Chapultepec Zoo," "Botticelli's Spring," "30th Year Dream," "Proximity," "When a Boy . . . ," "Getting to the Poem," "Spirit," "I Gave Away . . . ," "The Whole Mess . . . Almost"; "Last Night I Drove a Car," "The Mad Yak," "Hello," "Zizi's Lament," "Dementia in an African Apartment House," "Mortal Infliction," excerpt from "Bomb," "Poets Hitchhiking on the Highway," "Seed Journey," "The Saving Quality"; excerpt from "Friend," "Death Comes at Puberty"; "Nature's Gentleman," excerpt from "God? She's Black," "Second Night in N. Y. C. after 3 Years," "Writ on the Eve of My 32nd Birthday," "Proximity," "Many Have Fallen," "Sunrise," "Sunset," "I Met This Guy Who Died," "The Whole Mess . . . Almost," "Daydream"; and epilogue—the tape and its box misidentify a number of these titles and omit others; later printings of the videotape contain only the 1991 reading and edit the "Flu Ramblings" poem].

The Coney Island of Lawrence Ferlinghetti. Prod. Christopher Felver. New York: Mystic Fire, 1996 [Corso appears and comments briefly].

Couch. Prod. and dir. Andy Warhol. 1964 [Corso appears briefly in this silent, black-and-white film; Warhol ran the film at the Dom disco in New York City, but it was never released publicly].

Fried Shoes, Cooked Diamonds [1978]. Dir. by Costanza Allione. New York: Mystic Fire, 1980 [Corso comments and reads an excerpt from "Bomb"].

Gang of Souls. Prod. and dir. by Maria Beatty. Giorno Video Pak 4. New York: Giorno, 1990 [Corso comments and reads excerpt from "The Whole Mess . . . Almost," "Sea Chanty," excerpt from "Detective Frump's Spontaneous & Reflective Testament," excerpt from "Bomb," and "Spirit"].

The Godfather, Part III. Dir. and prod. Francis Ford Coppola. Paramount, 1990 [Corso has a bit role as an "unruly stockholder"].

Gregory Corso Reads from the U.S. Constitution and Bill of Rights. Prod. and dir. James Rasin and Jerry Poynton. 1992.

The Life and Times of Allen Ginsberg. Prod. Jerry Aronson. New York: First Run, 1993 [Corso appears sporadically but offers no comments].

The NY Beat Generation Show. Vol. 1. History and Overview: The Censorship Years. Prod. Mitch Corber. New York: Thin Air, 1994 [Corso reads "Birthplace Revisited" during the May 1994 Beat Generation Conference at New York University].

The NY Beat Generation Show. Vol. 3. Music Moves the Spirit. Prod. Mitch Corber. New York: Thin Air, 1995 ["Beat Coda" repeats from Vol. 1 Corso's reading of "Birthplace Revisited"].

Pull My Daisy. Dir. and prod. Robert Frank and Alfred Leslie. G-String Productions. New York, 1959 [based on third act of Kerouac's unpublished play "The Beat Generation"; Corso plays the character modeled on Kerouac himself].

This Song for Jack. Prod. Robert Frank. 1983 [Corso appears during anniversary celebration for publication of *On the Road* at Naropa Institute in Boulder, CO].

West Coast: Beat and Beyond. Prod. and dir. Chris Felver. Chicago: Facets, 1987 [Corso reads a brief manuscript passage on why people think he is "nuts," a manuscript poem entitled "Women," and "All Survived"].

What Happened to Kerouac? Dir. Richard Lerner and Lewis MacAdams. Prod. Richard Lerner. Vidmark, 1987 [Corso is interviewed throughout about the Beats and Kerouac].

Wholly Communion. Dir. Peter Whitehead. London: Lorrimer, 1966 [Corso reads excerpt from "Mutation of the Spirit"].

Index

Michael Skau is a professor of English at the University of Nebraska at Omaha. He has published a book on Lawrence Ferlinghetti and articles on Jack Kerouac, Ferlinghetti, Richard Brautigan, William Burroughs, and Gregory Corso. His poems have appeared in *Midwest Quarterly*, *Northwest Review*, *Kentucky Poetry Review*, *Sequoia*, *Carolina Quarterly*, *Paintbrush*, and *Passaic Review*, among others.